FACING **NORTH**

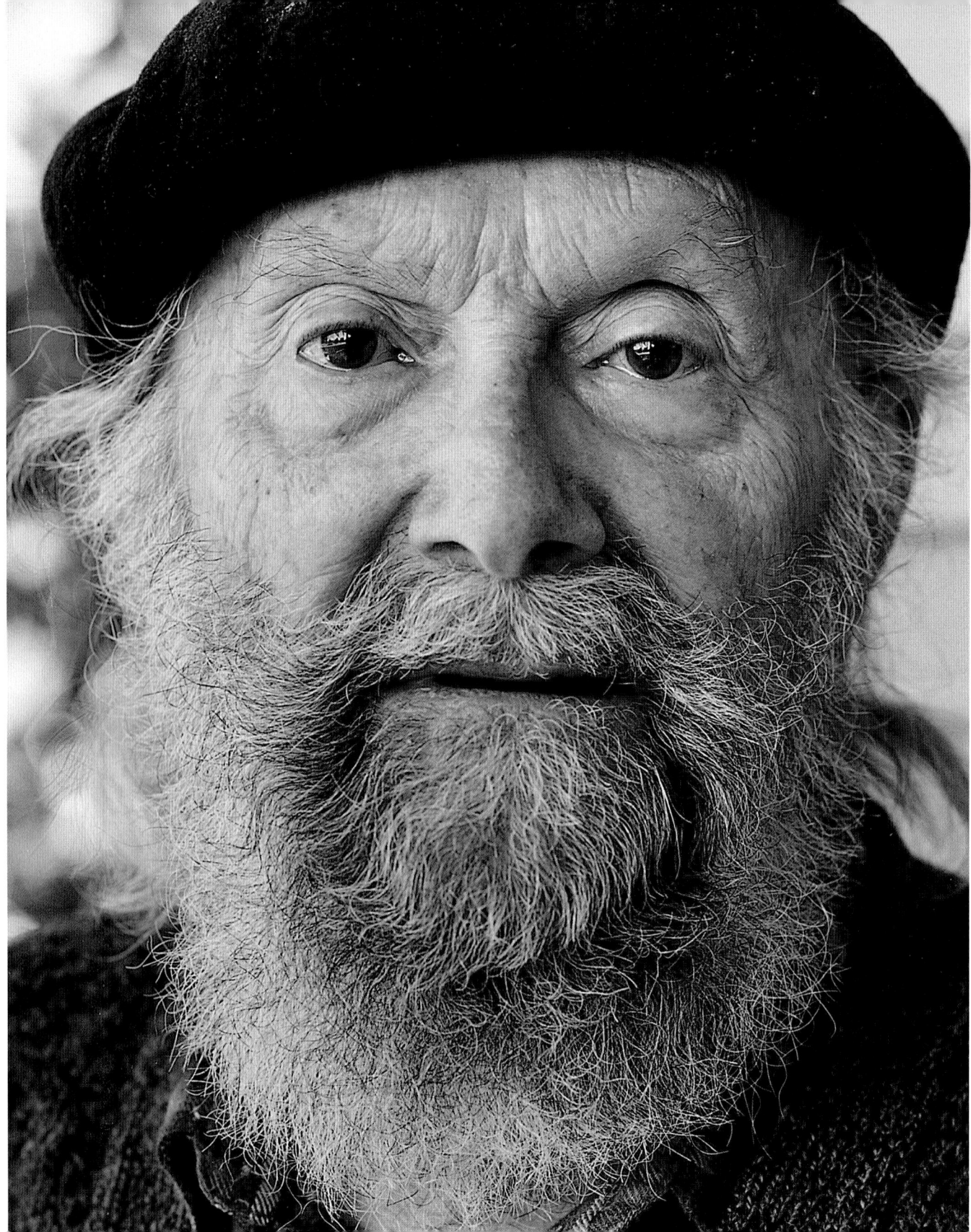

FACING NORTH

Portraits of Ely, Minnesota

Photographs by **Andrew Goldman**
Essays by **Ann Goldman**
Foreword by Jim Brandenburg

University of Minnesota Press
Minneapolis · London

This book is made possible in part by a grant from the Donald G. Gardner
Humanities Trust of Minnesota Community Foundation.

Copyright 2008 by Andrew and Ann Goldman
Foreword copyright 2008 by Jim Brandenburg

All rights reserved. No part of this publication may be reproduced, stored in a retrieval
system, or transmitted, in any form or by any means, electronic, mechanical, photocopying,
recording, or otherwise, without the prior written permission of the publisher.

Published by the University of Minnesota Press
111 Third Avenue South, Suite 290
Minneapolis, MN 55401-2520
http://www.upress.umn.edu

Library of Congress Cataloging-in-Publication Data
Goldman, Andrew and Ann.
  Facing north: portraits of Ely, Minnesota / photographs by Andrew Goldman; essays by
Ann Goldman; foreword by Jim Brandenburg.
     p. cm.
  ISBN: 978-0-8166-5147-4 (hc: alk. paper)   ISBN: 978-0-8166-5148-1 (pb: alk. paper)
  1. Ely (Minn.)–Pictorial works. 2. Ely (Minn.)–Social life and customs–Pictorial works.
I. Goldman, Andrew. II. Goldman, Ann. III. Title.
F614.E4G65 2008
977.6'77–dc22
                                                                        2007039033

Book design by Brian Donahue / bedesign, inc.

Printed in Italy on acid-free paper

The University of Minnesota is an equal-opportunity educator and employer.

15 14 13 12 11 10 09 08   10 9 8 7 6 5 4 3 2 1

Dedicated to

Reeder and Jack Goldman

whose youthful presence opened

many doors and many hearts

Ken Schlueter

who helped make the journey possible,

every step of the way

Nan and Gerry Snyder

who provided inspiration, encouragement,

and sustenance beyond measure

CONTENTS

Foreword JIM BRANDENBURG .... *ix*

Photographer's Preface .... *xiii*

Acknowledgments .... *xix*

A Northwoods Story: Ely, Minnesota .... *xxi*

Facing North *1*

    Green Ice *19*

    The Tinder Box *45*

    What Is in My Heart *67*

    Wild Neighbors *89*

    The Magic of It All *113*

Notes on the Portraits *133*

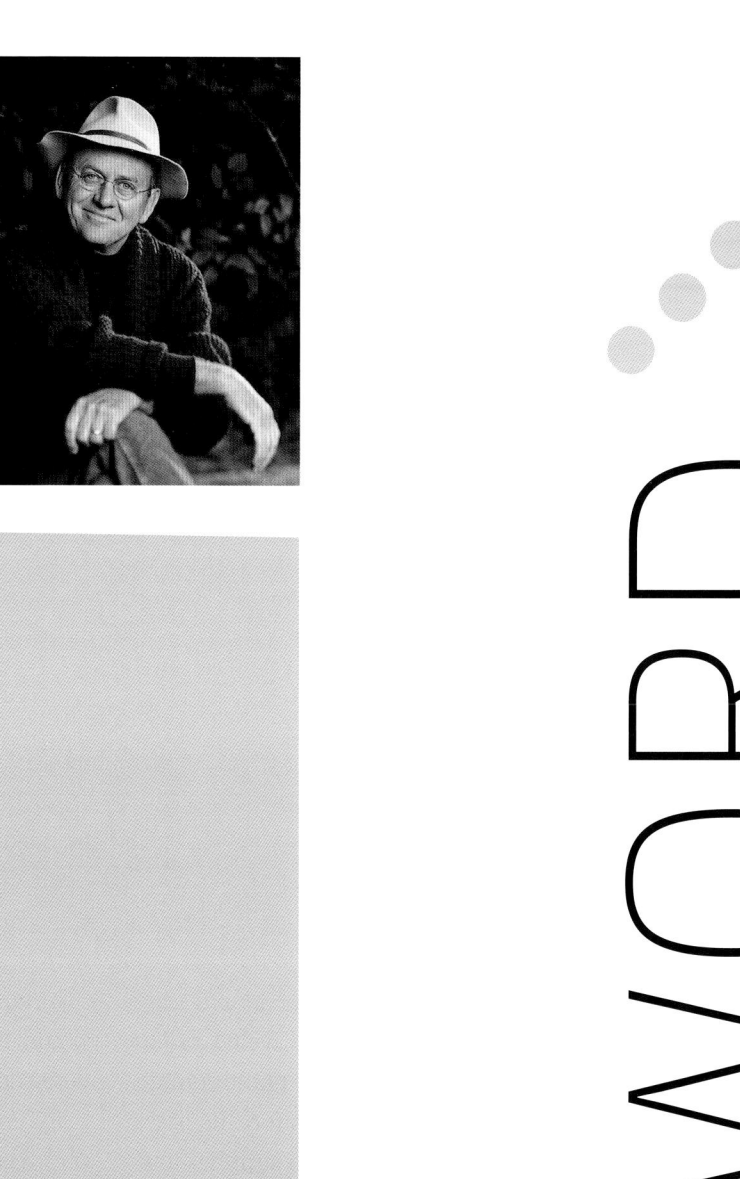

Foreword

FOREWORD

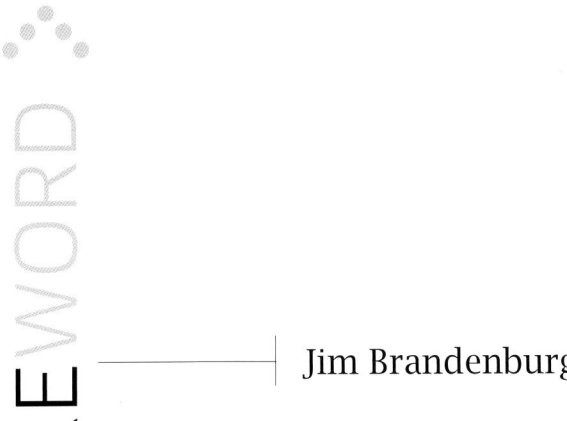

— Jim Brandenburg

First impressions can be powerful, but they don't always last. Thirty years ago I traveled to Ely on a *National Geographic* magazine photographic assignment. It was one of my first trips for this prestigious institution. I had just picked up supplies and loaded them into the back of my forest green, canoe-topped rented station wagon on Sheridan Street, the main drag of the town. I still remember its license plates with the letters ELY followed by three numbers, predating personalized plates; I was impressed with that random coincidence. Perhaps a good omen was attached, and my photographs would make a strong impression back at the Washington, D.C., headquarters.

As I pulled away from the curb, a sharply focused, dark, handsome man ran across the street and rapped on my window. "Are you from *National Geographic*?" he asked. Why, yes, I said proudly with a smile. Word sure gets around a small town in a hurry, I thought. He must want an autograph or would like to talk camera equipment. I felt important and flattered. "We don't need your type around here," he barked. He turned and walked back across the street.

I was confused, embarrassed, and hurt. I couldn't find the words to describe the feelings rolling around inside of me. I thought everyone loved *National Geographic*. It is a national icon, as American as the slice of apple pie I had just eaten at Vertin's Café. The magazine reaches millions and would certainly be good promotion for a small tourist town. Who was this angry man? What was his point? I grew up in a prairie town the same size as Ely on the far side of the state. I thought I understood small-town culture.

After twenty-five years of living here, I finally understand the meaning and reasons behind the outburst from that man (who, I discovered later, was the highly regarded mayor of the town). Ely had developed a personality, not unlike an individual who has endured the ups and downs of life's experiences. Turn the pages of Ely's colorful history and one finds plenty of epic and dramatic events that have shaped its distinctive persona.

Five hundred generations have passed since the first people walked into this area from the northwest. The land looked different then. A mile-thick continent of ice was melting and retreating north after pushing and scraping traces of previous life from its bed of greenstone, which was 2.7 billion years old. Saber-toothed tigers and wooly mammoths were among the resident animals that greeted those early packsackers.

Five hundred years ago, the Ojibwe came from the east to drive the Dakota out to the treeless prairie. Later, the first Europeans paddled through and claimed these lakes and rivers for Mother France. Then, for nearly two centuries, the voyageurs traded and carried untold fortunes in trapped animal furs back east for European consumption. False gold rushes and a real discovery of rich iron deposits opened this country to the industrial age, which scattered most of the native Ojibwe to the four winds. Slovenians, Finns, and Italians came to blast and dig iron ore from this stubborn ground. If the dangerous cold and dark underground mining did not break their spirits, the company bulls managed to drive them to the forty-odd bars that lined the downtown streets.

The tall pines were then logged in a blink of a historical eye. The prairies grew large red barns from the billions of board feet cut and floated to the local mills from the boundary waters around Ely. During the Depression my father came as a teenager from one of those prairie farms to cut some of the last virgin pine groves. He talked of numbing-cold forty-below days when he and his muscled partner hand-sawed through four-foot-thick white pines in waist-deep snow. The men worked, ate, and slept in remote bush camps—this was no place for family life. Like the mines, the logging companies ran a tight ship. Payday sent the thirsty, hungry, and fun lumberjacks to town to relieve themselves. The pioneer days produced stories of pain, company greed, and broken bones and hearts that could fill volumes.

Just as the iron ore and the big trees were running too thin for profit in the 1960s, the federal government declared the lakes and forests around Ely a canoe park to be preserved and shared with the rest of the country. Locally, this was taken as grand theft of the town's own backyard paradise. One of the nation's longest and most bitter environmental battles began, and the flame still flickers. Never mind that my beloved *National Geographic* named the Boundary Waters Canoe Area Wilderness one of the fifty most scenic places in the world: "We don't need your type around here." Well, now I know a little about why the aggravated mayor barked those painful words at me. I was a modern-day "packsacker," and he didn't think I belonged here, especially if I would be telling a "tree hugger" magazine story of why this land should change hands. His nine generations of French voyageur (via Montreal) and Native American ancestors were speaking. He was a proud and protective chief speaking for his village.

The wolves I came to photograph also didn't welcome me, and they certainly didn't enjoy my poking cameras around in their space—but I stayed. I went on to tour the world for the magazine, and I saw more than anyone could absorb in a lifetime. One thing that kept me grounded all those years was the thought of my log cabin nestled in the woods near Ely. I eventually reached the conclusion that the secrets hidden in my cabin's backyard woods were more interesting than the exotic far-off places so many people yearn to visit. I am glad I stayed, even more deeply now.

I have built my life and photographic career around wild animals, especially the wolf. That elusive animal is what originally drew me to Ely. Truth be known, though, I enjoy making pictures of people as much as of wildlife: I find it just as rewarding. My work as a photojournalist has involved assignments about people and faraway cultures as often as about raw nature. Alas, I always felt there were more stories per square foot in Ely as anywhere else I have been. I have talked of making a book like this, and now Andrew Goldman has beaten me to it. Look into these Ely faces he has captured with his razor-sharp lens and read the stories in their eyes.

Oh, by the way, *packsacker* is the term the locals called newcomers around here, the label you wore if your grandparents were not born here (well, at least your parents). Are you able to pick out the packsackers in these portraits?

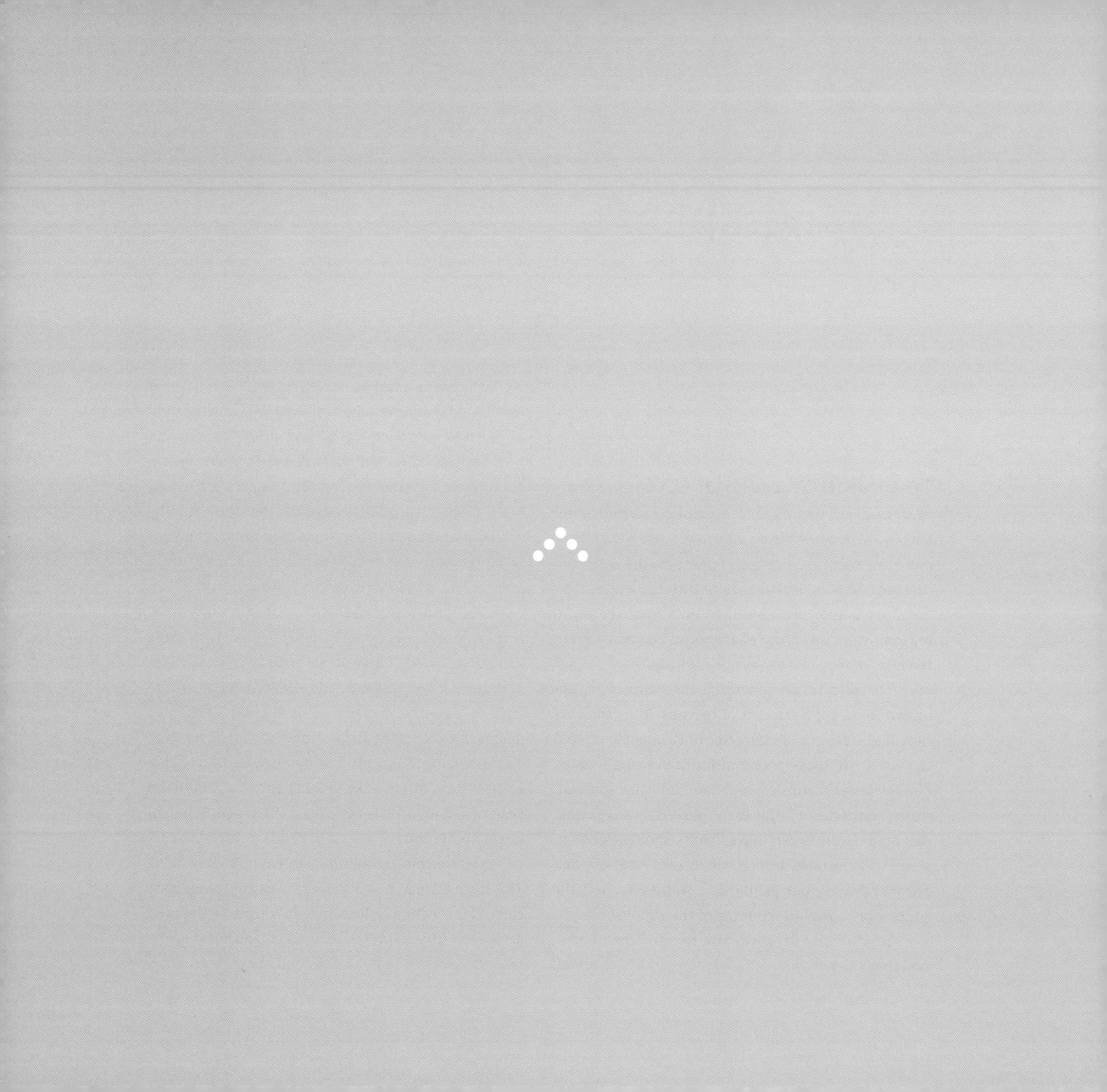

Photographer's Preface

The value of a visual record changes over time. One photograph can capture an individual and an environment in a moment yet also tell a larger, more lasting story. A group of photographs goes even further, offering deeper insight into the whole. How the story is interpreted will change from season to season, year to year, but elements and expressions in the human face will always be familiar.

The idea of documenting Ely, Minnesota, appealed to me for a number of reasons. The visual variety and strength of character in the people offered seemingly limitless potential for interesting images. The town has a timelessness, an enduring spirit directly connected to the early pioneers who settled this area barely one hundred years ago. The context of the Northwoods is present in every person and every endeavor, but primarily I wanted to find the larger story through the faces of the people here.

Driving into Ely gives you the distinct impression that you have arrived at the very end of the road. And you pretty much have. Perched on the brink of the Boundary Waters Canoe Area Wilderness, just fifteen miles from the Canadian border, Ely is a comfortable destination for anyone who likes the woods. There are no fast-food restaurants, there is no Wal-Mart. Instead, you will find outfitters and family-run restaurants, gift shops and galleries, and lodges along the shores of pristine lakes. All of this attracts more than 200,000 tourists every year.

The year-round residents number only 3,700 and represent a surprising diversity of experience and background. They are the children and grandchildren of loggers and iron ore miners; they are Ojibwe, forestry workers, artisans, trappers, students, environmentalists, hunters, retirees, and entrepreneurs. Many of their names date back to the earliest days of Ely. A seamless connection between yesterday and today is easier to decipher here than in larger communities.

I started photographing the people of Ely in 2002. The large-format 4 × 5 camera was my immediate choice for the project. It affords subtle play with focus across the film plane, enabling a controlled exaggeration in the depth of field. The unique grain structure

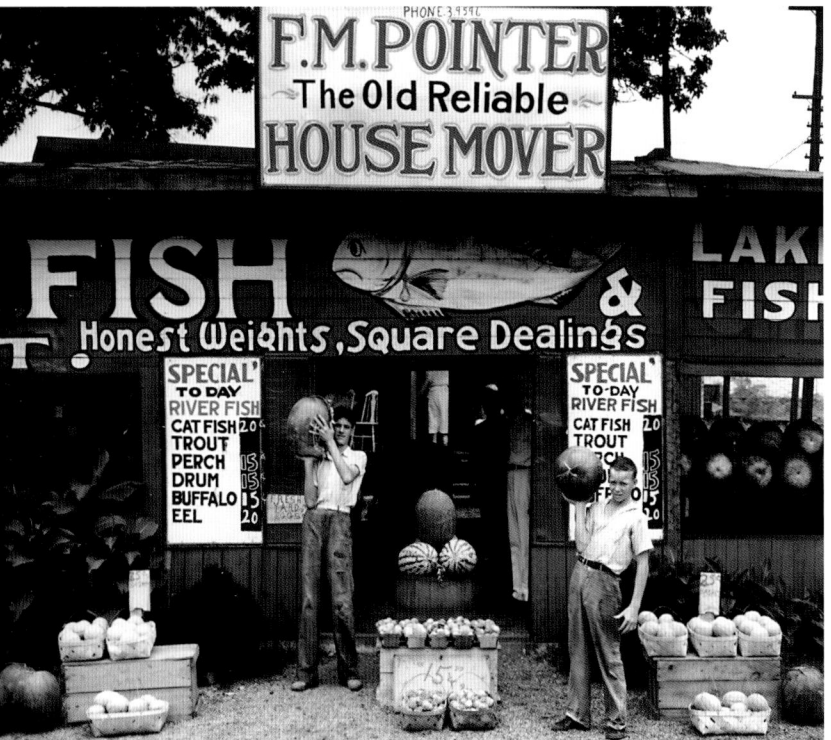

This Ely project was inspired in part by the Farm Security Administration photographs that captured people in their unique settings at a specific moment in time. Walker Evans took this picture of a roadside stand near Birmingham, Alabama, in 1936. Courtesy of the Library of Congress.

to this format results in a rich and elegant texture in the final print. Yet it is a restricting choice of equipment. I cannot walk around the subject at will, cannot capture movement; the range of focus is tricky, and the depth of field is shallow. These characteristics slow the picture-making process considerably, forcing a deliberateness between myself and the subject that lends itself to an almost ceremonial result.

I cannot be an anonymous observer in this format, and the subject is definitely aware every time the shutter closes. The trick is to make the person seem at ease when actually the process is anything but relaxed. When confronted with an "old-fashioned" camera and a photographer under the focusing cloth, subjects usually become extremely aware of themselves in the moment. Some people stiffen, some stand a little taller, and others—well, it pays to just let them get bored and open the shutter when they are distracted.

I believe that the subjects' self-awareness contributes to an honest and dignified representation of the core of these individuals. I never tell them what clothes or facial expression to wear, seeking to capture their own perception of themselves, framed in a formality of lines and placement that lend artistry to the photograph and that magnify the eternal aspects of the moment. I have always been inspired by the documentary work of the Farm Security Administration photographers Walker Evans and

Dorothea Lange. Yet the 4 × 5 camera and the collaborative approach resulted in the more formal compositions of this book, recalling the structured images of Civil War photographers that also inspire me.

The first photograph I took confirmed that this formal approach was the one most suited to how I wanted to explore Ely. I had been sitting on the deck of the Chocolate Moose restaurant when I saw a guy drive down Sheridan Street in an old army jeep with a machine gun mounted on the back. I asked my friend Ken Schlueter about him. Ken, a fishing guide and retired conservation officer from Babbitt, immediately said, "Oh, sure, that's Sludge. He used to work in the mines." As he would do so many times throughout this project, Ken made the connection, setting up a time for me to drop by and talk to Sludge, whose real name is Seraphine Rolando.

Even though Sludge had a working cannon in his front yard, I knew that his oil-stained garage with the "Coffee Shop" sign above it was the ideal spot in which to photograph him. This is where he built his replica Willys jeep out of oil drums and mounted it on an original chassis. I set up three or four flash heads and played around with the film plane to throw different parts of the image out of focus. When I looked at the Polaroid, the picture seemed like it might have been taken in the 1930s.

So we committed ourselves to the project, but we had no idea of the scale into which it would

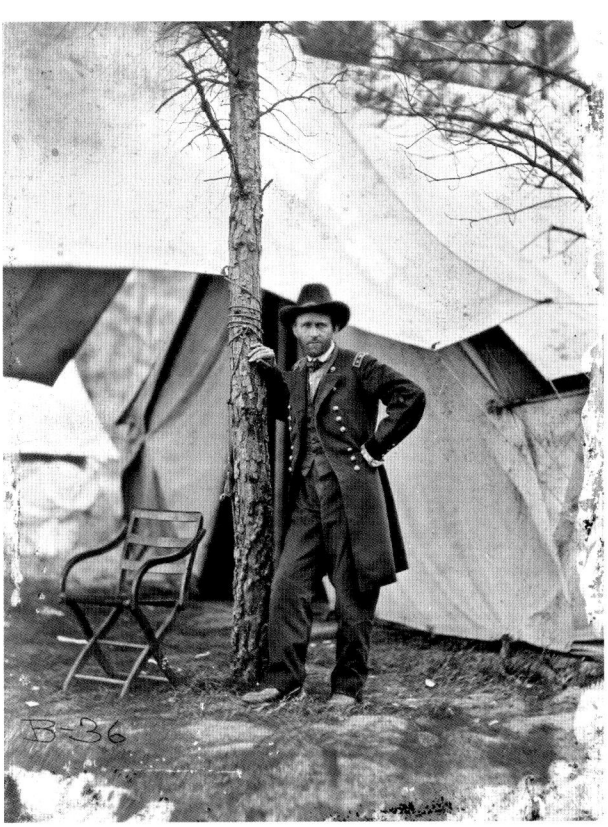

A large format camera, like the one used for *Facing North*, slows the picture-making process, resulting in a formality much like we see in Civil War photographs. This image of Ulysses S. Grant was taken in 1864 at Cold Harbor, Virginia, by E. G. Fox. Courtesy of U.S. National Archives.

eventually grow. Not until we amassed more pictures and the work really took on a life of its own did we recognize the potential for a book. Everyone we photographed would suggest additional subjects, and then those people would make suggestions, too. We covered pages and pages of notepaper with phone numbers and names and location ideas. At home in Chicago, my wife, Ann, and I would plan a trip to Ely and set a schedule of three portraits per day. The pace was hectic, and our list was getting longer and longer. Plus, Ann had started interviewing the subjects with a handheld tape recorder, and the length of each sitting was getting longer, too.

We decided to really invest in the work and rented an apartment on Chapman Street one summer. This enabled us to slow down and not feel so pressed. We learned that it was better to underschedule our days and let things happen more naturally. We would book one, maybe two, sittings and then see what else came up. A great example is the afternoon when we had just finished photographing Trader Craig at his shop and were loading our equipment into the car. Sylvio Boulanger pulled his motorcycle into the parking lot, looking for directions to the Echo Trail; we knew the way. Amazed by his wonderful face, we asked him to sit for a portrait, and he agreed on the spot.

The first winter I photographed in Ely I discovered what it is like to work in subzero temperatures. One morning I photographed "Jackpine" Bob Cary out on Miners Lake. It was forty degrees below zero, and my strobe lights failed. They weren't broken—they just wouldn't work. I pulled out my meter, and the button shattered when I pressed it. The Polaroids wouldn't develop even when I stuck them inside my coat. All I had left that would work was a tungsten 1,000-watt light, so I used it and hoped for the best.

These kinds of temperatures were hard on the film. In fact, working with sheets of 4 × 5 film required much care and maintenance in every season. During a shoot, we had to be careful not to double-expose any of the sheets. Each night, I would unload the film in a changing bag, clean out the holders, and reload. Keeping the holders clean was always a challenge when we were outside all the time. It took a while to get a system down. Ken Schlueter, Ann, and even our kids became impromptu photo assistants. They kept the film straight, the generator running, and the subjects entertained, and nobody got out of holding a light stand in the wind when forty pounds of sandbags wouldn't stop it from blowing over. This project obviously had to be a family enterprise, because Ann and I were working on it together, and for the most part our two boys were with us. They helped in many ways, learned and saw a lot of new things, hindered us occasionally, but mostly they made people feel more relaxed and trusting.

Trust was essential to making the pictures in this book, and I am still impressed by how willing

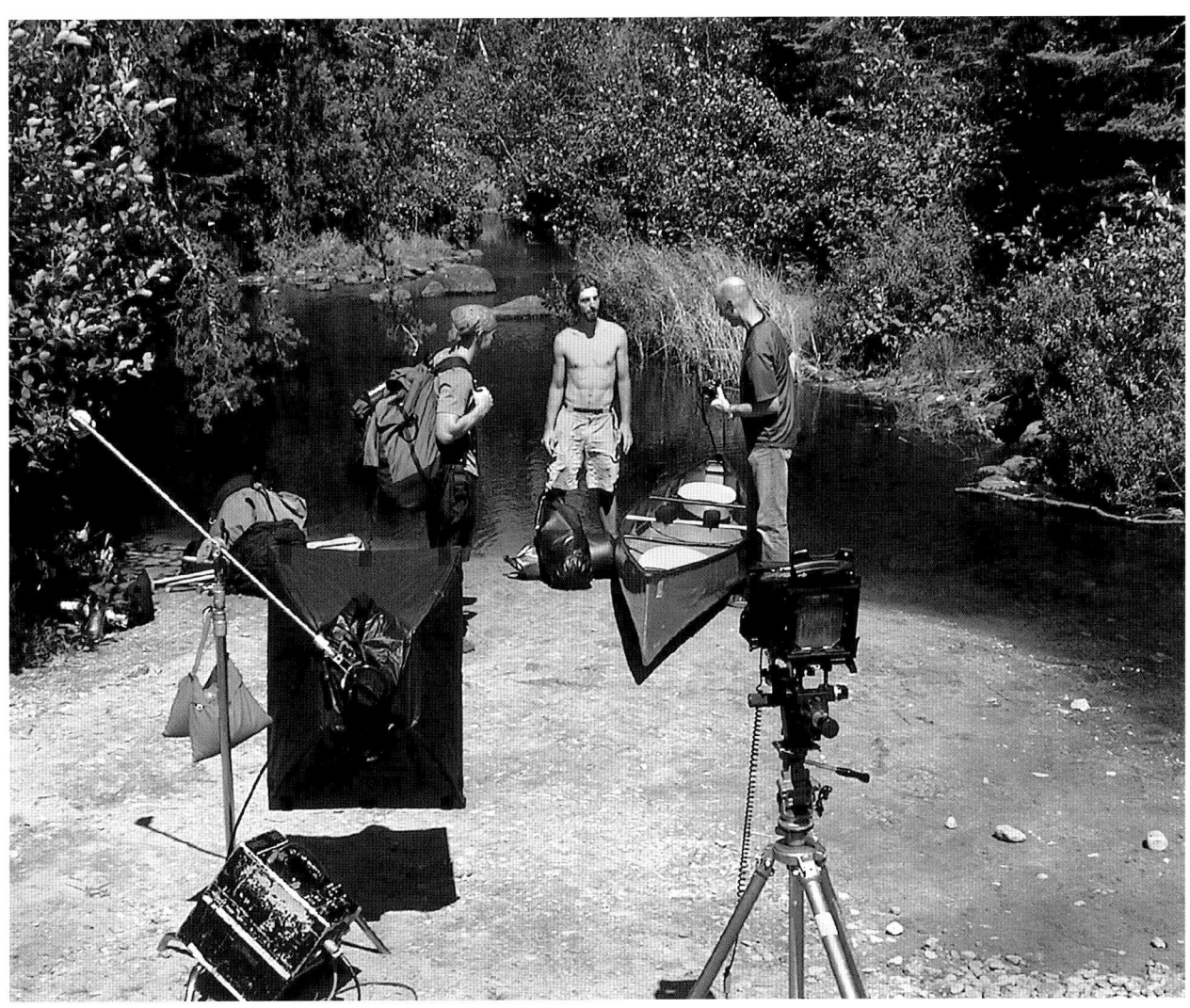

Andrew Goldman *(right)* photographs James Kurzdorfer and Ryan Jones as they exit the Boundary Waters Canoe Area Wilderness at Mudro Lake Access Point. The resulting image can be seen as Plate 20.

the people of Ely, Winton, and Babbitt were to participate. We would call people out of the blue, and they would invite us into their homes, to their places of work, or to their favorite fishing holes. One winter when we were staying in a cabin on Garden Lake, we decided to try to get a shot of someone emerging from a sauna—a notable tradition in the area. Someone suggested Kim McCluskey, so Ann called him and told him what we were thinking. He said, "Let me get this straight. I've never heard of you, and you're calling me and asking me if I'll get naked in the snow for a photograph tomorrow afternoon." When Ann confirmed that, yes, he had that right, Kim said, "Sure. I'll do it."

The added element of a tape-recorded interview intensified the need for trust. Ann's essays provide important context to the images in the book and were shaped partly out of our own perspective on Ely and its people. Even more, they emerged from Ann's interactions with individuals and their oral histories, perceptions, and opinions they offered so generously.

In the end, I photographed and Ann interviewed more than one hundred people. I exposed between eight and sixteen sheets of film on each person, for a total of about 1,600 negatives. Every picture was individually tray-developed at The Print Lab in Chicago, then I did all the printing in my home darkroom. The only exceptions are a few of the scenic shots. I finally and reluctantly traded in my old 8 × 10 Deardorff camera for a Fuji digital camera, which ended up being convenient for some of the landscape pictures.

As outsiders, we were in a unique position to move among residents with ease, relatively free of affiliation or bias. We made no attempt to judge, rank, or stratify the subjects, nor did we try to make a political statement or call to action. Our guidelines in making choices about whom to document were twofold: first, to capture the aesthetic value of the individual and the setting; and second, to represent the larger picture of the community and its history. Given the politics of a small town, this work attracted an astonishing unity. To a person, the subjects of *Facing North* understood and supported the project totally. Our only regret is that the project must necessarily come to an end, leaving so many interesting individuals unphotographed.

We spent five years creating *Facing North: Portraits of Ely, Minnesota*. During that time, much changed in the community. Businesses came and went. People died, moved away, grew up. The story is different today from what it was the day I took the first picture, and it will be different again tomorrow. In the end, I hope that the collective and lasting story these images tell reflects the unique and ageless spirit of the Northwoods.

ACKNOWLEDGMENTS

This project graced us with an unending flow of generosity from the people of Ely, Babbitt, and Winton. Our greatest appreciation goes to the individuals who posed for portraits. We are humbled by the frankness and integrity with which they approached their sittings.

We thank the following people for their contributions to the project: Ken Schlueter for every imaginable thing, including but not limited to time, connections, stories, ideas, generator, truck, and excellent fishing; Nan and Gerry Snyder for inviting us to Ely and Whitshell Island in the first place and encouraging this project every step of the way; John and Norma Wood for their generous and careful reading of the manuscript and for watching the kids when Ely beckoned us back; Wendy Schlueter for sharing Ken with us and for countless hours of entertaining our children with puppies, kittens, chickens, horses, and every conceivable stray animal; Paul and Susan Schurke and their family for opening their lodge and home to us; Jim Brandenburg and Heidi Brandenburg for advice and encouragement; Amy Yates for her invaluable counsel; Dayna Mase for her artistic point of view; our friends at Piragis Northwoods Company, especially Steve, Nancy, and Lisa, for their commitment to the project from the earliest days; everyone at Jackpine Lodge for treating us more like family than guests; Bert and Johnnie Hyde for their many suggestions and for getting us "off the grid" for a few heavenly afternoons; and Jeanne Peshel for letting us use her office as our personal P.O. box. And last but certainly not least, thanks to Deb Pettit for her undying support.

Thanks to the team at the University of Minnesota Press, especially to Todd Orjala for his shared love of the North Country.

The work of several writers contributed to our understanding of and appreciation for the community: Emma Bissonett, Lee Brownell, Miron "Bud" Heinselman, Johnnie Hyde, Lynn Maria Laitala, Marvin Lamppa, Dan Schmiechen, Jeff Forrester, and the many editors and contributors to the *Ely Echo*.

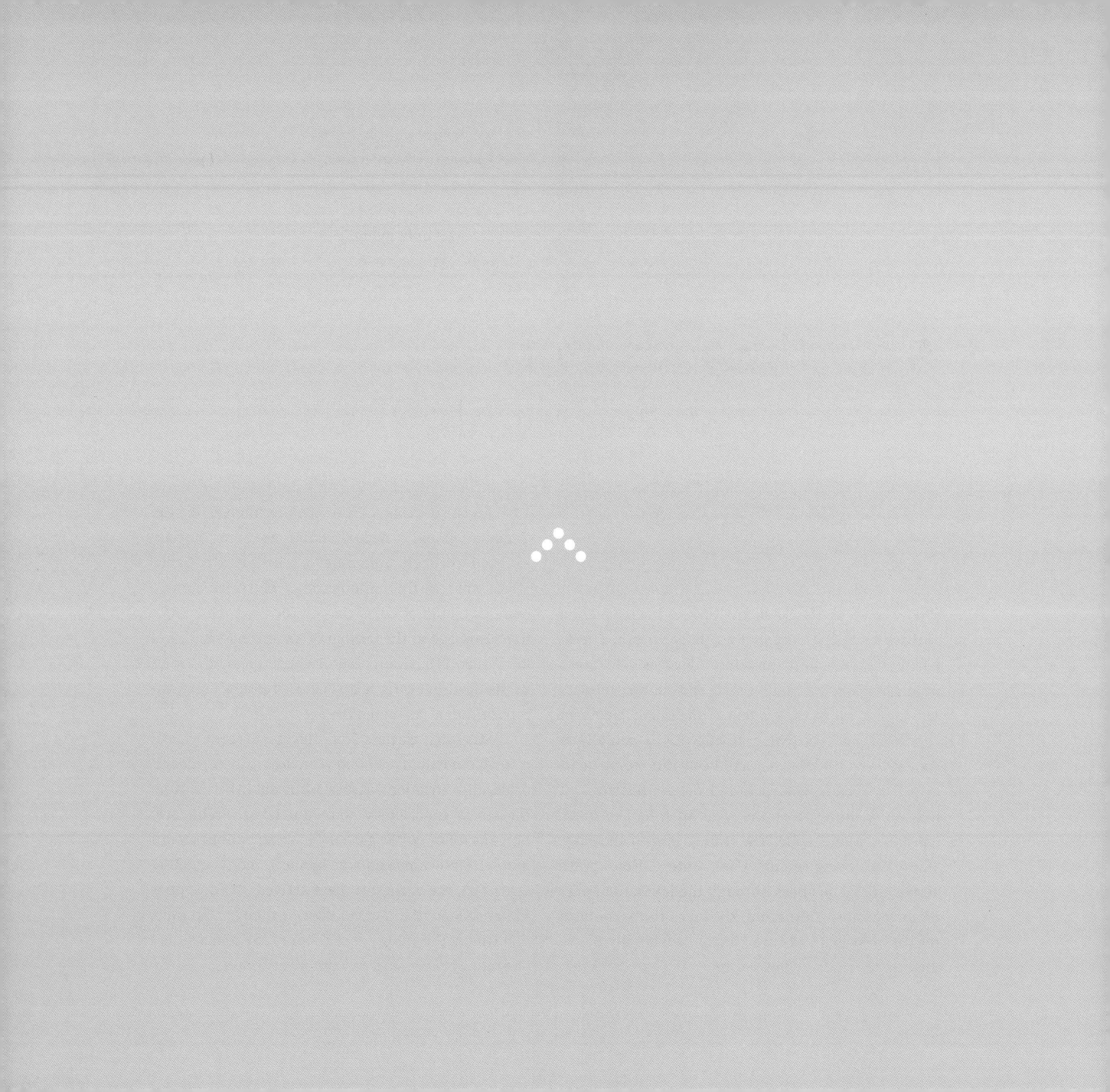

We primeval forests felling,
We the rivers stemming, vexing we and piercing deep the mines within,
We the surface broad surveying, we the virgin soil upheaving,
Pioneers! O pioneers!
—WALT WHITMAN

A Northwoods Story
ELY, MINNESOTA

Pull out a map of the United States and you will see that Ely is situated north. Far north. It feels particularly northerly on a forty-degrees-below-zero day in January. But remove state and country borders and look at Ely in the context of the North American continent, and you will find that Ely is actually at the *southern* tip of a vast and beautiful region characterized by ancient rock and deep wilderness. It lies along the edge of the ridge of hills that form the Laurentian Divide. The Ojibwe named the ridge Mesabi—sleeping giant. Cool waters flow north across the giant's back through the lakes and rivers of northeastern Minnesota, known as the Arrowhead region, past Ely, and into Canada, eventually draining into icy Hudson Bay.

Ely also rests at the southern edge of the Canadian Shield, a bed of Earth's most ancient rock exposed through millennia of erosion. On Camp Street you will find an outcrop of Ely greenstone, a bulbous chunk of moss-colored rock formed 2.7 billion years ago at the bottom of an ancient sea. Local log builder Brian Kainz found a huge spear of granite in his yard; he calls it a slice of "mother earth" in recognition of its incredible age.

Mile-high glaciers from the most recent ice age retreated north just 12,000 years ago, leaving a band of parallel striations across Minnesota that became the state's notoriously abundant lakes. Prehistoric humans followed the glaciers' melting path in search of food. First came nomadic hunters, and then, 3,000 years ago, the earliest miners arrived—"Old Copper Indians." Mound-builders followed, then the Dakotas, and finally the Ojibwe laid claim to the area as they were forced westward by European settlers.

The Ojibwe, also called Chippewa, call themselves *Anishinabe*, which means *original person*. From their new Northwoods home, the Ojibwe continued a thriving trade with the chanson-singing voyageurs, who kept London in beaver hats and Canada's Hudson's Bay Company prosperous for nearly two centuries. Their tradition of ornately decorated birchbark canoes continues today under the care of Native artisans and others, like Eric Mase, who have learned their beautiful craft. An 1866 treaty established a reservation for the Bois Forte Band of Ojibwe on Lake Vermilion, twenty miles west of Ely, and even farther west on Nett Lake. The life of the Bois Forte—"Strong Men of the Woods"—is interwoven with everyone's story in these parts.

After the Civil War, prospectors arrived in the Ely area looking for gold. They even built a road through the deep woods and started a little town called Eviston. But no gold was found and Eviston disappeared. Instead, the earth provided a high-grade hematite iron ore—a vermilion-colored treasure that would transform this wooded landscape into the Iron Range and feed the massive steel furnaces of a growing nation.

> *Ukko, maker of the heavens,*
> *Cut apart the air and water,*
> *Ere was born the metal, iron.*
> *Ukko, maker of the heavens,*
> *Firmly rubbed his hands together,*
> *Firmly pressed them on his knee-cap,*
> *Then arose three lovely maidens,*
> *Three most beautiful of daughters;*
> *These were mothers of the iron,*
> *And of steel of bright-blue color.*
> (*The Kalevala*, an ancient epic of Finland)

Not long ago, two men were wandering in the woods near Section Thirty, one of the old iron ore pits near Ely, when a seventy-foot white pine tree disappeared before their eyes. It plummeted through the forest floor and was gone, leaving only a dark, deep hole and a chill down their spines. The man to call when something like this happens is local historian Marvin Lamppa, whose life's work has been discovering and describing the vast network of abandoned mines and ghost towns across Minnesota's Iron Range. Shafts like the one the tree fell through are numerous. Miners covered retired shafts with cedar trees. The forest took over and grew aspen, pine, and brush across the logs, and then, over time, the cedar rotted. This is not a comforting thought as we trudge through the rainy woods with Marv, looking for Section Thirty. Once we find it, he cautions us as we stand at the edge of the pit: "If you fall in, there's really no way to get out." Trees and moss cling to the rusty red cliffs, and a murky bluish green pond rests about 100 feet below, concealing an additional 700 feet of the pit's depth.

Along the upper edge, only a few stone foundations remain of the settlement that included a school, dance hall, hotel, post office, hospital, and general store—a settlement that existed at the pit's edge for fourteen years but was never given a name by the people who lived there. Why name it when it will dissolve in an instant, when it will collapse and disappear like the white pine?

Ely was unusual. Unlike the 130 ghost towns on the Range, it was not only named quickly—in honor of Samuel Ely, a mining magnate from Michigan who never actually saw his namesake town in person—it thrived and proved a lasting settlement. Its initial success owed to the amazing output of the Chandler Mine. In 1888, the railroad arrived and started hauling out iron and carrying in workers. Ely was ultimately home to seven major underground mines, with the granddaddy of them all, the Pioneer Mine, yielding more than 41 million tons of ore before it closed in 1967. The town's population started at 177 people in 1889, peaked in 1930 at 6,151, and has been declining ever since. Today, Ely is home to 3,700 souls.

The first mines in Ely were opened and supervised by Cornish men who had experience with underground mines along the coast of Britain. To this day, you can get a darned good pasty anywhere along the Iron Range. Finns came afterward, many of them fleeing the clutches of the Russian army and the overpopulation and poverty of their home country. Slovenians came too, and Germans, Italians, and more. Walk through Ely's graveyard and the names reveal this immigrant heritage—Oreskovich, Indehar, Sayatovich, Skue, Pryatel, Ojala, Koski, Jarvenpää, Haapala, Thompson, Anderson, Guisippina, Mariani, Ambrogio, Benko, Antio, Nauha.

Life in Ely today is directly connected to those pioneer families. Zup's Grocery, first run by Slovenian settlers, has been here almost since the beginning. The business has progressed from a general store, and the Zupancich family has grown, but some things never change—hot bologna on Thursdays is a perennial favorite and a gift we have received gratefully from Pat, the current family patriarch. The local radio station, WELY "end of the road radio," is owned by the Bois Forte Band of Ojibwe, and for many years you could catch a Finnish radio show hosted on Sunday mornings by Milli Salmela Bissonett, whose grandparents settled on the Pipe River near Tower when they first arrived from Finland. Joe Seliga's family arrived in 1890, just two years after the Chandler Mine started production, and three generations worked the ore veins before Joe's canoe-building became viable full-time work.

A strapping young immigrant who appeared fit could easily get a job in the mines and would often be hired on the spot. But they might last only a short time. Fatalities were common, and it was dark, wet, miserable work with little or no opportunity for advancement. Pay came in the form of a contract for production—you depended on your crewmates and a good "place" on the ore vein for your money. And Ely's numerous saloons and blind pigs—illegal liquor houses—gave you plenty of opportunity to spend your cash rather than save it. Most of the miners lived in boarding houses, often renting beds in shifts.

To read the demands the miners made during the famous and bloody strike of 1916 is shocking—they were so minimal, so basic, so grounded in human decency. Yet their requests for an eight-hour day, the elimination of the Saturday night shift, two paychecks per month, back pay upon severance, employer-funded mining equipment, and on and on, went largely unmet in the face of the powerful steel companies. Losing the strike, many of the miners, particularly the Finns, were blacklisted and moved to the logging camps in search of work.

Indeed, it was mining that finally opened up the infrastructure for logging in these parts. The railroads and roads paved the way, and even the first sawmill in Ely was powered by steam from the Chandler Mine boilers. Lumberjacks worked the long northern winter felling trees and living in deep-wood camps where the cook was king and the dinner hour near silent as the ravished men devoured their salted meat and doughnuts. Their brightly colored woolen clothing called "mackinaws" kept them safely visible to each other as they worked in gangs of choppers, skidders, and sawyers to gather the highly prized white pine. They would drag huge sled loads of harvested timber along ingeniously crafted ice roads to "banking grounds" along the nearest lake or river. This work accelerated in the spring as ice-out approached because any logs left behind after the ice roads melted would be stranded until next season.

And then the spring drive commenced. Mountains of timber rushed down the waterways to Winton's sawmills, just down the road from Ely. Dodging log jams and eating on the run, lumberjacks finished the season in a blur of danger and exhaustion. The minute it was over, a forest-worth of men descended on Winton and Ely, many to the brothels. The early days of the timber trade were the most raucous here, and the towns had plenty of "bawdy houses." Scrappy characters like Stoney Slim, the best fighter in the area, who could kick "high and fast," are still the stuff of legend. But as industry grew and families with children arrived, the saloons were relegated to the outskirts of town, and both Ely and Winton settled into respectable townhood.

The old forest cut was finished fairly quickly, and the life of the lumberjack declined rapidly. Poor conditions, poor wages, and exploitive employment practices were rampant. The lumber companies owned *everything* in Winton, including real estate, general stores, and water and electrical sources. Even the post office was run by company officers. There were ongoing efforts to unionize, but the militia and rough-tactic Pinkertons helped the lumber companies squelch every lumberjack's hope. It was not until 1936 that the Timber Workers Union won a place in the Ely area. But it was too late. The pine was gone, and the last major log drive took place in 1937, just a year after workers gained their much-needed protections.

All that remained was new-growth "pulp" wood, fit for papermaking and Popsicle sticks. A different economic model of logging emerged with logger-owners like the Kainz family, using high-tech equipment and a small workforce. A third generation of Kainz men still works with lumber in the area—two are loggers, one is a carpenter, and two others build log homes. Their father always told them to focus their work on fulfilling human needs, and the forest remains their means of doing just that.

Many of the immigrants who came to work the timber were left with nothing. Despite the richness of the ore and timber resource, the rocky land around Ely is virtually useless for agriculture. While other Minnesotans were able to set up farms and dairies on the healthier "cutover land" to the south and west, the people of the Arrowhead turned to the Civilian Conservation Corps (CCC) for relief. They replanted the forest and brought home a government allotment of $30 a month to feed their families. They carved the Echo, Fernberg, and Kawishiwi trails atop the original Ojibwe and Dakota tracks. And some learned new trades, like Joe Prijatel, son of Yugoslavian immigrants, who became adept at making rawhide snowshoes. "Times were tough then," he says. "The CCC hired all the young folk in the area from the age of sixteen up. That's when I learned to make Ojibwe-style snowshoes from a guy I knew. Now I make twenty to twenty-five different kinds."

After the "CCC days," Joe found work in the mines. And, indeed, the mines kept a few generations employed through two steel-hungry world wars and well into the 1960s. Rooster Lekatz was destined for a life in the mines, but he first tried a different tack. He landed a job in Cleveland but became so totally homesick that after only one week he high-tailed it home to join his Croatian-born father in the Pioneer Mine. He never again considered leaving Ely. "People are friendly," he says. "They get along with everyone else." He was middle-aged by the time the mine closed, destiny pulled out from under his feet. The underground Pioneer Mine finally became cost prohibitive, and alternate processing techniques made the high quality of Ely's iron ore unnecessary to the steelmakers. The last miner in Ely was laid off in 1967. The older guys retired, the young ones took jobs at a taconite plant in Babbitt, and Rooster found work as a propane delivery man. When he eventually retired, he lived in a house just a block from the one in which he was raised.

Frana Cherico was raised in Ely during the "good days" of mining. Her father came to Ely from Yugoslavia by himself at the age of fourteen and eventually served as the deputy sheriff of St. Louis County for more than forty years. "I feel really blessed that I lived in the era that the mines were going," says Frana. "We had so much fun as children growing up in the woodsy area—canoeing, boating, saunas, and all the better things in life."

Down the road, the small town of Babbitt was born and died through unsuccessful attempts to process and market taconite, a very low-grade iron ore encased in rock. But in 1956 taconite found a market with the large steel conglomerates, and the town of Babbitt was reborn as a planned mining community. Families moved in and jobs were plentiful. Tommy Helm's dad was an automotive engineer for the mine, and Tommy followed in his footsteps, working as an exploration miner for thirty-three years. But as the taconite mining process became more sophisticated, fewer and fewer workers were required to produce the same yield. Tommy retired early in 2001 when his job was made defunct and spends his days inventing a menagerie of gadgets and toys, including more than thirty different styles of kites and some amazing vehicles. "My winters get a little long," he says. "But now that I've been working on my ski bike, it's gone really fast." Tommy's son found work by leaving Babbitt, becoming a robot engineer in the Twin Cities.

While the glory days of mining and logging may indeed be over, the region's partial reliance on the extraction of natural resources is likely to continue for some time. Speculators hire miners like Aaron Mellgren and Ronald Tokela to send drills a mile below the lakes and surface rocks in search of base metals like nickel and copper and the precious metals unsuccessfully sought during the gold rush. Backed by large multinational corporations, the Arrowhead's potential to give up more of its bounty is a promise that might eventually prove lucrative—and perhaps environmentally costly.

People often long for the clarity of a linear story, but the real life of a community defies such a simplistic approach. Tourism is often painted as being the "new" market after Ely's ore mines closed, but in fact tourism has been a mainstay of the economy here since early in the 1900s. The rise of the automobile and the establishment of the Superior National Forest in 1909 brought Americans flocking to the area, bringing more money than logging ever did. In 1913, the Ely Chamber of Commerce and the Superior National Forest started marketing the wilderness together and attracted a growing number of visitors.

By 1948, Ely had the largest freshwater seaplane base in the country, whisking fishermen deep into the heart of the wilderness. Can you imagine the heyday of the fly-in fishing and big-game hunting lodges? Gangsters and bootleggers, blue bloods from the East, writers and philosophers, but mostly average folk would find privacy and paradise deep in the forest. But there were others who preferred to find the forest more slowly, by canoe and portage and sweat of the brow. Their successful lobby resulted in a permanent ban on air traffic below 4,000 feet over the Boundary Waters after January 1952, putting an end to the thrill and glamour—and ruckus—of the fly-in lodges.

Nevertheless, the 1978 establishment of the Boundary Waters Canoe Area as a protected wilderness sealed Ely's fate as a tourist town. Almost 200,000 people per year come through the area on their way to paddle the lakes, providing a major economic boon to the community. While you cannot be airlifted to your ultimate destination, Ely is an easy and delightful place from which to launch a wilderness experience. There are plenty of lodges and cabins accessible by road or boat, and outfitters and guides who will help you pitch a tent or catch the perfect fish. Generations of tourists come back every year to stay at resorts that have likewise been run by generations of locals. Many are like an extended family.

On the shores of Moose Lake, Jeep LaTourell runs the resort his father started, "where everything has the fisherman in mind." His twin daughters, Mindy and Missy, run the motor portage to legendary Basswood Lake. A third generation of kids follows in the tracks of the eighteenth-century voyageurs when they launch their annual summer camp canoe trips from the likes of Camp Widjiwagan and Camp Voyageur. And the Baby Boomer generation has produced its own slew of outfitting entrepreneurs, like Steve and Nancy Piragis whose Piragis Northwoods Company presides over the western entrance to town.

The community has a growing arts reputation and attracts upwards of 40,000 people each year for the Blueberry Arts Festival, which features more than 150 local artisans. The galleries and shops along Sheridan Street offer a rainy-day alternative to a hike in the woods and are more than just a collection of mom-and-pop establishments. Patti Steger's Steger Mukluks and Susan Schurke's Wintergreen Designs together employ more than a hundred locals in the manufacture of quality Northwoods shoes and apparel that are shipped all over the globe. The Brandenburg Gallery offers the world-class images of *National Geographic* magazine photographer and filmmaker Jim Brandenburg in a stunning setting that rivals the best galleries in Manhattan or L.A.

By far the majority of jobs in Ely are tourism related. But thanks to new technologies, employment opportunities have expanded into industries like data management and telecommunications. Near Tower, the Soudan Underground Mine is now home to particle physics experiments a half mile underground—a U.S. Department of Energy project that has brought jobs and millions of dollars to the region. Yet, the unemployment rate in Ely is still above the state average.

People live here because they love it, not because there is a thriving job market. They love the town and they love the wilderness. "A bad day in the woods is better than a good day at the office," says Chris Maher, who was first attracted to the place when he attended Camp Widjiwagan as a boy. Like so many in Ely, Chris sews together a patchwork career—canoe outfitting, guiding, trapping, chopping wood, running dogs, painting houses. "You gotta be flexible," he says. "You need a lot of different skills, but most importantly you need to have good networking skills."

Folks rely on each other here. Wilderness ranger Bert Hyde and his family are able to live "off the grid" in a home deep in the woods with no running water or electricity precisely because there are others here who do the same. They barter, trade, and share annual chores like rice harvesting and ice cutting among a community of people who, as Bert says, "are committed to working this way." The weekly paper and the radio station are essential links in the chain of shared resources. Every weekday morning Trader Craig hosts the *End of the Road Trading Post* on WELY, offering bargains and making connections. Someone's looking for a black piano bench or maybe a purebred dachshund. Craig is a natural radio talent and a consummate salesman, combining charm and poetry with a darned good deal. He is always sure to include "free stuff" that is yours for the taking— women's ice skates (size 8), a truck liner (good as new). The *Ely Echo* offers free classifieds for individuals to post their offerings but politely requests that once something becomes your "year-round business," you please be kind enough to pay for the space.

The seasons dictate much of the work. The summers offer jobs like log peeling, where you can make a few dollars a foot scraping the bark off recently felled fifty-foot trees using a razor-sharp drawknife to create the unique contours prized by log-home builders. Theresa Moreland can finish up a tree like that in about four hours; her husband, Leonard, can do it in two. Either way, it allows the mostly retired pair to make a few bucks and enjoy a sunny afternoon together. Dan Olson has been running the Ely Ice Center for sixteen winters but spends summers doing masonry work and guiding. "There's an exchange," he says. "I don't make the money I could in the cities, but I want to be in the woods."

I asked Anne Swenson, publisher of the *Ely Echo*, how this period in the town's history would be characterized. She said, "Tourism and the influx of money." A land rush is on in these parts. Lakefront property is outrageously expensive, and even the tiny houses in town are quickly being priced out of reach for third- and fourth-generation Ely residents. As one person said, "We're going to have more of these million-dollar houses that are used only two weeks of the year, and the locals won't be able to afford to live here." Success as a tourist town, it seems, has a cost. The premium land on which many of the lodges sit has become more valuable than the continued running of them could ever be. Many owners are now facing the agonizing decision of whether to pass on a high-maintenance but much-beloved property or cold hard cash to their children. Lodges like Jackpine on Snowbank Lake are closing their doors after more than fifty years of family operation.

One day, I picked up an inexpensive cassette recorder from the Radio Shack on Chapman Street and started to capture the voices of the people

Andrew photographed for this project. At first I was amazed, but over time I grew accustomed to how many people were moved to tears when talking about their lives in Ely. I would switch off the tape recorder and let them tell me more about their passion for this place. Here at the southern edge of a vast wilderness, barely a century after a few immigrant families braved an inhospitable climate to make a new life and a new town, I find it a privilege to give witness to these accounts. A privilege to hear these new pioneers reflect on the myriad stories that brought them here, the magical beauty that keeps them here, and the resolution of spirit that somehow, someway will ensure them a lasting foothold in their beloved Northwoods.

FACING NORTH

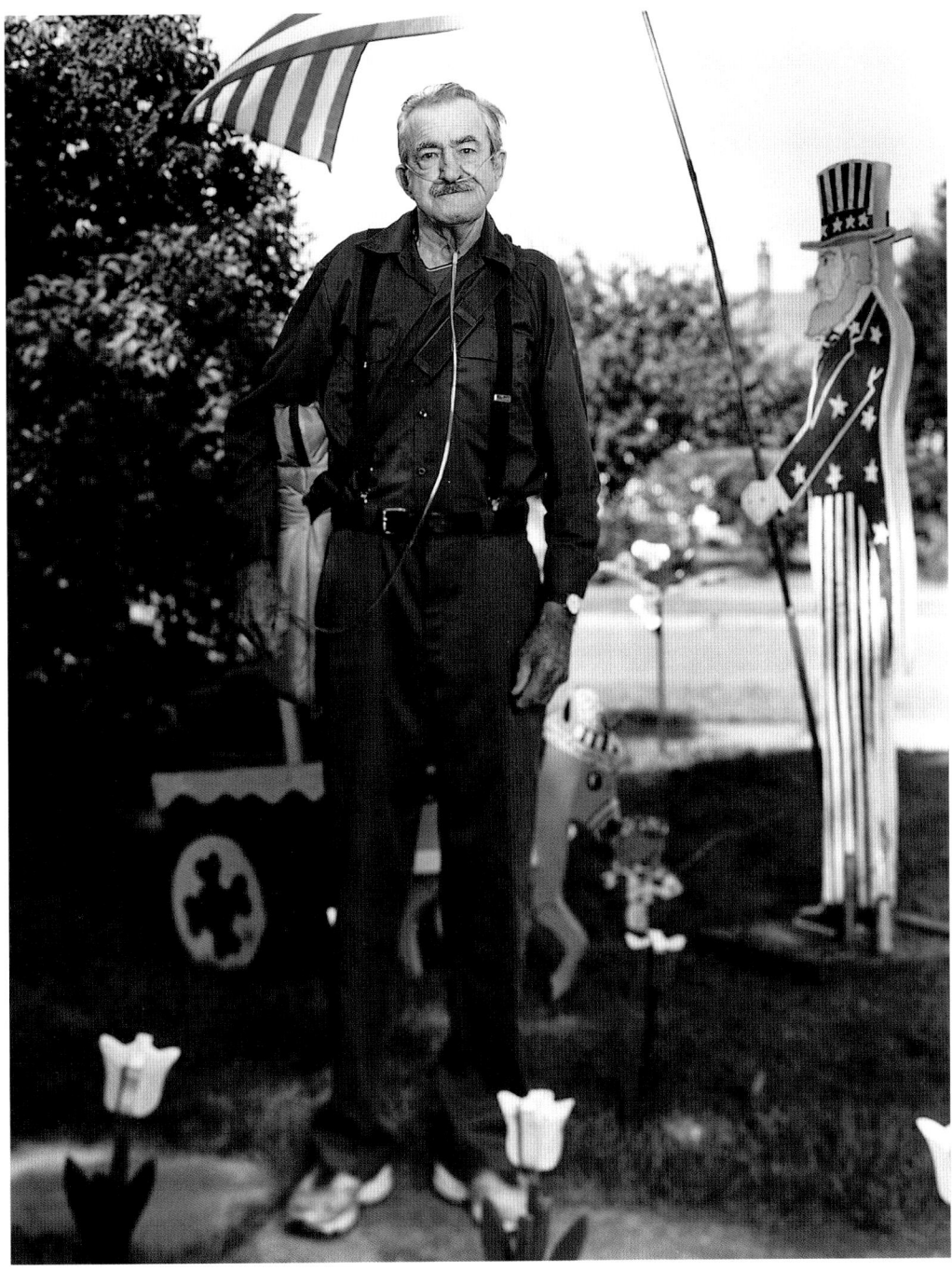

PLATE 1. Steve "Rooster" Lekatz, retired miner

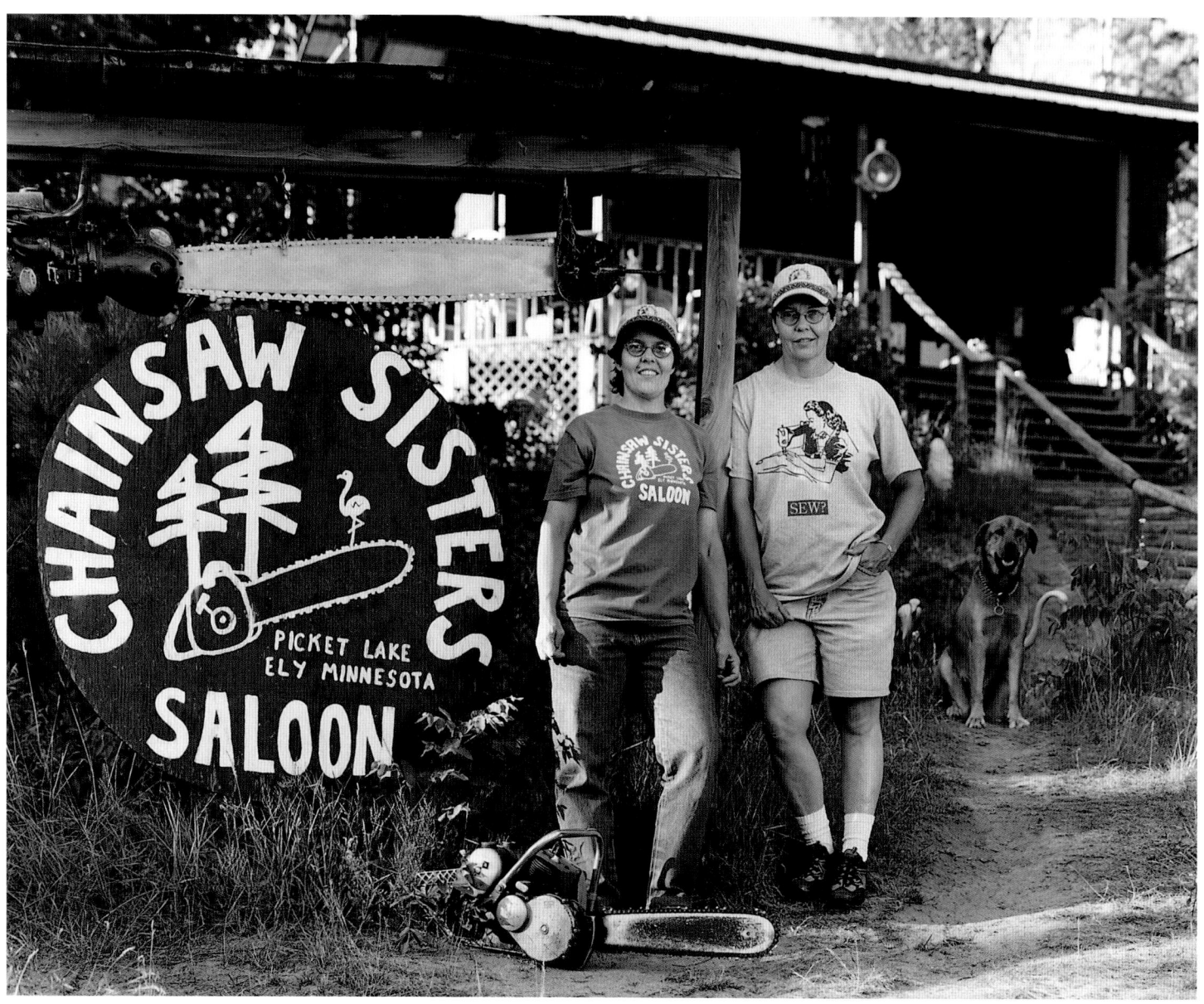

PLATE 2. Michele Richards and Marlene Zorman, the Chainsaw Sisters

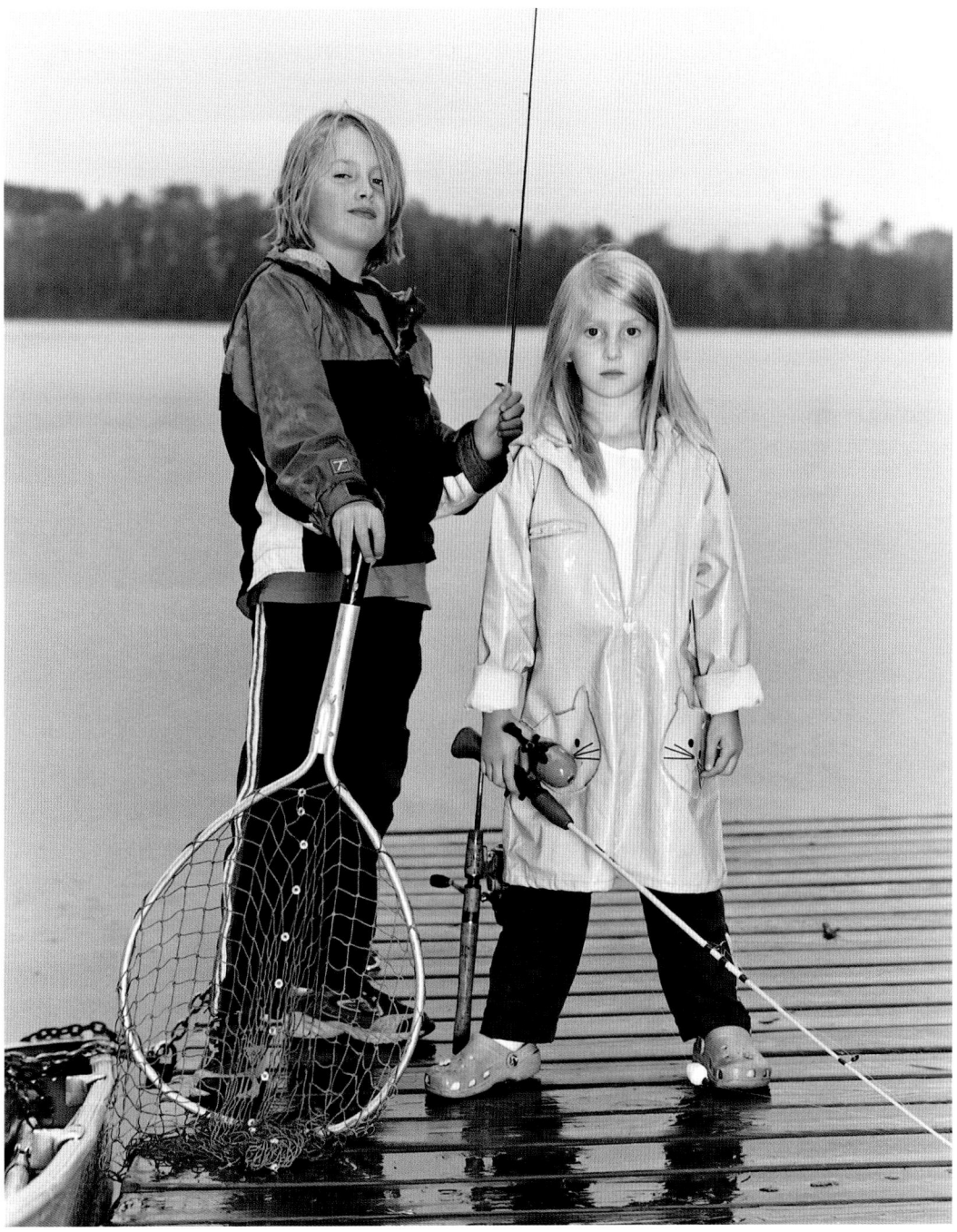

PLATE 3. Simon and Lucy, Ely residents

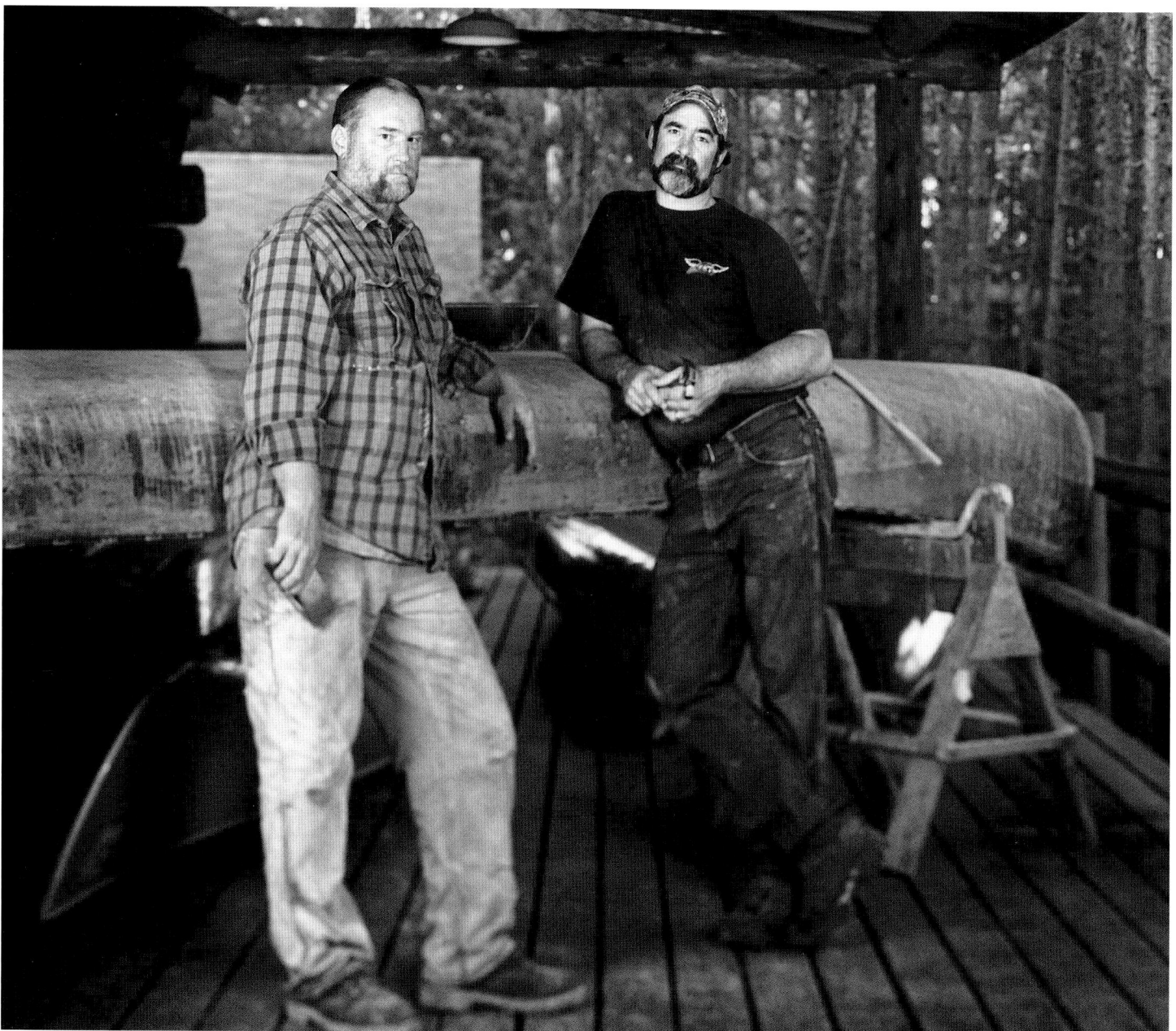
PLATE 4. Joe Smith and Jim Schwartz, Camp Widjiwagan

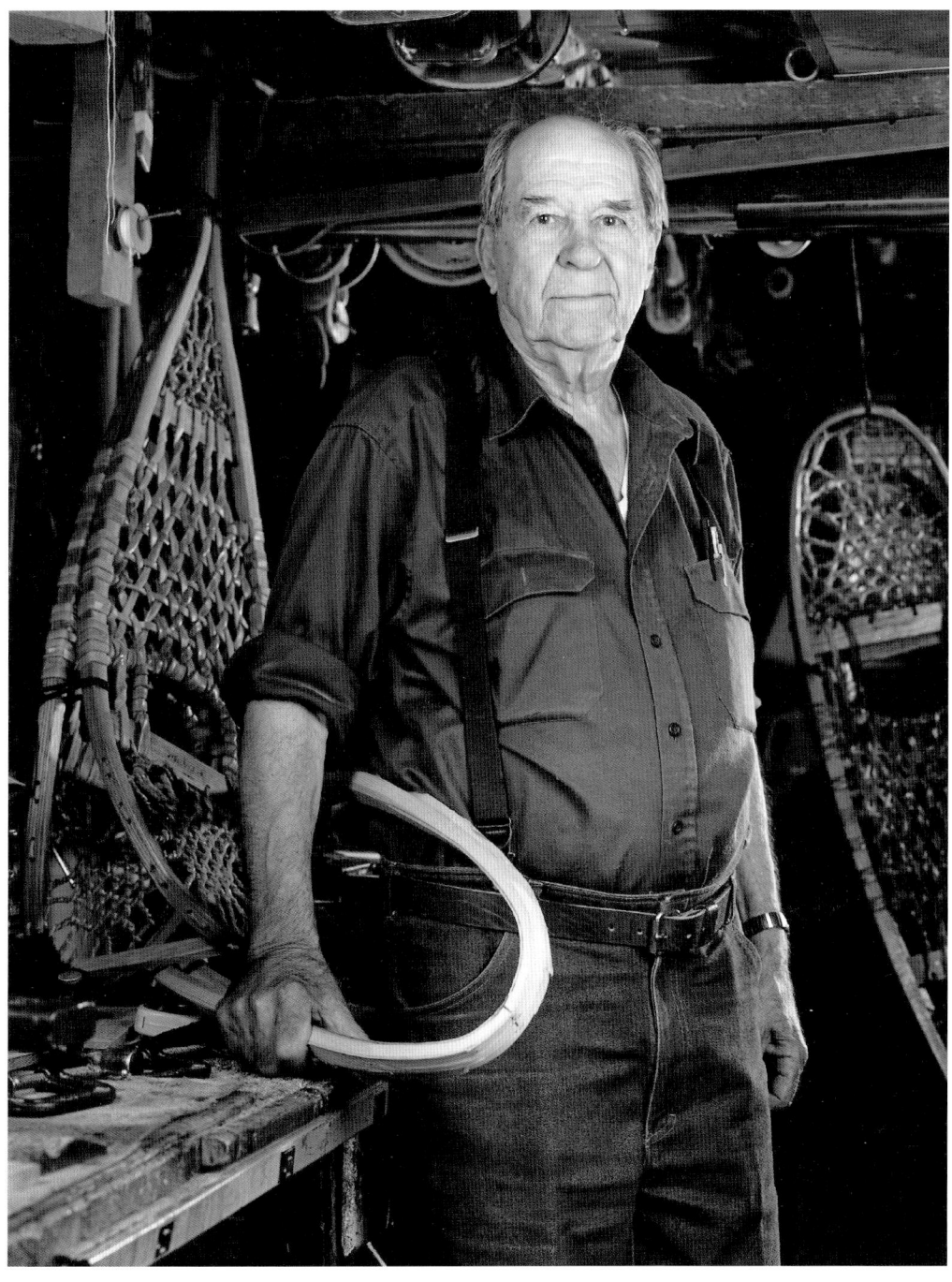

PLATE 5. Joe Prijatel, retired miner and snowshoe maker

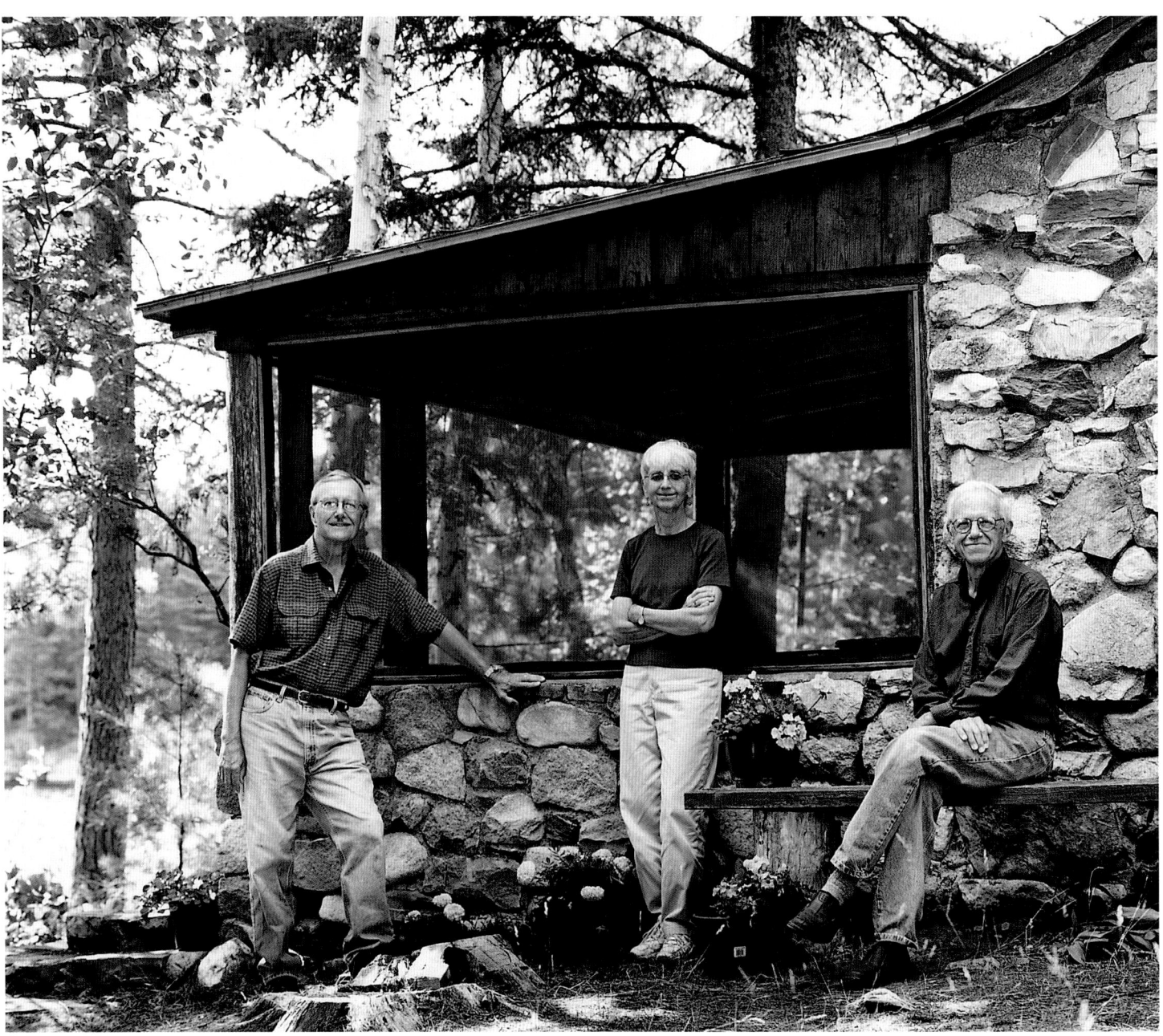

PLATE 6. Peter Schmiechen, Abbie Bahnemann, and Daniel Schmiechen, Burntside Lake

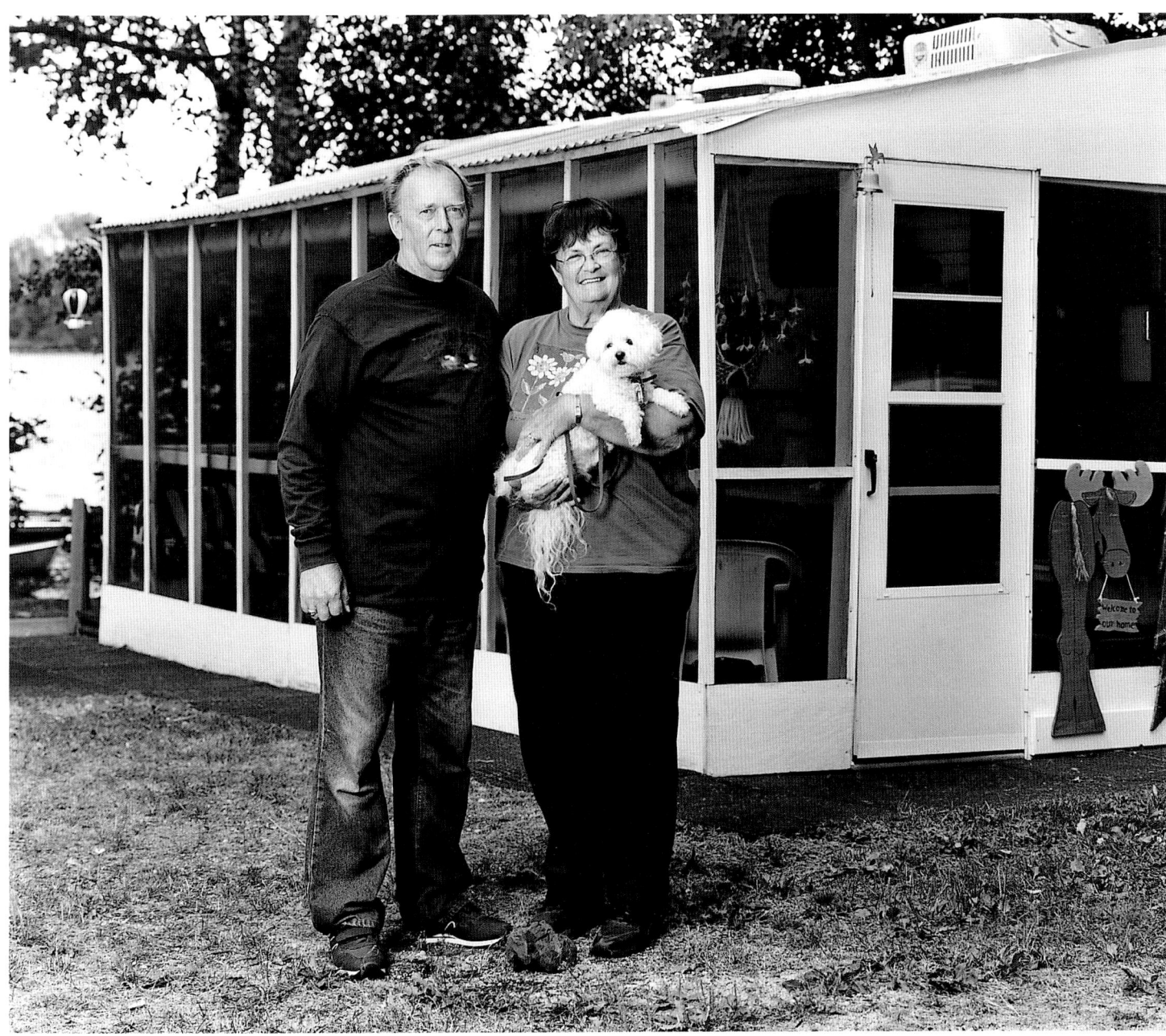

PLATE 7. Dennis and Bonnie Orn, Bear Island Lake

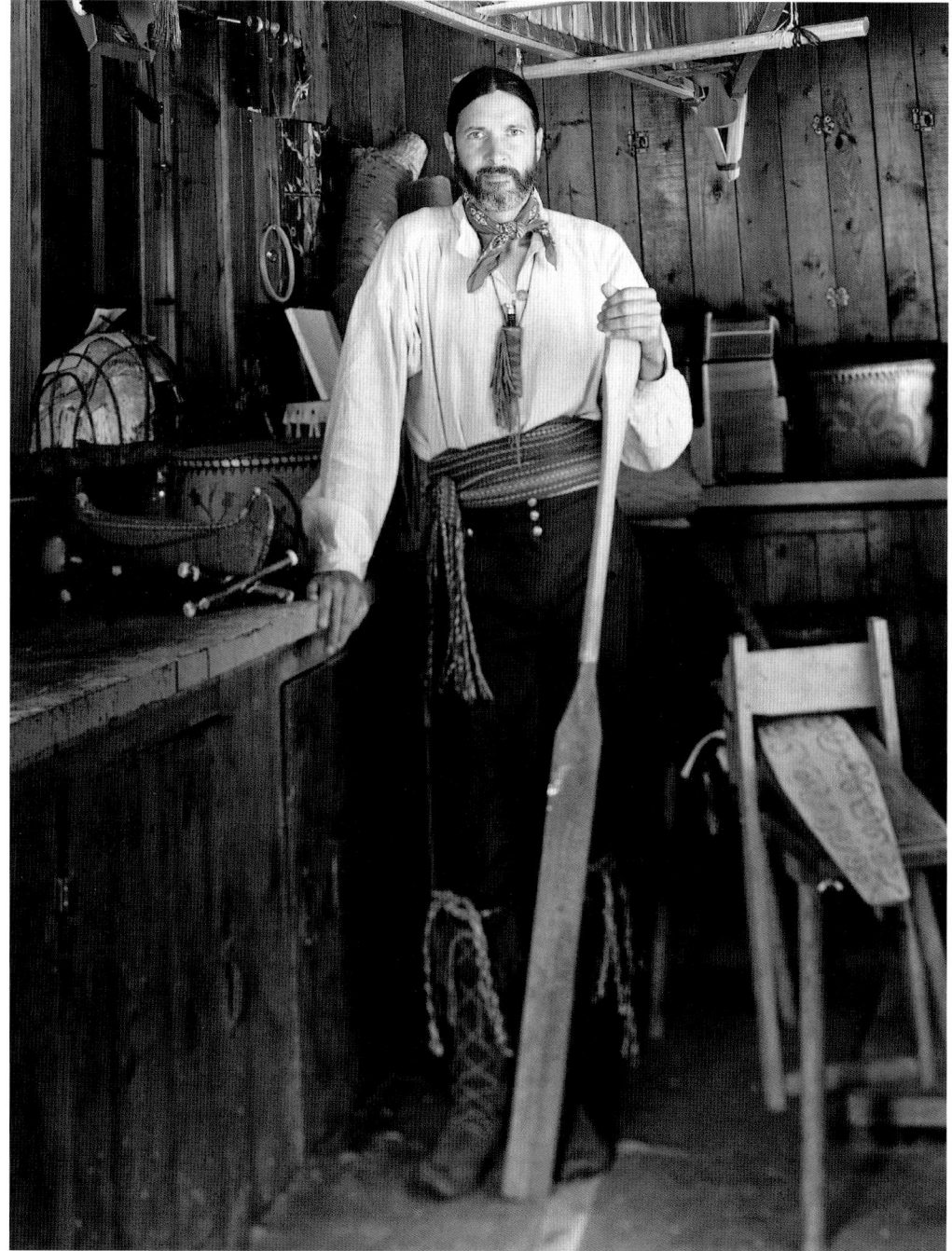

PLATE 8. Eric Mase, Northwoods artist, Wee Cabin Company

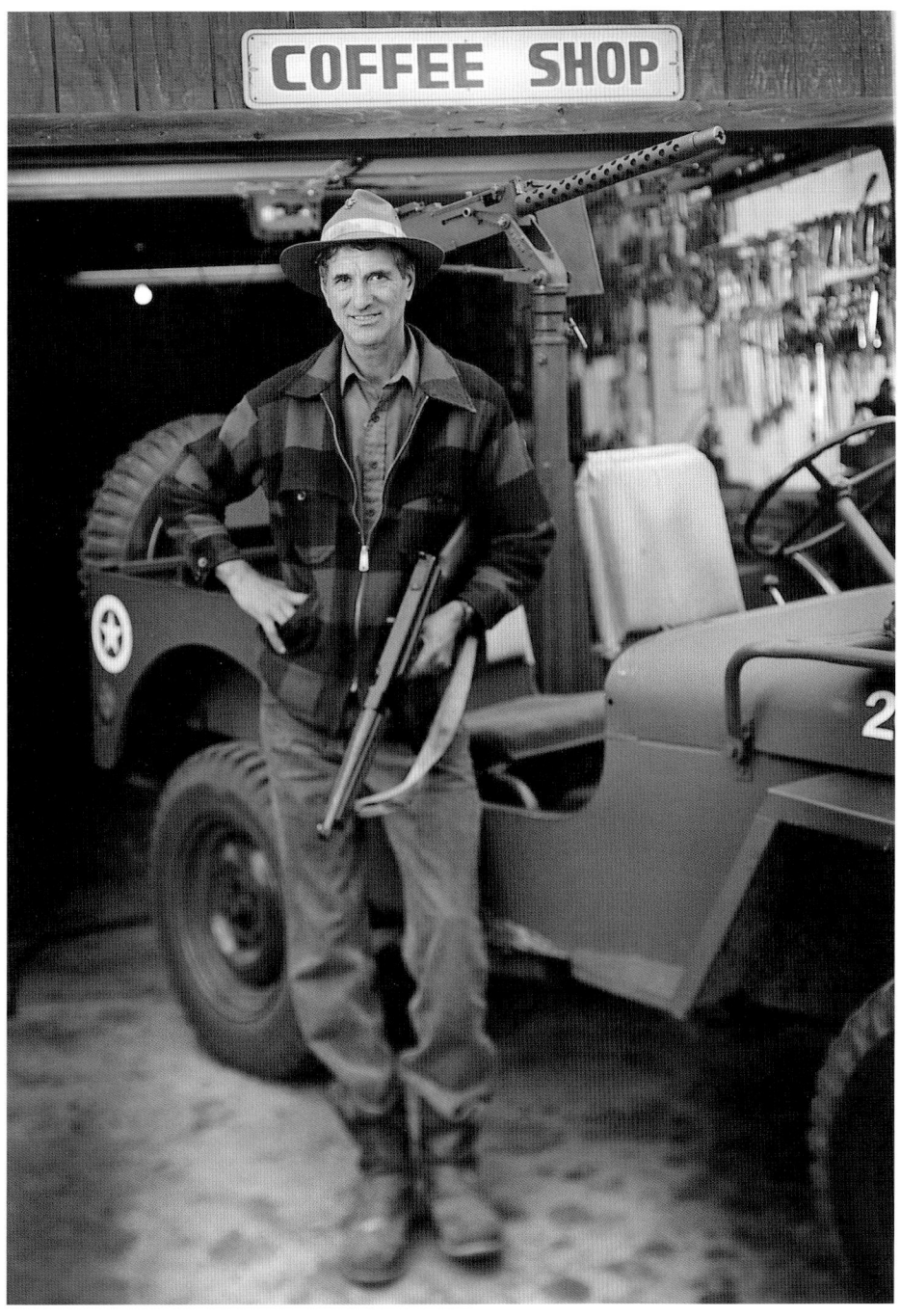

PLATE 9. Seraphine "Sludge" Rolando, retired miner, welder, and artist

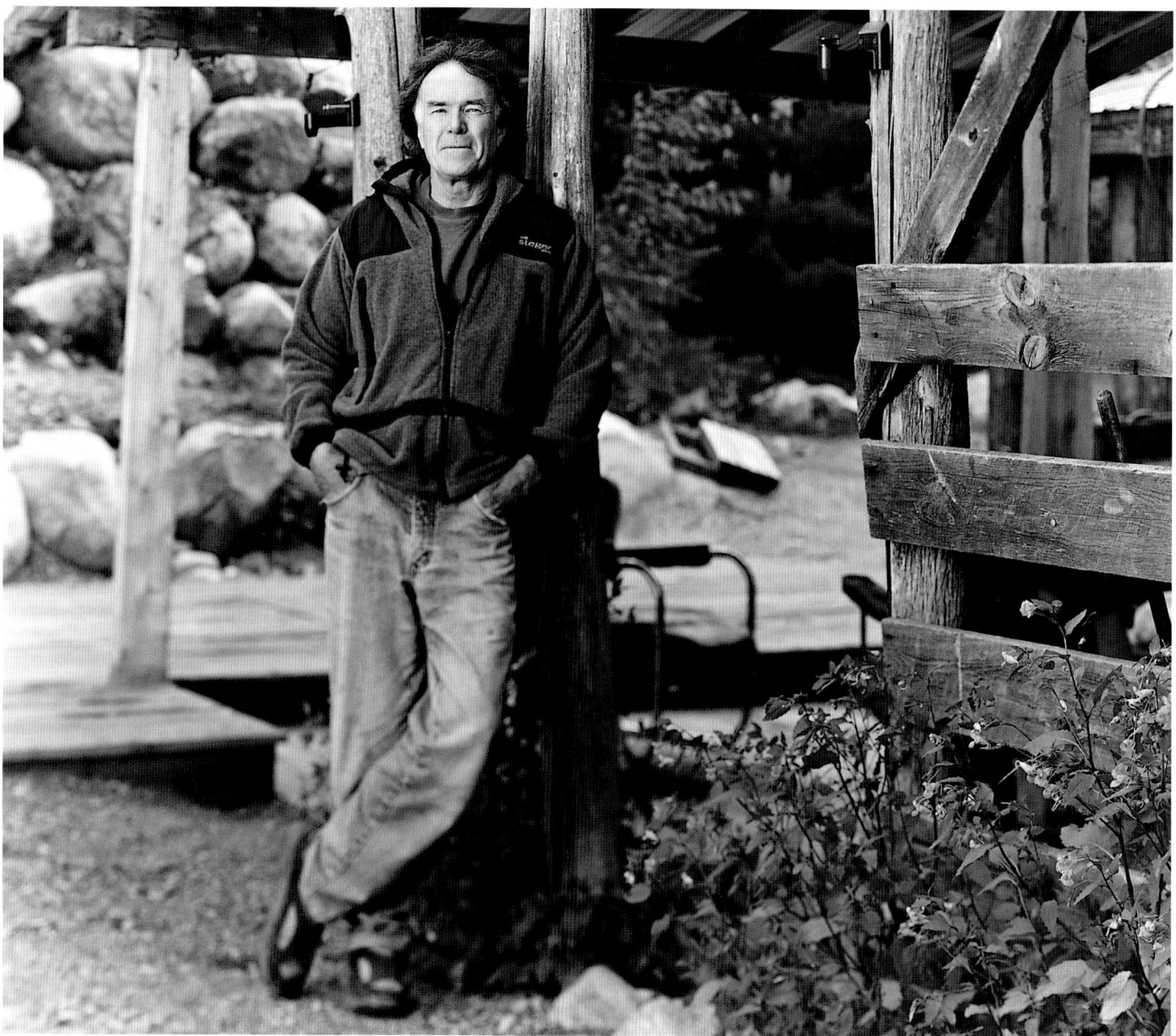

PLATE 10. Will Steger, polar explorer, educator, and environmentalist

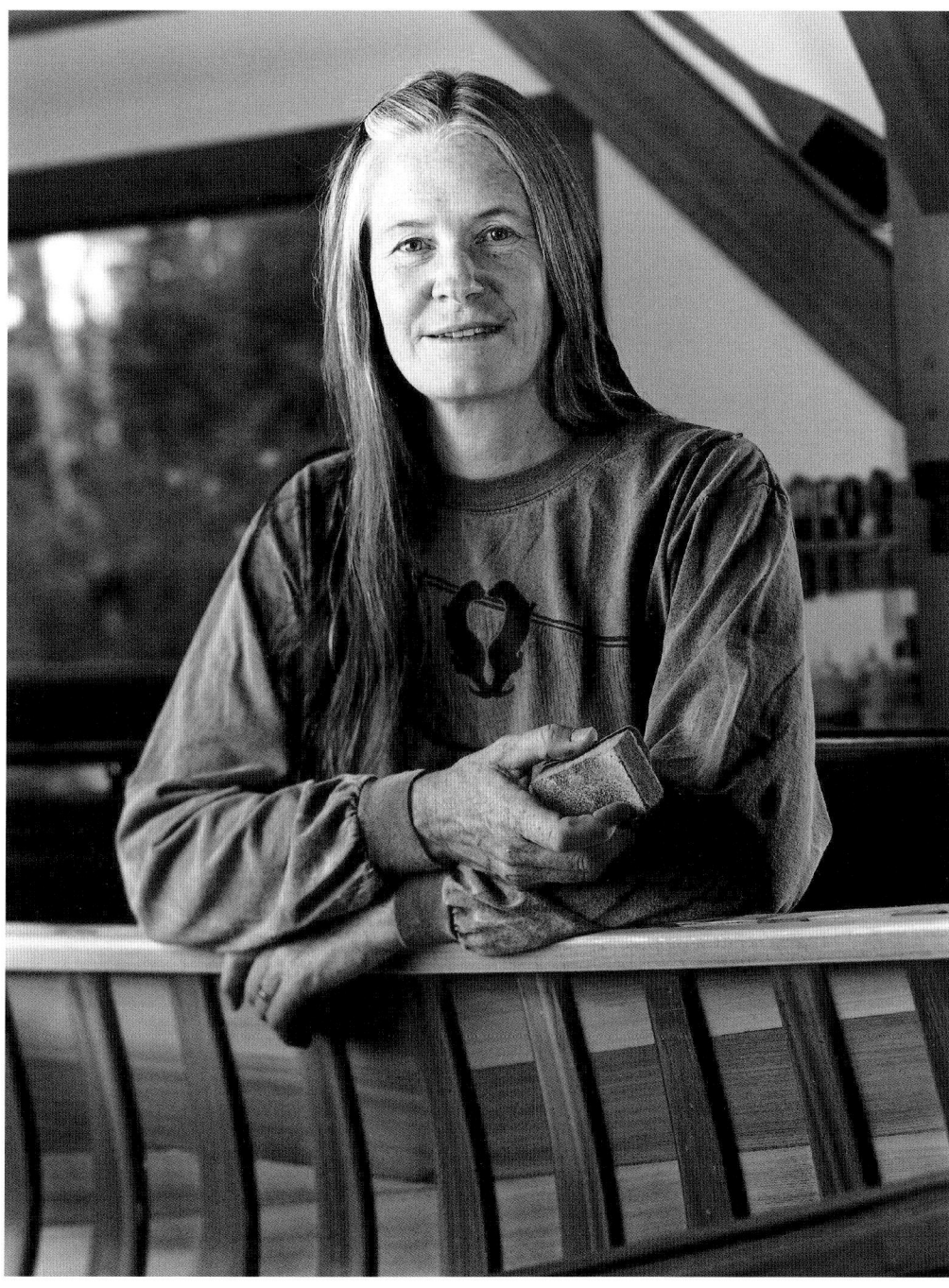

PLATE 11. Jeanne Bourquin, canoe builder

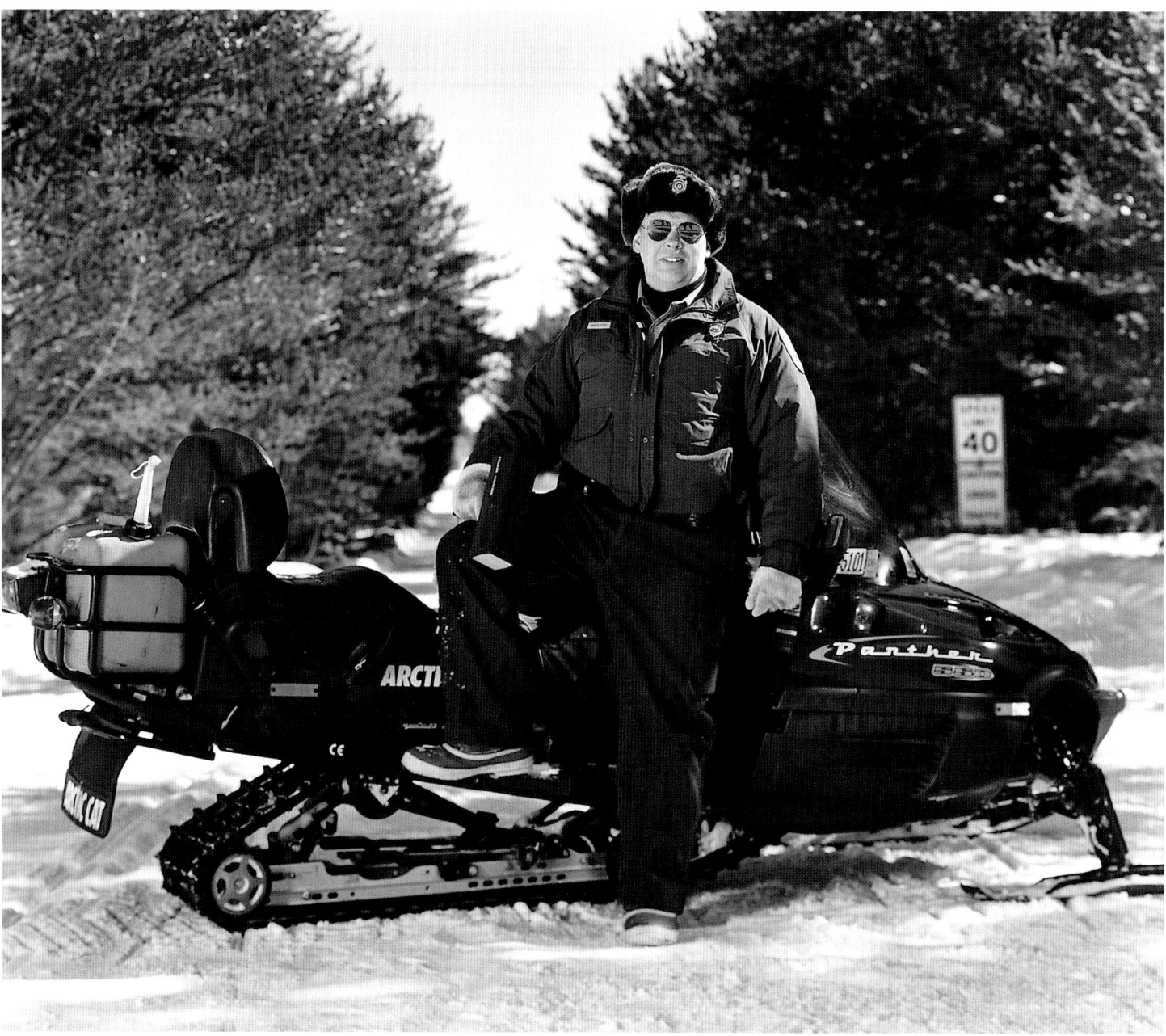

PLATE 12. Marty Stage, conservation officer, Babbitt

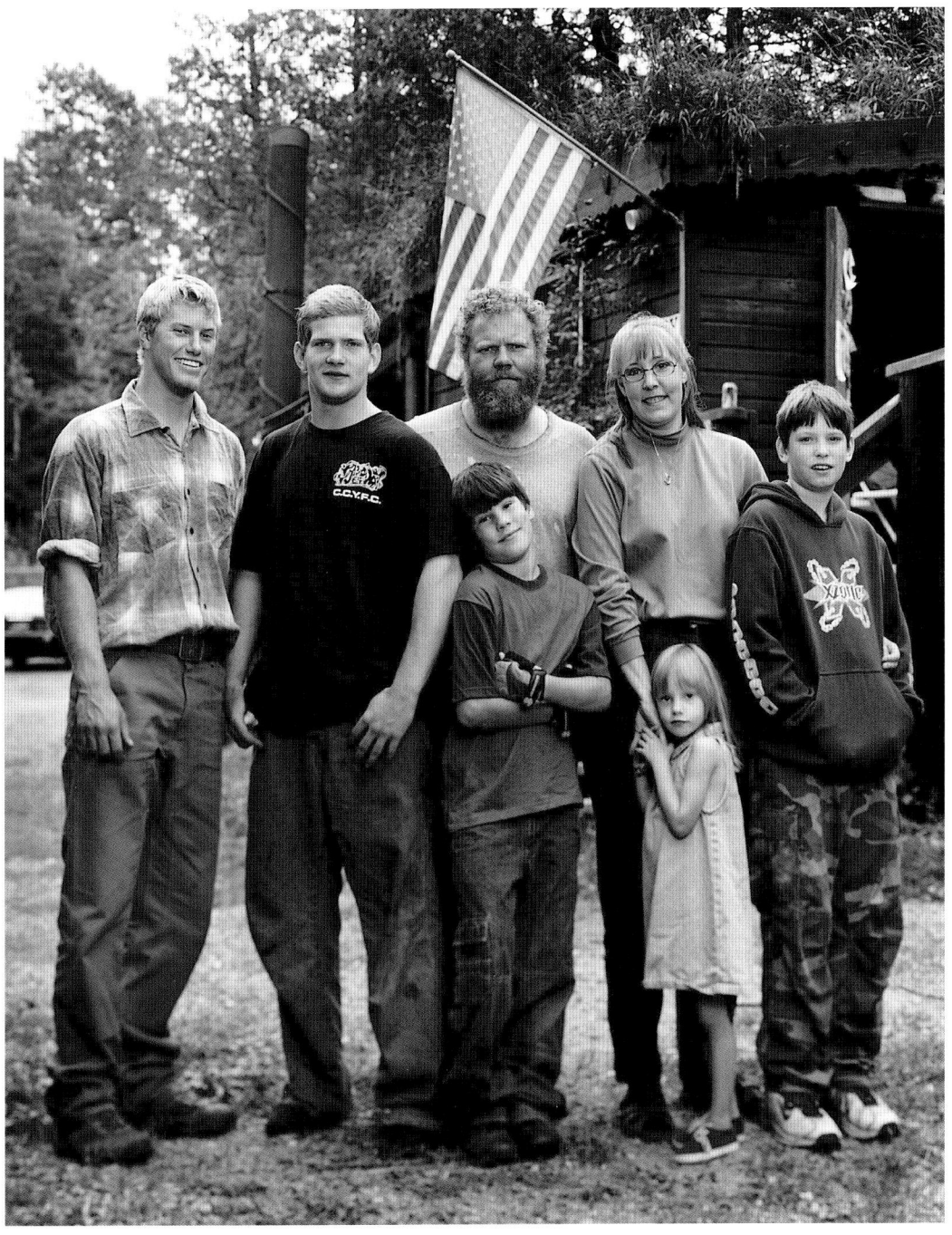

PLATE 13. Heather and Dale "Limey" Tweit and family, Cedar Creek Mini-Golf Course

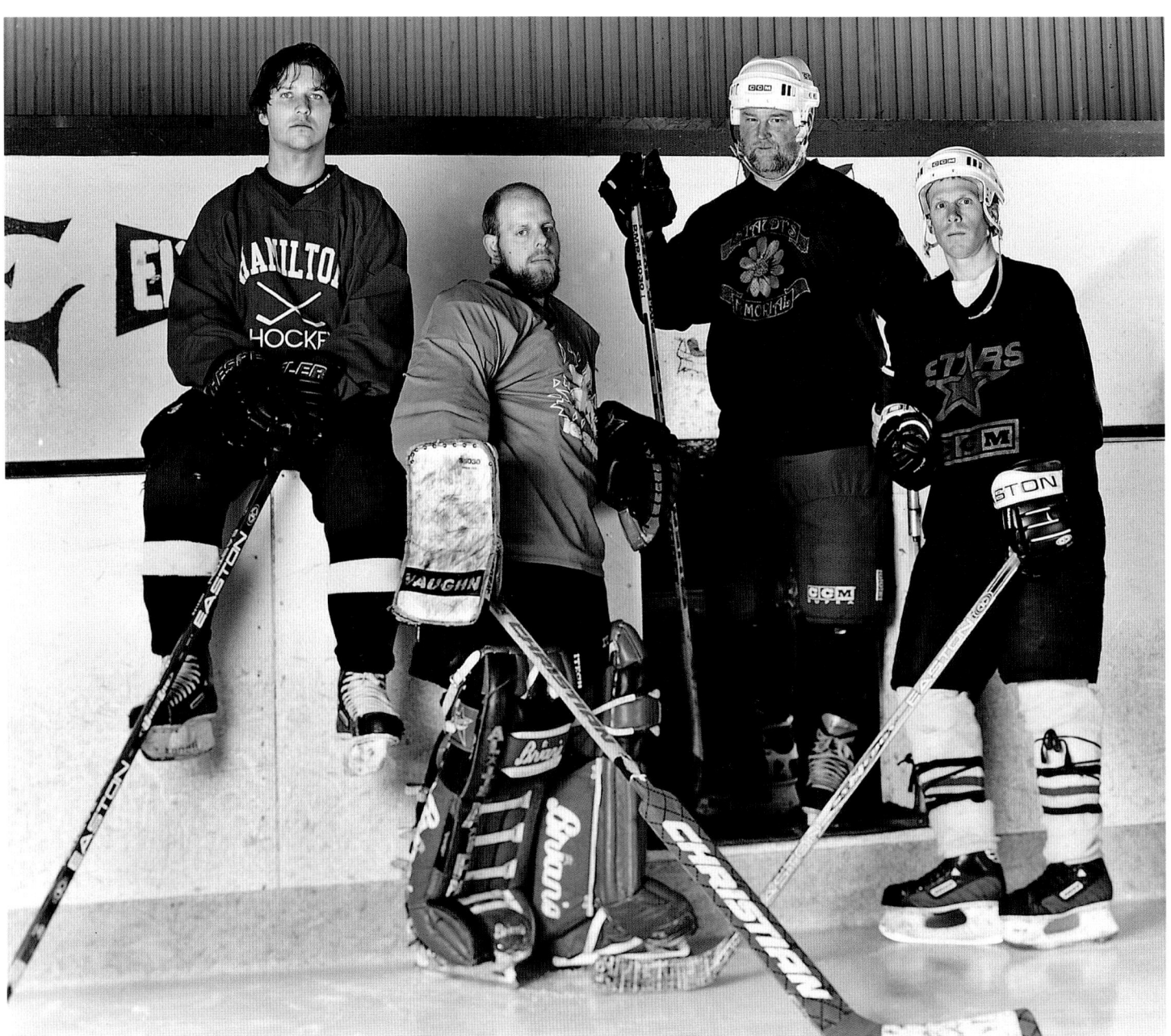

PLATE 14. Kurt Simer, Noah Lucarelli, Joe Smith, and Dan Olson, men's hockey league

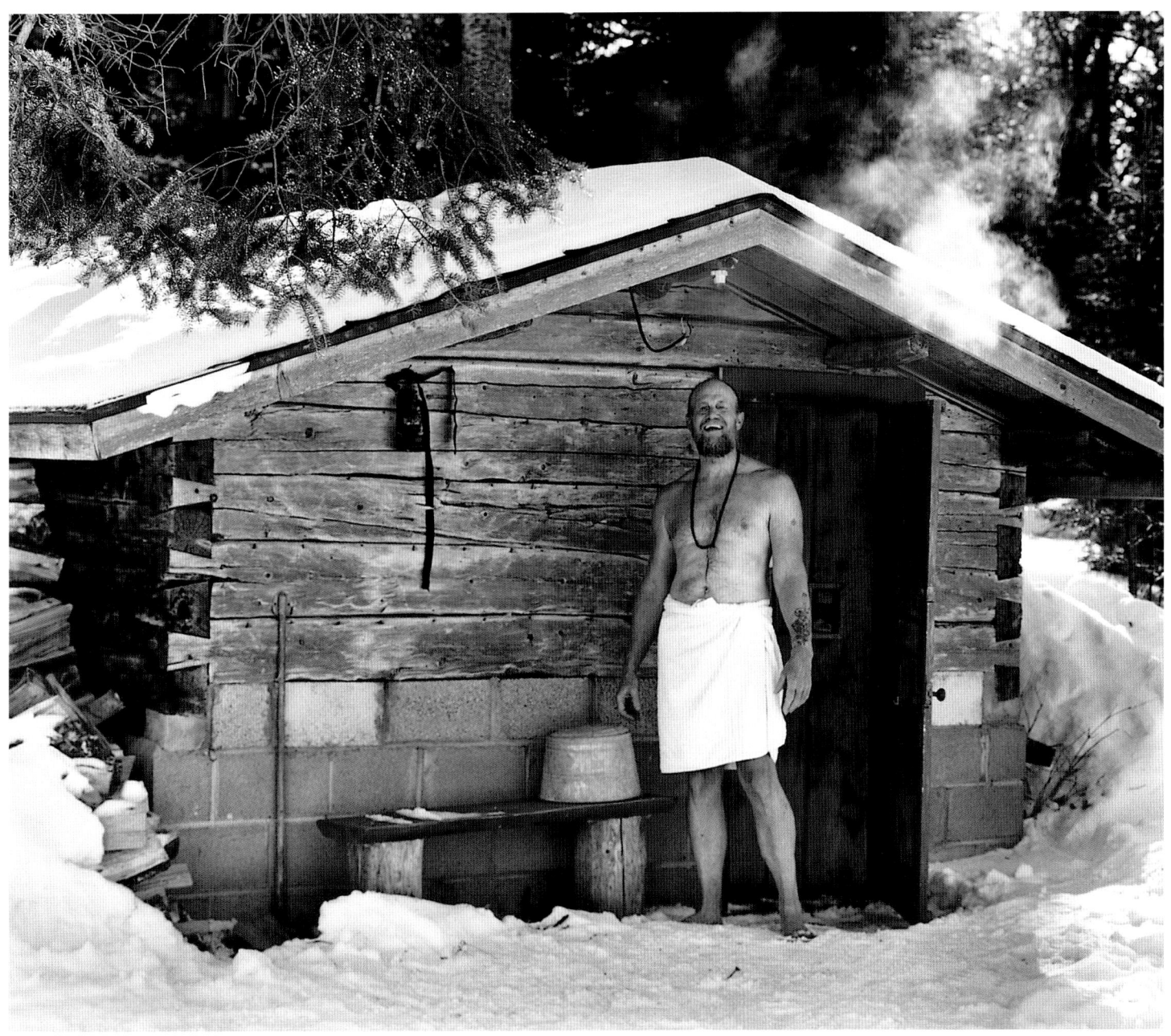

PLATE 15. Kim McCluskey, owner/explorer, Worldwide Paddling Adventures

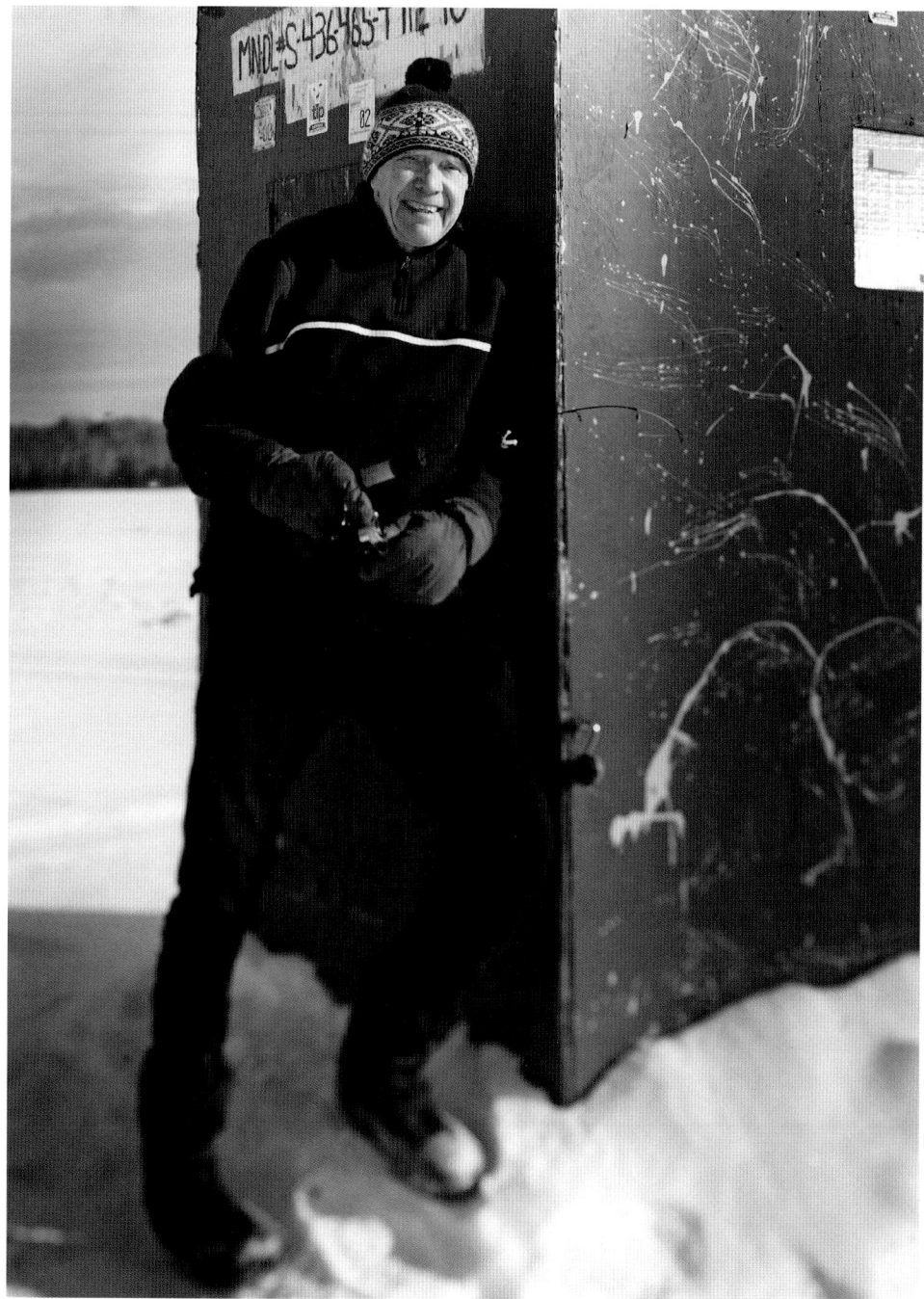

PLATE 16. "Jackpine" Bob Cary, author, artist, and one-time presidential candidate

Green ICE

In summer you could dive from a dock into the still-cold waters of Garden Lake, a few miles east of Ely. As you rose up from the green, you would scatter the winter footprints we made there on a lunar landscape of ice and snow. You might float on your back and disperse the dotted path made by white-tailed deer in February as they made their way single file across the frozen lake in search of nourishment on opposite shores. As you rolled over and submerged again, the last ghostly traces of a transient winter terrain would slide away across your body.

Our host assures us it is safe to walk on the frozen lake. "You could drive your car on it," he says. "We're definitely lighter than a car," I think, as I venture the first steps with my young sons into the undefined zone between land and lake, a seamless border smoothed by a mantle of white.

In a heart-stopping moment, our legs plummet. A thin layer of ice, formed in a recent warm spell, rests about two inches beneath the top layer of dry, soft snow. This fragile, unseen crust cracks, and our feet sink quickly into more soft snow. We are knee-deep, but the soles of our boots rest safely on at least another foot of snow above the ice. We proceed to do what we thought only mystics could do. We walk on water.

To anyone south of Milwaukee, walking on an icy lake seems a foolhardy venture. But to the people of Ely, ice is a way of life, a winter heaven of beauty, sport, and sustenance. After all, their forebears settled this land on the heels of receding glaciers.

The people here fish through the ice; they sled, snowmobile, snowshoe, and ski on it. They cut and store huge chunks of it to preserve their summer food, they trap beaver through it, and they even camp on it. In neighboring Wisconsin, it has recently been ruled illegal to drive drunk on a frozen lake. Who would be so doubly risky?

In such a lake-rich landscape, winter means an opening up and easing of formerly impassable areas, a smoothing of the topography. For the Native Americans, the ice signaled a time to travel. Winter migrations were far easier than the summer portages. Ojibwe Mary Anderson was born on Burntside Lake as her family traveled to their wintering grounds near Lake Vermilion. She lived along Burntside for ninety-eight years, and her children and grandchildren and great-grandchildren are there still today, running Anderson's Resort. In January they plow a circle of snow, brush the ice smooth, and plant torches in the drifts to light up the faces of the family's youngest children as they skate on the lake in the setting sun.

Today, tourists enjoy the exhilaration and freedom of the ice, many of them choosing to travel across it by dogsled, guided by hardy mushers. Carving a six-foot hole on White Iron Lake and jumping in is a rite of passage for the mushers at Paul and Susan Schurke's Wintergreen Dog Sledding Lodge. Bob Nass is one who had to prove that he could grasp his ski poles at the base and use them as picks to pull himself up and out of the frigid water. His reward was an immediate sauna and a good winter job.

We follow our friend and fishing guide Ken Schlueter along the Fernberg Trail to the last resort accessible by car before you reach the road-free Boundary Waters. Smitty's cabins are closed for the winter, but this former Chicagoan maintains a modest income by keeping a makeshift snowy road plowed onto pristine, spring-fed Snowbank Lake. An old coffee tin sits on his counter with a slip of paper that reads, "Road Donations Welcome."

"Follow my truck onto the lake, and we'll drive out to the fish house," says Ken.

"In our car?" is our incredulous response.

"Yup. Smitty's road is like the highway only better. No potholes."

So, we drive our long-suffering station wagon down the shore and onto Snowbank Lake with nearly everything we care about aboard—including our children. And Ken is right, the road is smooth and clear with three-foot banks on either side. It feels like we are on the moon—our tire tracks might be here forever.

Ken's fish house is high end except for the words he has scribbled on the door with a marker: "Fish Stories Inside." Unlike the guys who use handheld augers and sit in lawn chairs, Ken has got himself a six-hole trailer with kitchen cabinets and counters, a submersible camera, a heater, and a carbon-monoxide-spewing power auger.

There is a flurry of activity by Ken and his two pals, brothers Dave and Tony Serena. Holes are drilled through two feet of ice, the submersible camera is dropped, and we get a look at the murky cold water thirty feet below, for what actual purpose still remains unclear despite a detailed explanation by Tony. Fishing lines are dropped, the reels attached to holders on the wall, the heater stoked, and the powdered doughnuts distributed. And then, nothing.

The men spend five or six days a year sitting in this fish house. Sometimes they even camp in it. How many fish do they catch? A few. Ken caught an eleven-pound lake trout a week after we were there. Why do they do it?

"When you get a fish on," says Tony, "you've got yourself some fun."

You cannot see through this ice, even if you brush away the snow. It is green and bumpy and cloudy and thick. It is a window nevertheless, a spyglass onto the creatures that also benefit from the increased mobility that winter brings. The black bears lie hidden in their dens, but other animals are more readily observed in the open expanse of a frozen lake. Even the least experienced tracker can find evidence of moose, marten, mink, fox, deer, snowshoe hare, and the most elusive of animals, the wolf, in the telltale snow across the lakes. The ice keeps no secrets.

As we emerge from a surround of sugar-dusted trees, our boots crunch onto another frozen lake, this time with increased confidence. We are in the company of two trappers, Aaron Chick and Chris Maher, who lead us toward a snow-covered beaver lodge swelling along the lakeshore like an ancient Indian mound or an igloo. "Be careful!" they cry. The ice is fragile near the lodge, weakened by the motion of active beavers as they enter and exit their home via an underwater passage. What? We thought this stuff was safe. The rules keep changing.

Fanning out from the beaver lodge are three sticks planted vertically in the snow, marking the location of rusty old underwater traps held in place with crossbar sticks set across holes chipped in the ice. Aaron ladles new slush from one of the holes, formed since he placed his snare, pulls up a trap, and finds he has caught a young beaver, perhaps a year old, now drowned. He tosses it into the snow to dry it and fluffs its rich, oily fur. We are in awe of this creature's amber-colored teeth and webbed feet. The tail would have been a fatty treat to the voyageurs, and Aaron pounds it on the snow to demonstrate its impressive noise-making power.

Nothing has changed here in two hundred years. Time is elastic. Aaron turns to us in his mackinaw wool trousers, his rusty beard and beaver hat creating a wreath of shiny reddish gold, and he says, "This is my soul. It's all here."

"Ice-in" starts in early December, and a period of near total impassability ensues. If you are rich and perhaps you live on an island, you get yourself an Argo or some other amphibious vehicle. Otherwise you wait. The expanding water moans and groans as it solidifies, an eerie and surprising sound in the otherwise silent woods. Ice can form more crystalline structures than any other known substance—miniature hexagons and squares multiply before our unseeing eyes during ice-in.

Around the third week of December, the ice should be thick enough to venture forth. But how do you know? The trouble is that there is simply no predicting it. Dan Schmiechen has measured the ice on Burntside Lake for decades and come up with an erratic record ranging from eight inches to four feet from year to year. So, you drill or hack a hole and measure the thickness of the ice for yourself. Ken Schlueter tells us that at three inches the ice is safe enough to walk on and at four to six inches you can take your snowmobile or ATV on it.

"Eight to twelve inches is green ice, and you can drive a car or truck on it, but of course, you never know if the whole lake is the same as where you drilled it, so the best thing to do is wait 'til you see a bunch of cars out there." Hmmmmm.

"Ice-out" starts in late March, the fish houses are removed, and the trails closed. The ice gets "rotten," honeycombed at the surface, and only the foolish proceed onto its tenuous surface. This is the time of year when accidents happen.

For all the pleasure and sustenance the frozen lakes provide, for all the reassurances we receive, the truth is that people do fall through, and you are wise indeed to give the ice some respect. Trapper Aaron Chick says, "I fell through the ice one time with a pair of snowshoes on in about three feet of water, and since I was buckled in with my boots, I had to go down and release my boots out of the bindings. As soon as I was out, I stripped down to my underwear and ran back to the car." Aaron was lucky to have a car nearby. Jack London's story *To Build a Fire* tells the story of a man who simply gets one foot wet on a break-through and dies quickly of hypothermia. It is, no pun intended, a chilling tale.

Every season a few people near Ely drown when they fall through the ice over deeper water. One winter a man went through the ice on a nearby lake and, with his backpack weighing him down, paused long enough at the surface to throw his hat as far as he could across the ice so his family might find his body. Would you think of doing that in your final moment? He must surely have rehearsed just such a scenario in his mind, as have many others who hope never to enact a similar scene. Snowmobiles are particularly susceptible to all kinds of accidents—they are involved in more fatalities than firearms in this part of the world—and falling through the ice on them is not an unusual occurrence.

One common piece of advice in the event you do fall through is to carry a long pole to use like you would if you fell in quicksand, throwing it across the hole and using it to steady you as you climb out. This assumes that two opposing sides of your hole are solid enough to hold you—not a bet I would take. Another frequent suggestion is to carry a sharp object like a pick, screwdriver, or even a set of keys to use as leverage to pull yourself out. Most people drown in the first minute, even in still water, because of "cold shock," during which the body responds in part by hyperventilating, not a good thing to be doing if your head dips underwater. Hypothermia is the next danger, so once your breathing is calm you should get yourself out fast!

A friend told us of an acquaintance who was uncertain about the ice but drove on it anyway. As a precaution, he undid his seatbelt and rolled down his window. Good thing, because he was able to slip through the window and swim up to the surface when his truck did in fact go through. I kid you not.

Will Steger, famed polar explorer and educator, has pulled many a dog and expedition member from stunning ice crevasses in Antarctica and has traversed the most hazardous of ice floes at the North Pole. Here at home in Ely he makes a party out of the ice on Picket Lake. More than sixty people gather for the annual "Ice Ball" on a sunny February day to fill up Steger's ice house, where he will keep his vegetables in perfect cool humidity all summer long.

With the promise of a feast and a heel-kicking music concert, partygoers first chip through the ice with hammer and chisel. Once the first hole is dug, a chainsaw is used to carve enormous blocks of quartz-like ice, which are loaded onto a Bobcat and driven up the hill for storage in the ice house—a five-foot-by-seven-foot vault. By the end of the day, the revelers are knee-deep in slush with mist rising from their shins, the unseasonable warmth turning their ice party into a watery enterprise. Only water has the capacity to move so easily between solid, liquid, and vapor.

As my sons and I step onto a small island in Garden Lake, we cannot help but breathe a little easier. We are on solid ground. A week later, we are unafraid of this shiny landscape, dreading instead our return to a different, grayer kind of winter in Chicago.

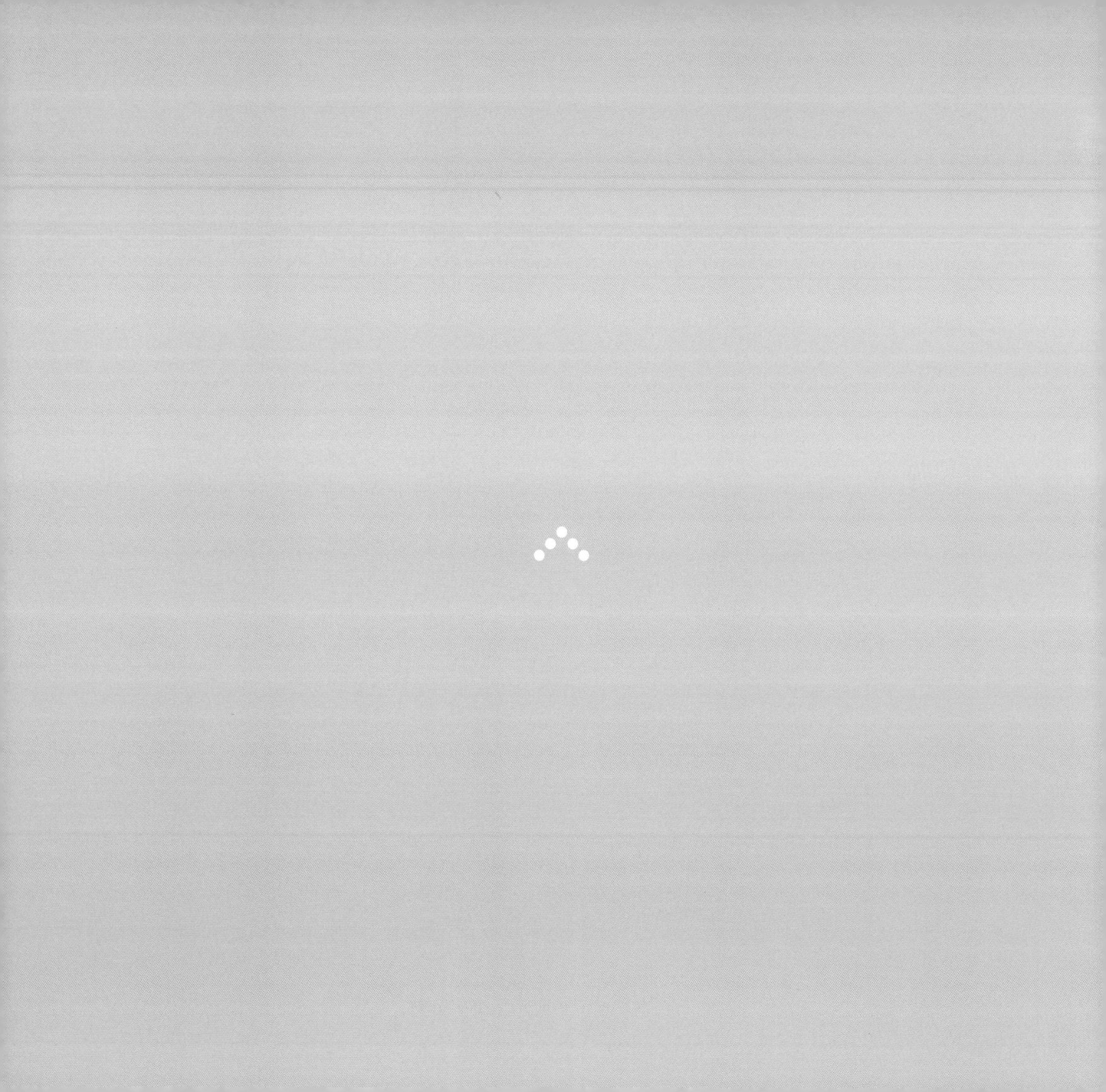

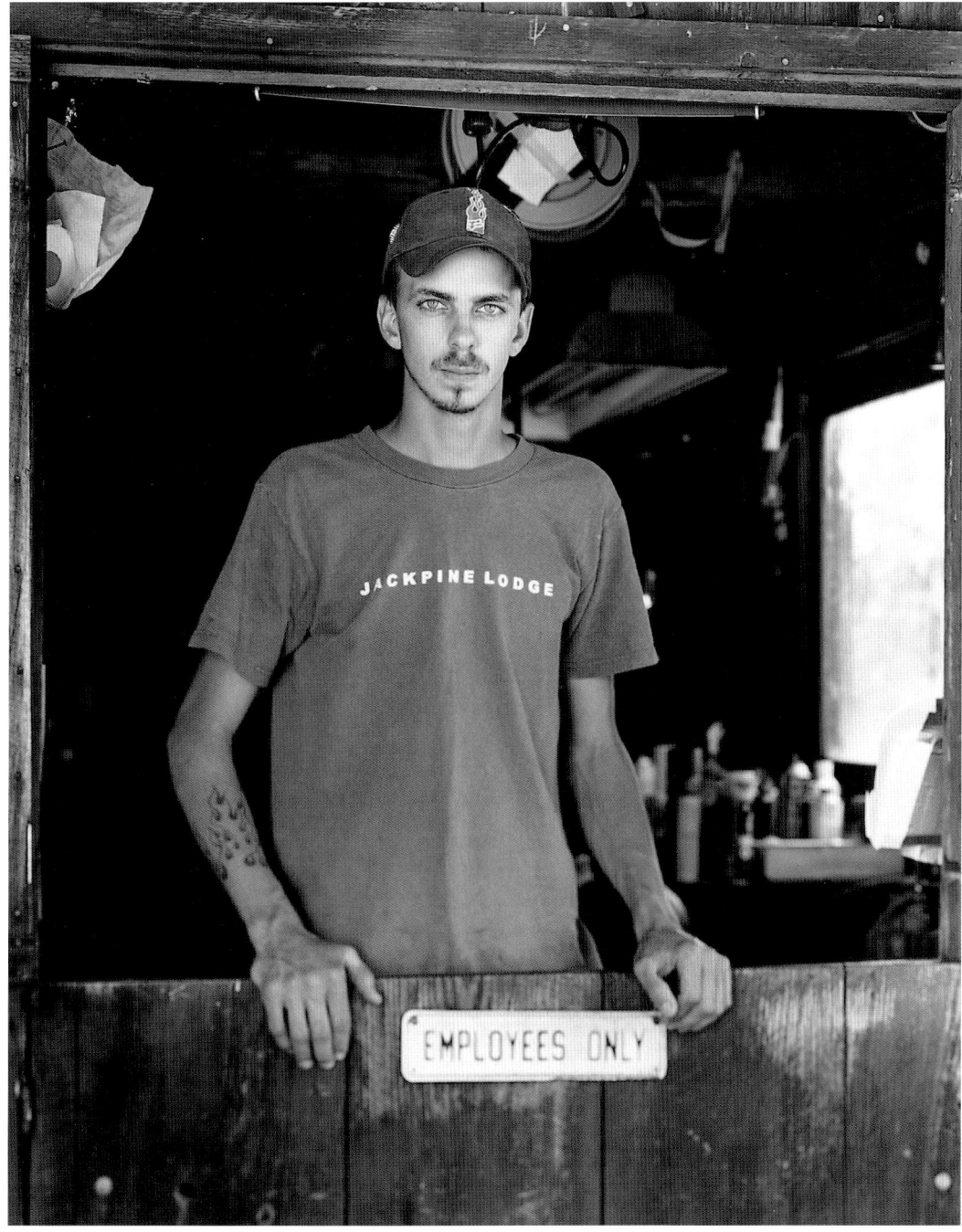

PLATE 17. Roger Nyquist, Jackpine Lodge

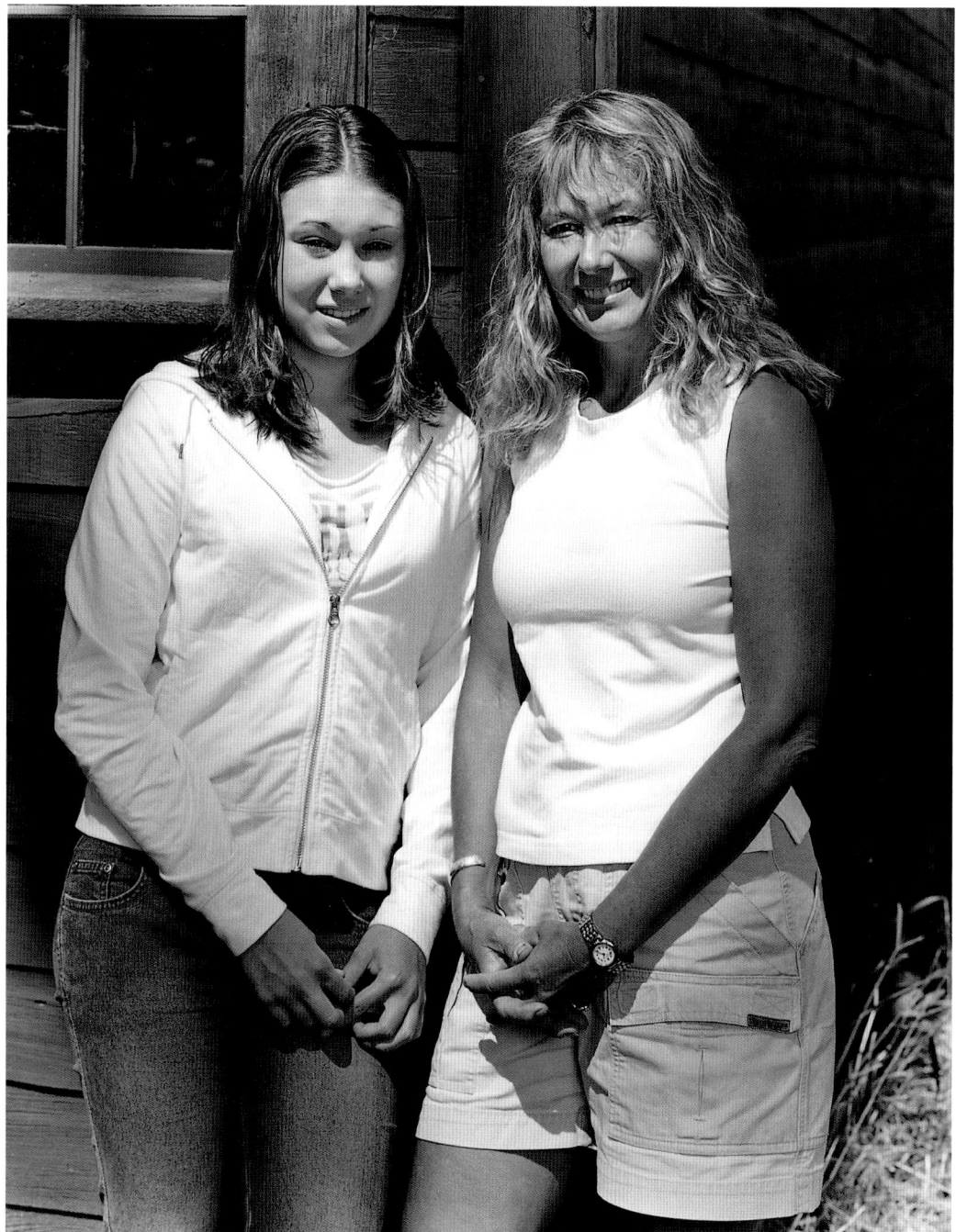

PLATE 18. Elli and Nancy Piragis, Ely residents

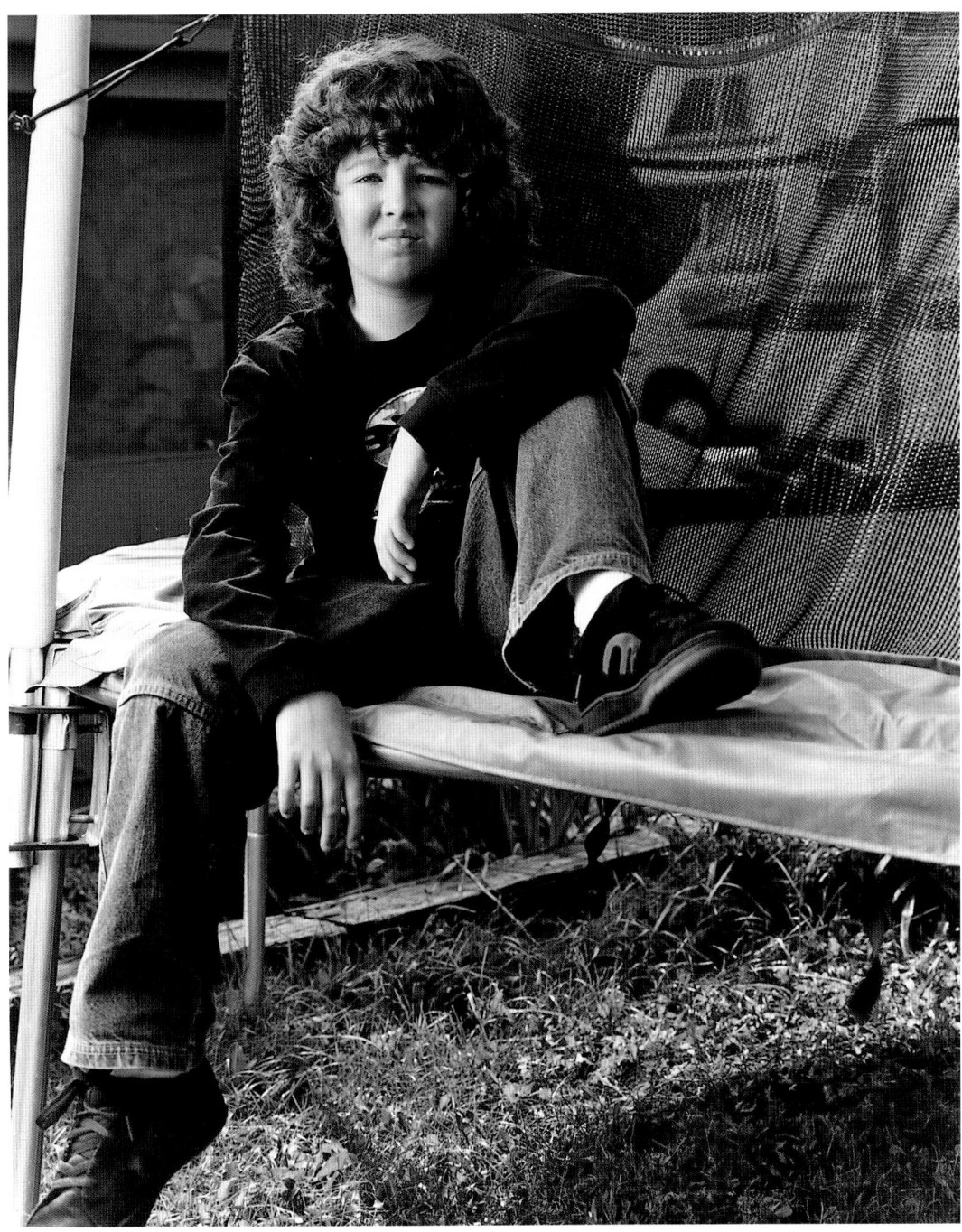

PLATE 19. Colton, Ely resident

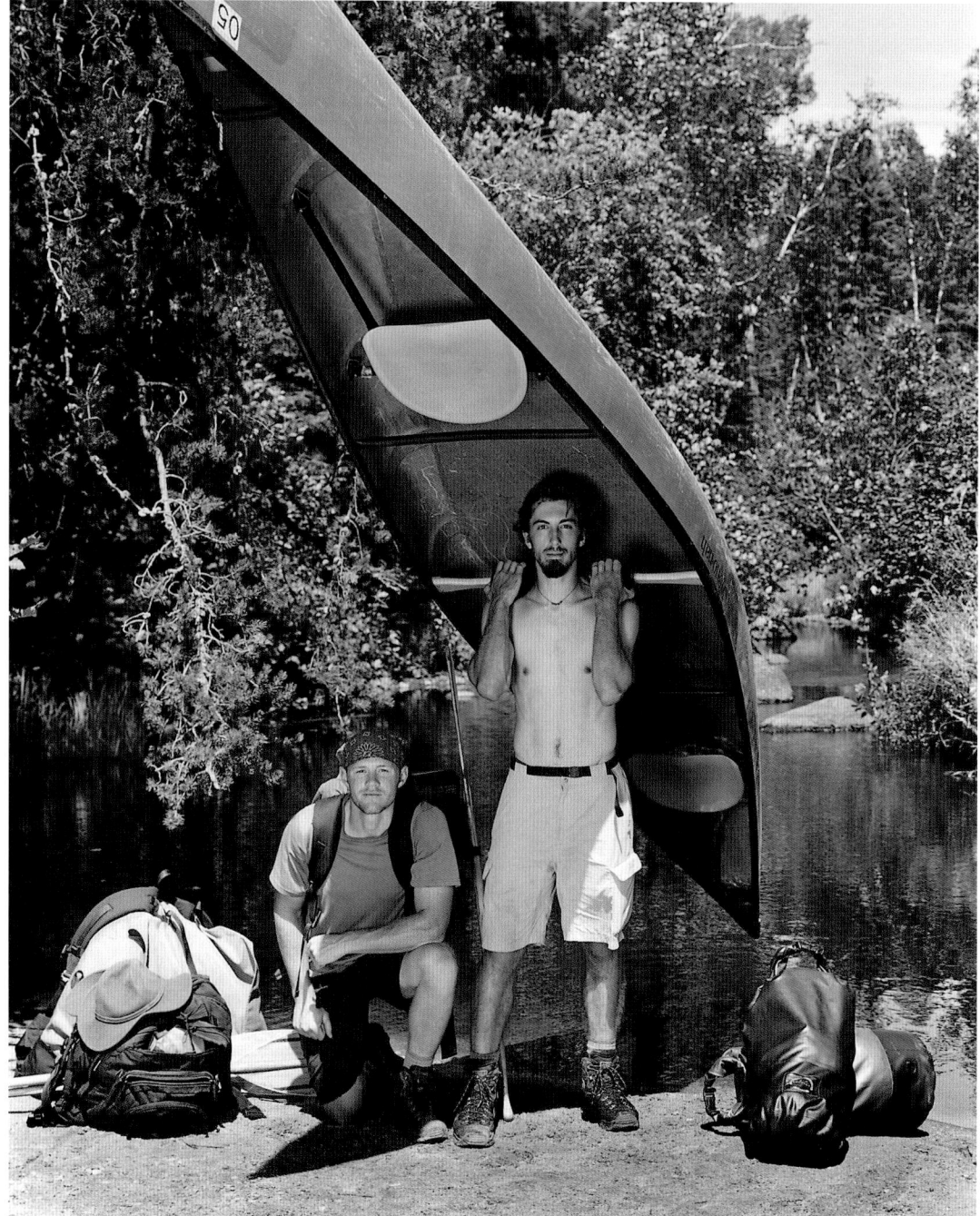

PLATE 20. James Kurzdorfer and Ryan Jones, Mudro Lake Access Point, Boundary Waters Canoe Area Wilderness

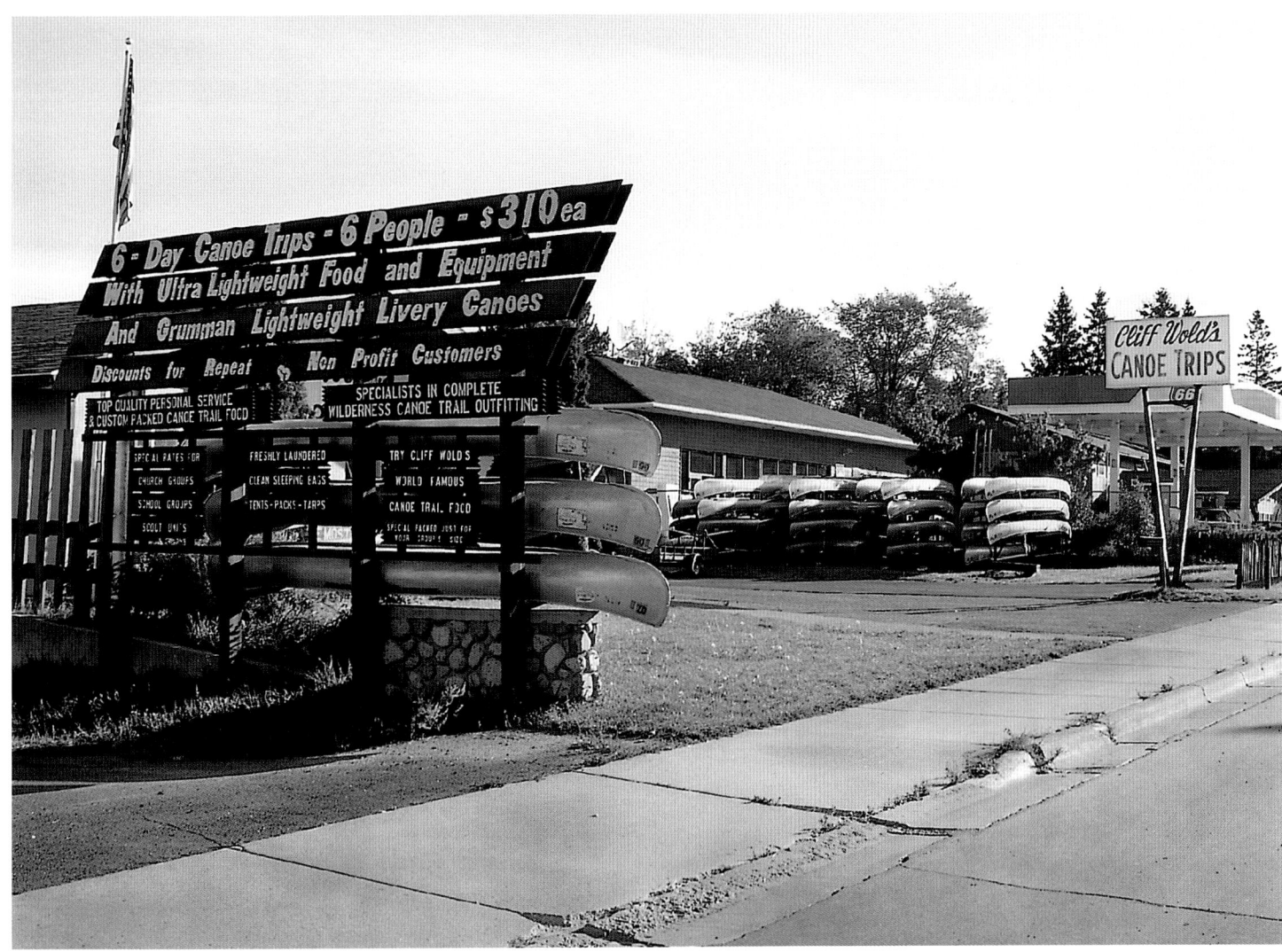

PLATE 21. East Sheridan Street, Ely

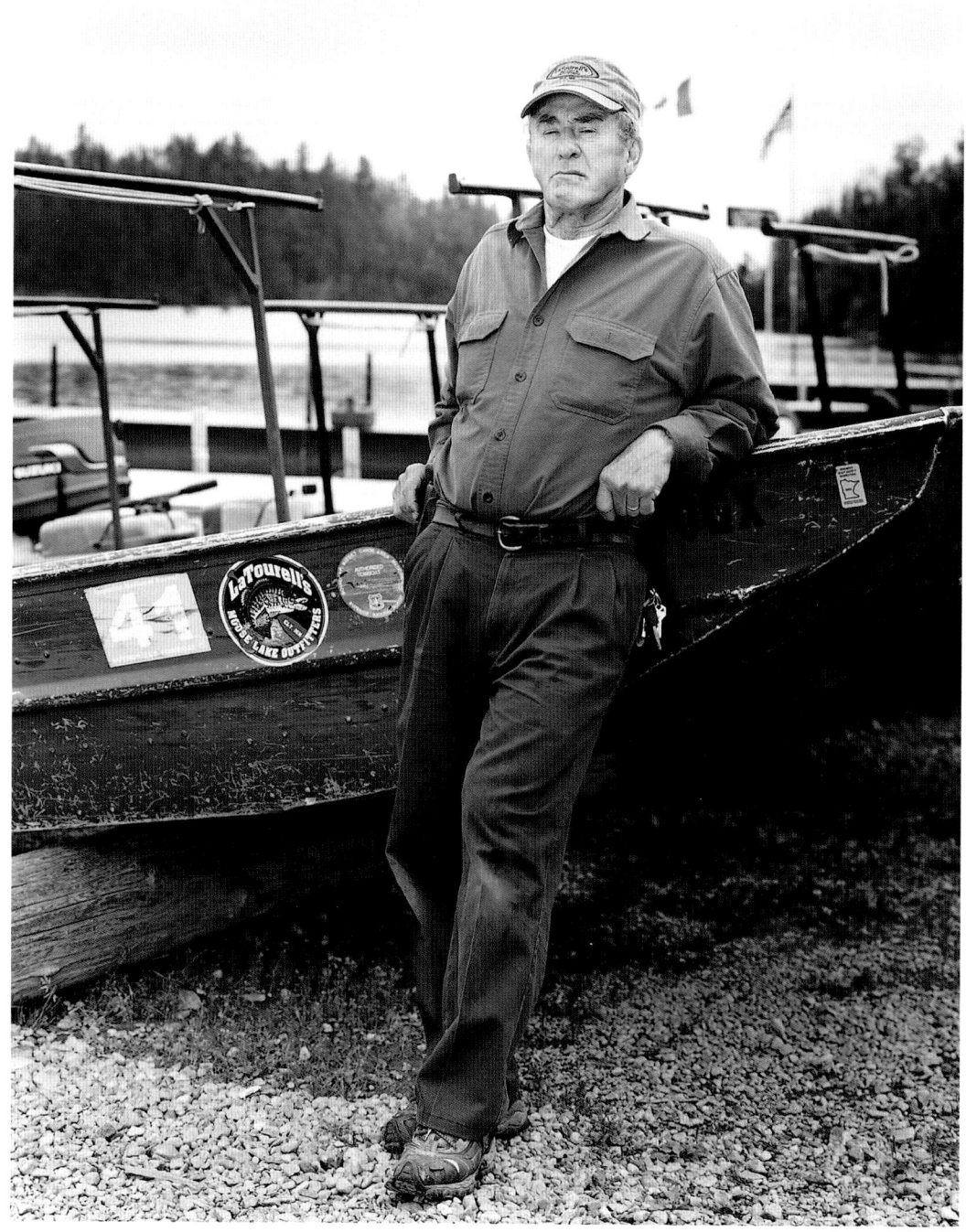

PLATE 22. Robert "Jeep" LaTourell, LaTourell's Moose Lake Resort

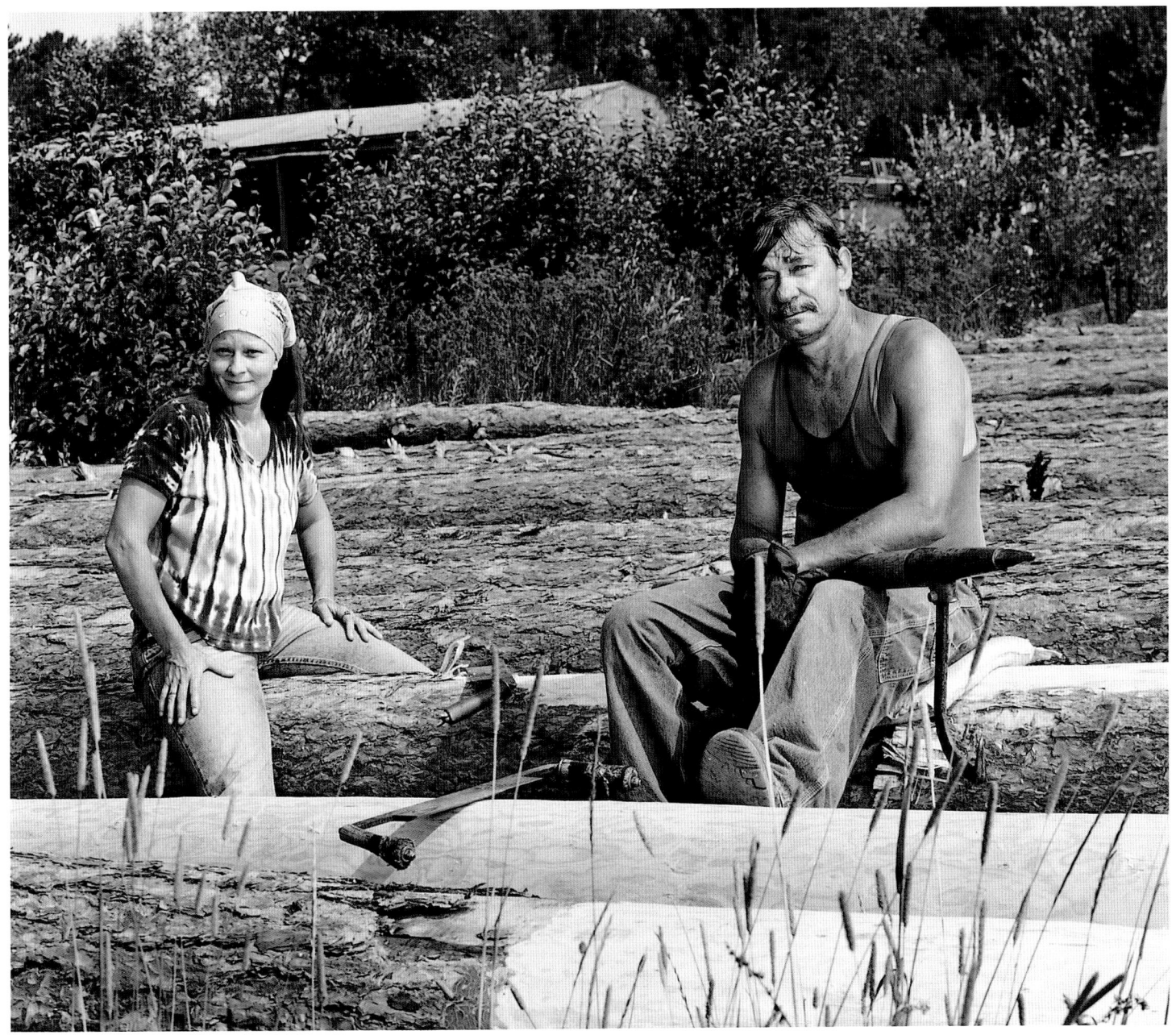

PLATE 23. Theresa and Leonard Moreland, log peelers

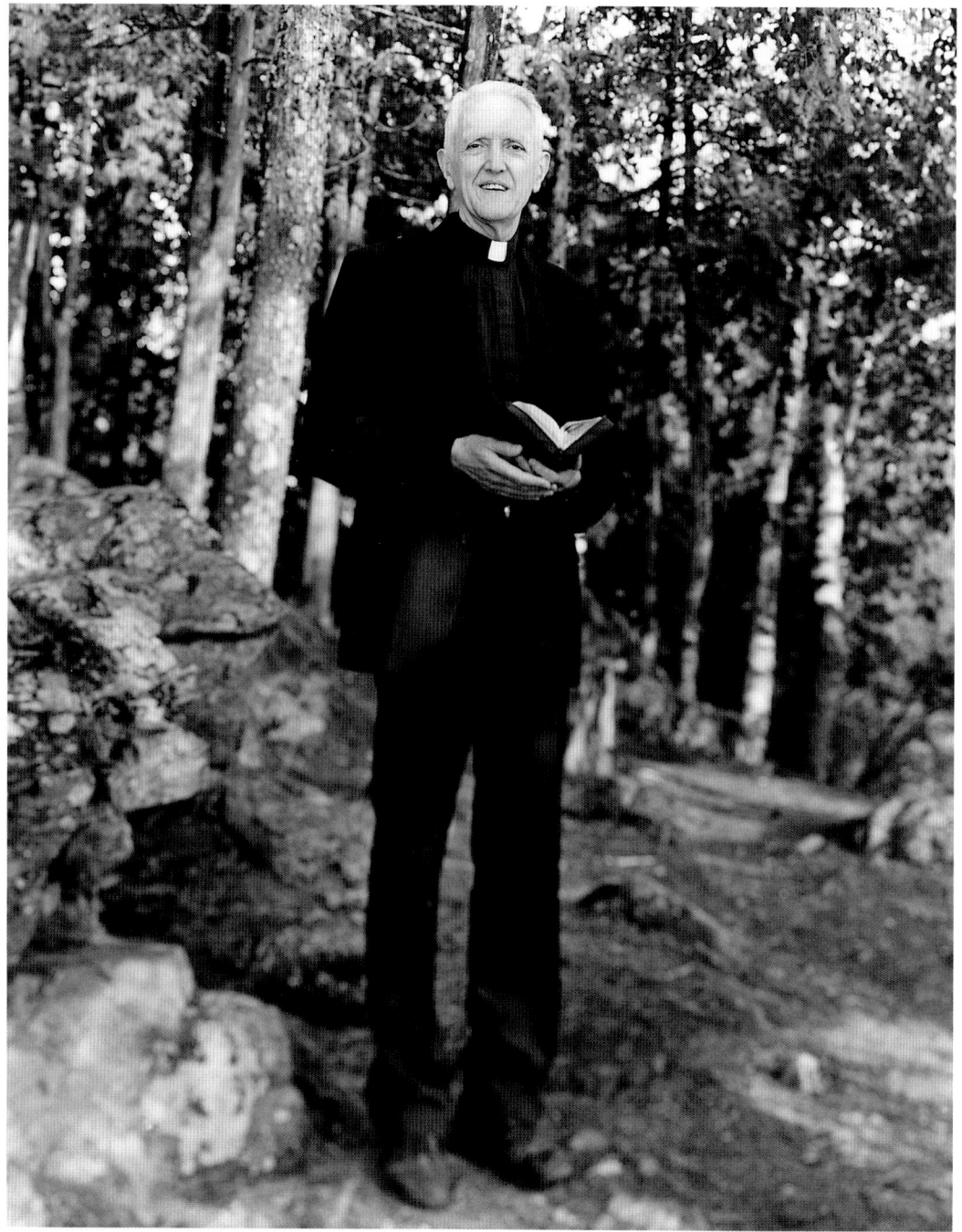

PLATE 24. Father James Scheuer, St. Anthony's Catholic Church

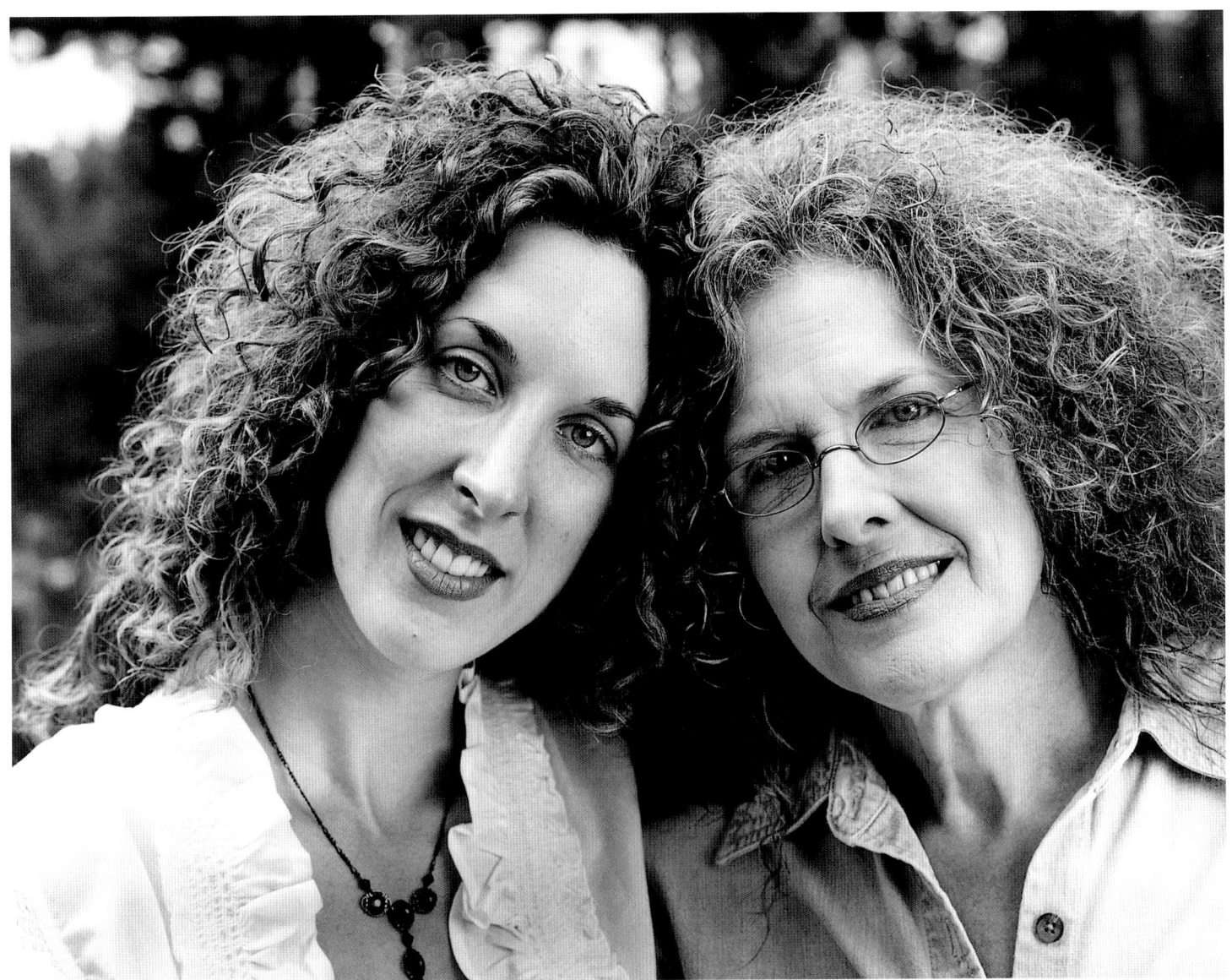

PLATE 25. Rebecca and Carol Stouffer, Ely residents

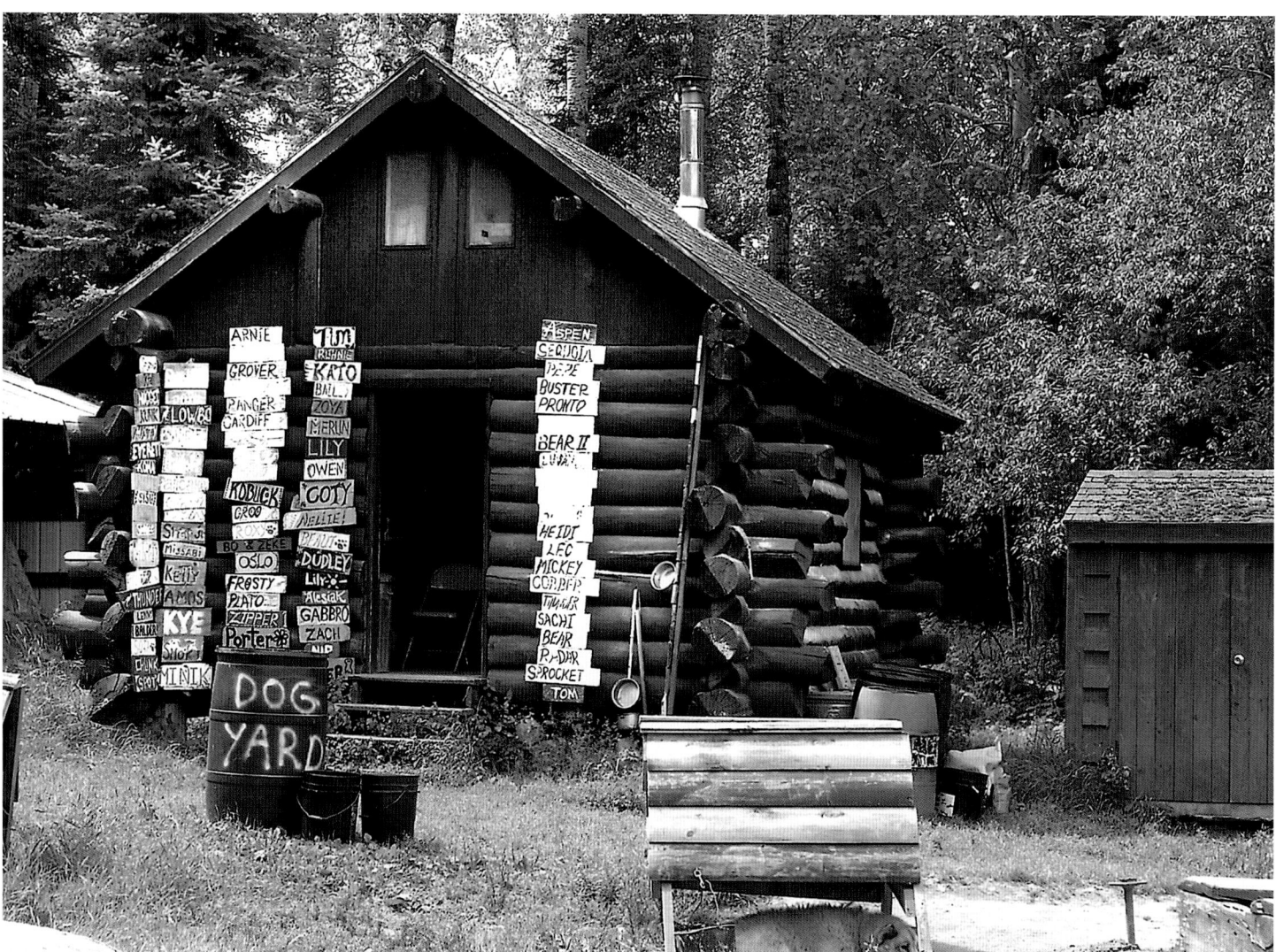
PLATE 26. Dog yard, Voyageur Outward Bound School

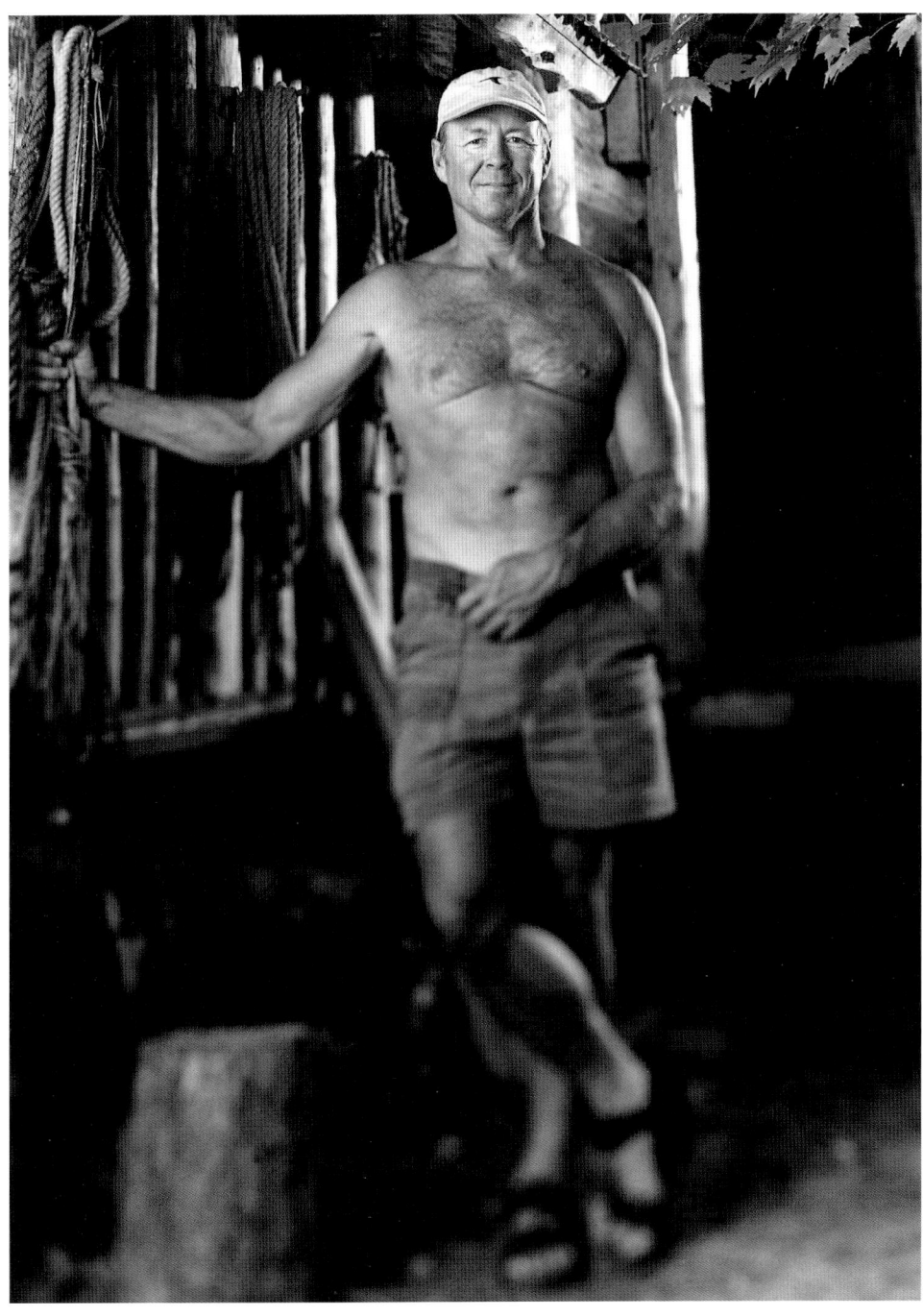

PLATE 27. Steve Johnson, wilderness guide, High Lake

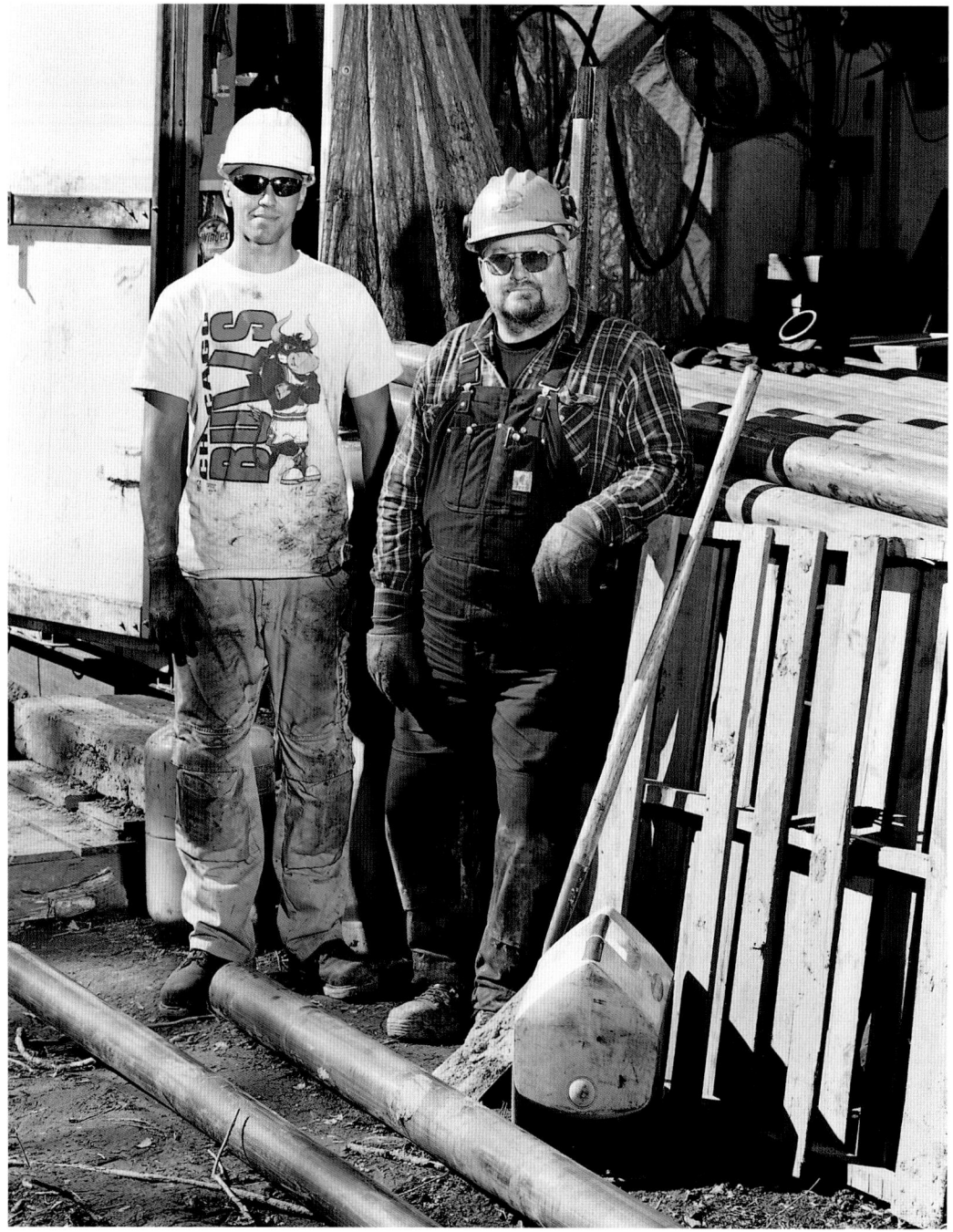

PLATE 28. Aaron Mellgren and Ronald Tokela, miners exploring for copper, nickel, and precious metals

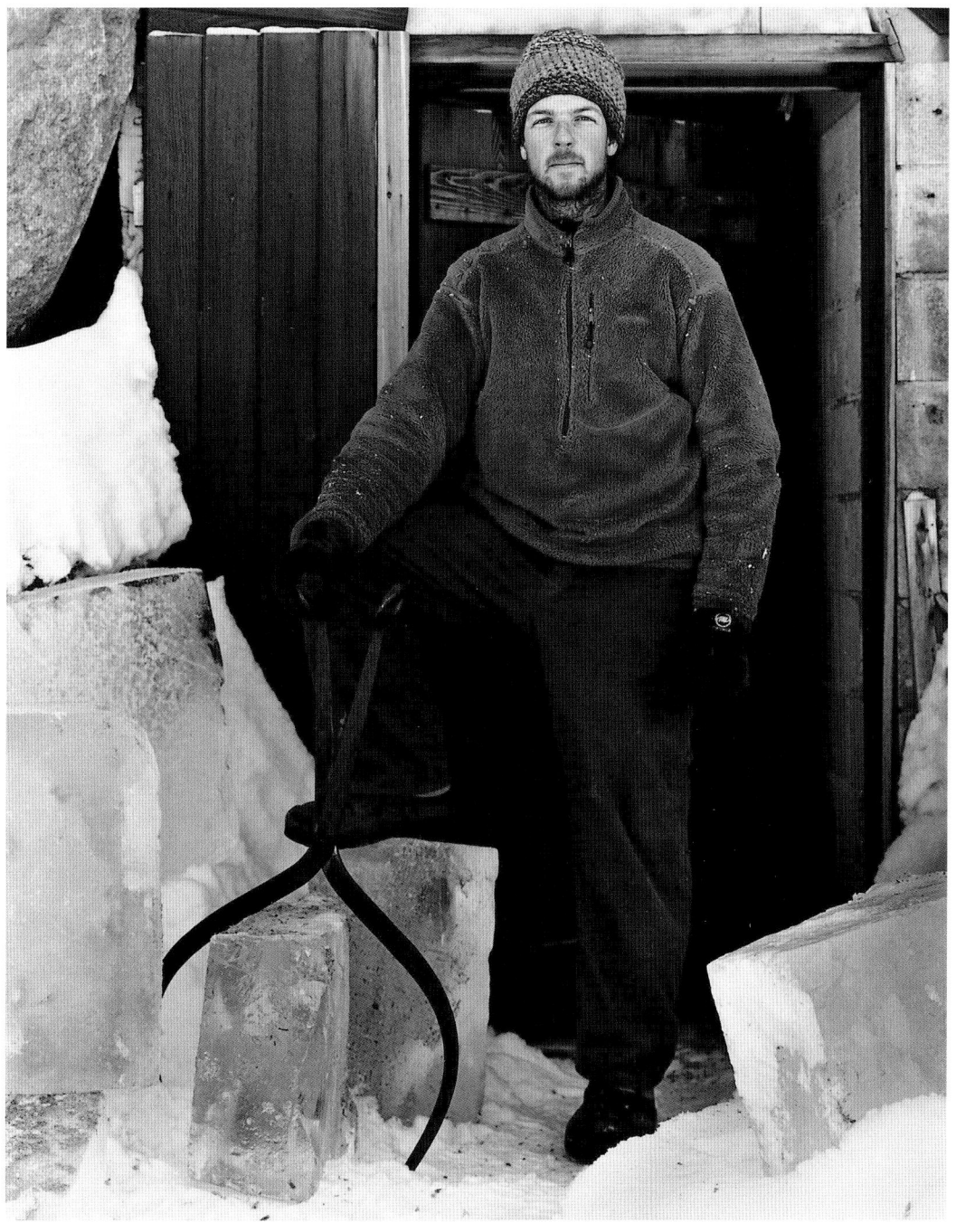

PLATE 29. Van Conrad, at Will Steger's icehouse

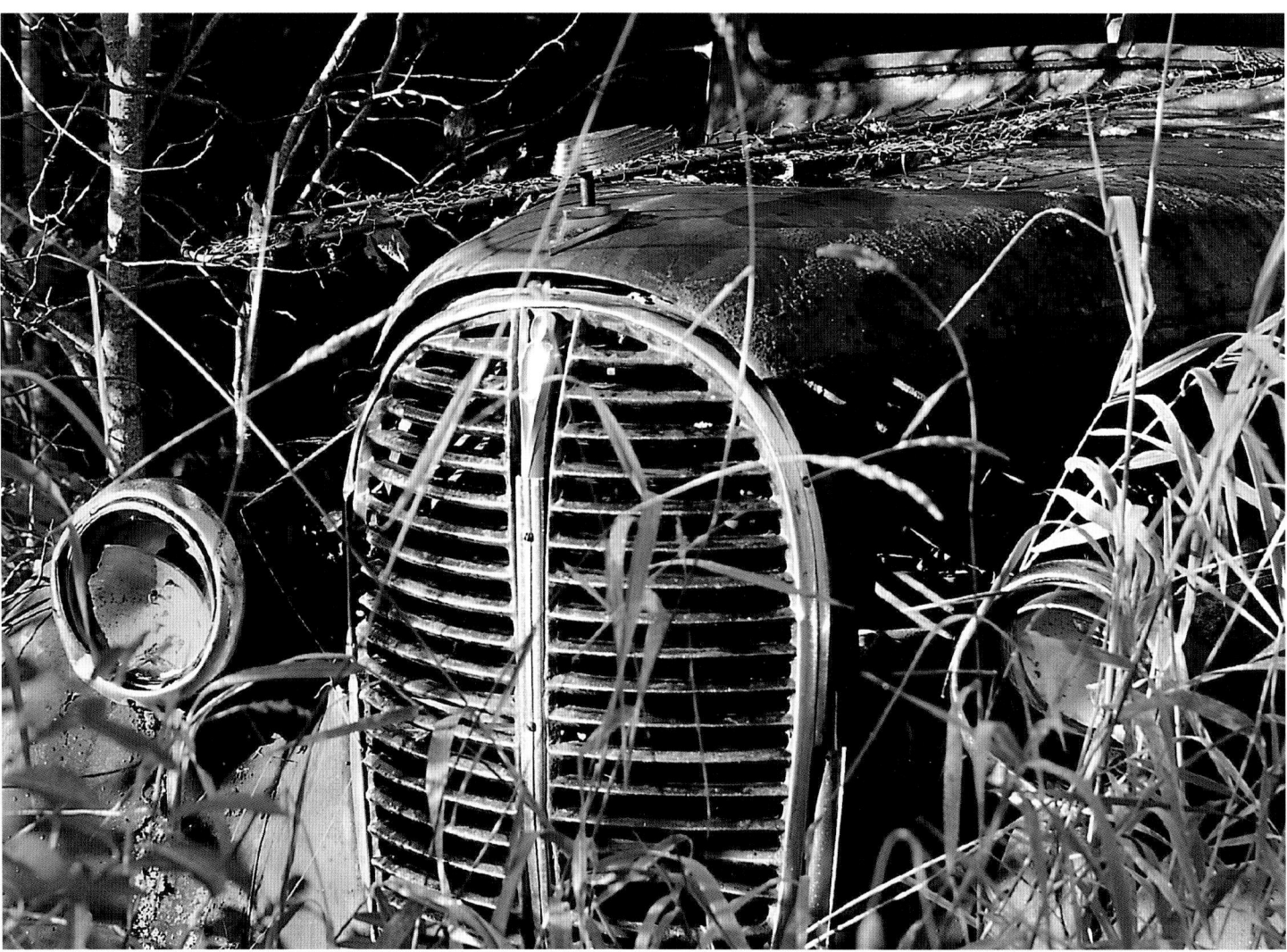

PLATE 30. Cedar Creek Mini-Golf Course

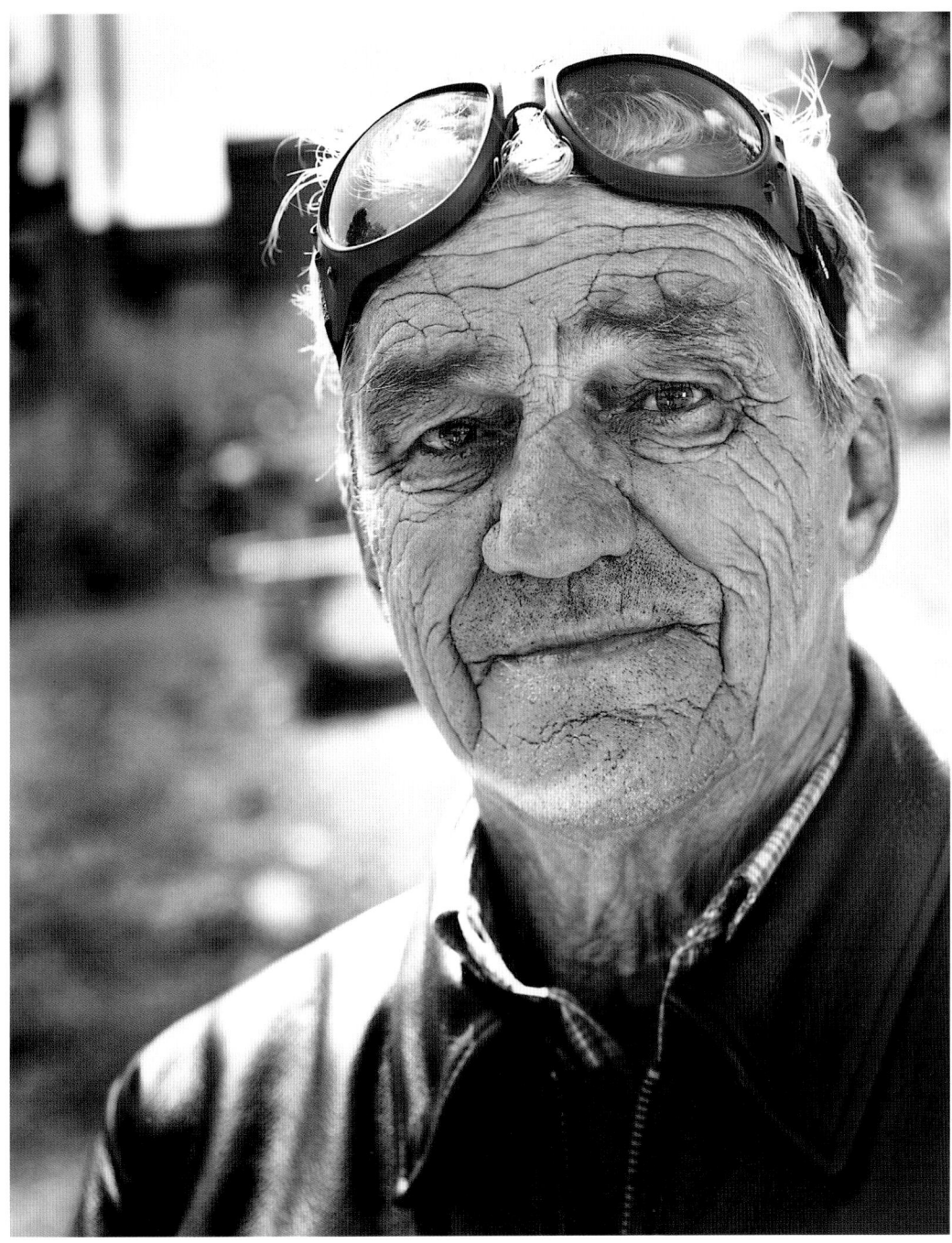

PLATE 31. Sylvio Boulanger, motorcycle traveler

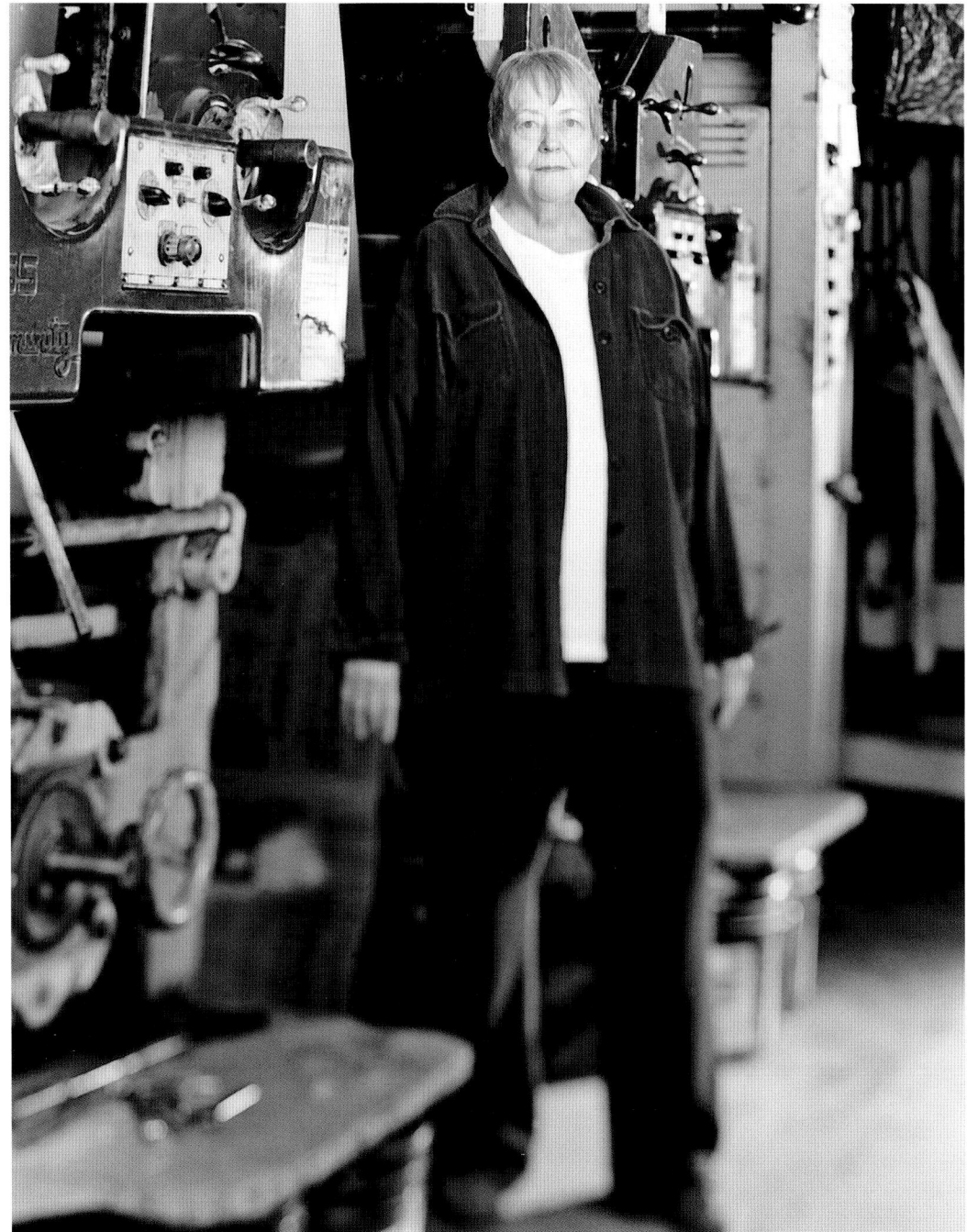

PLATE 32. Anne Swenson, owner and publisher of the *Ely Echo*

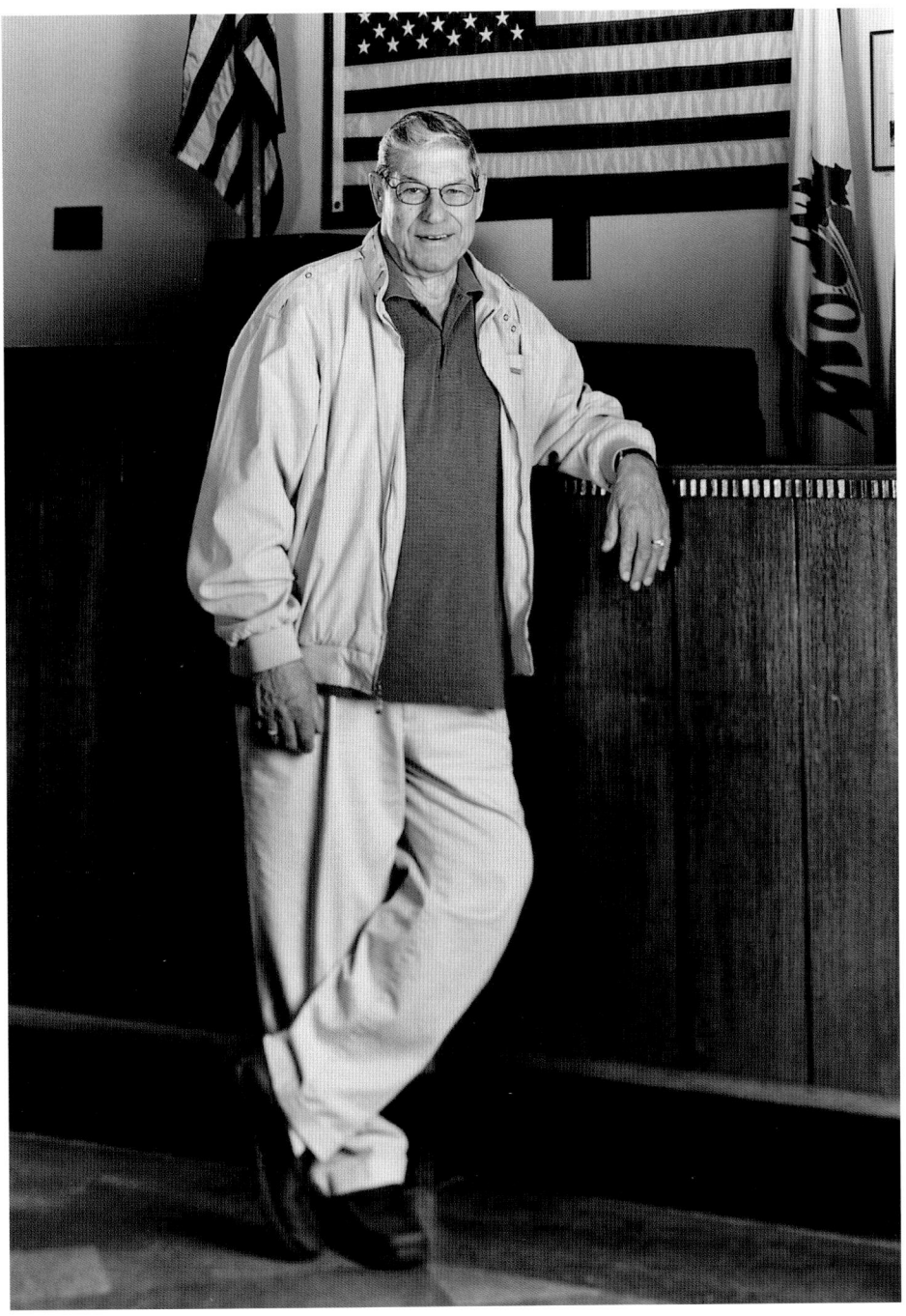

PLATE 33. Frank Salerno, mayor of Ely

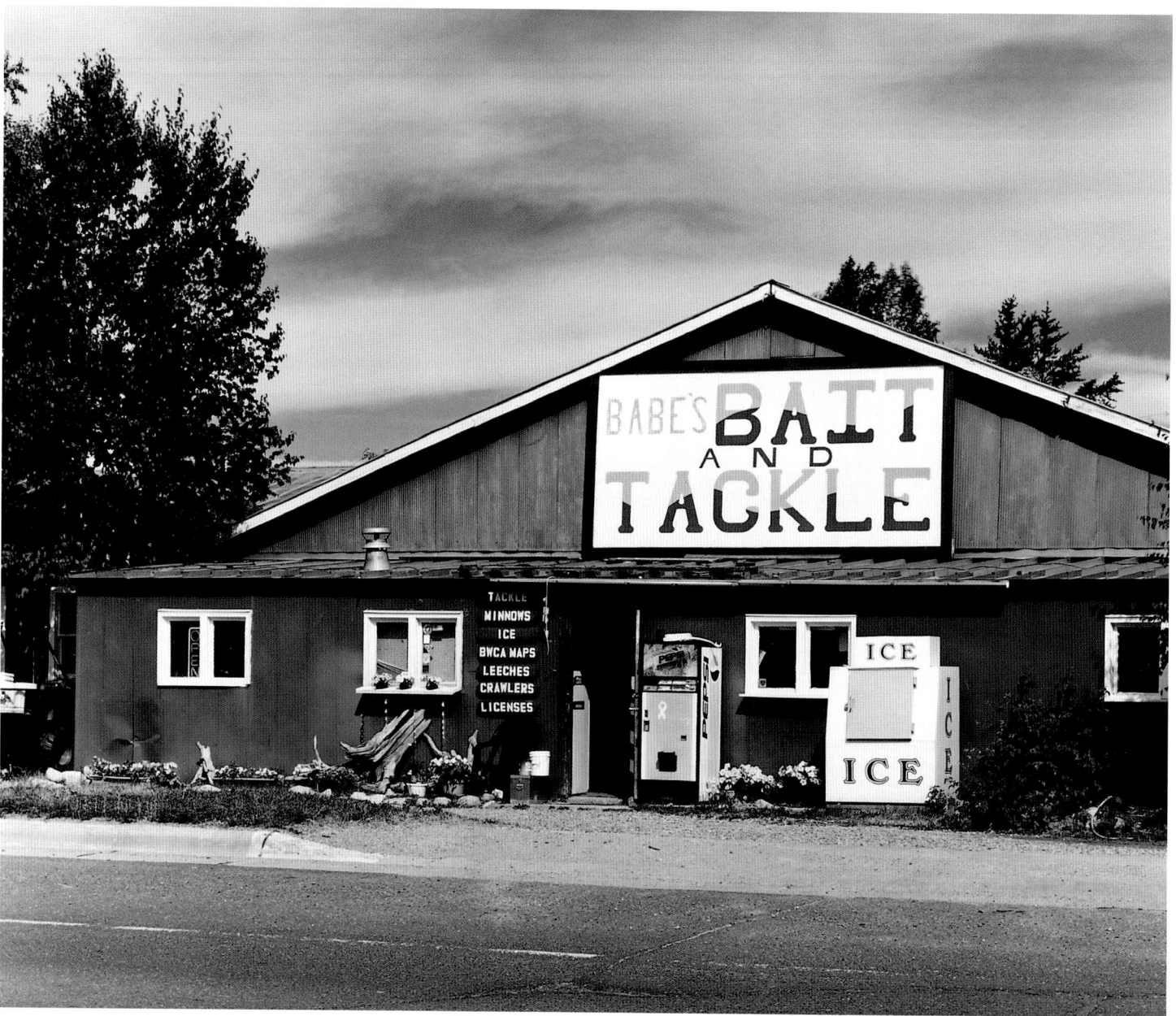

PLATE 34. Bait shop, West Sheridan Street, Ely

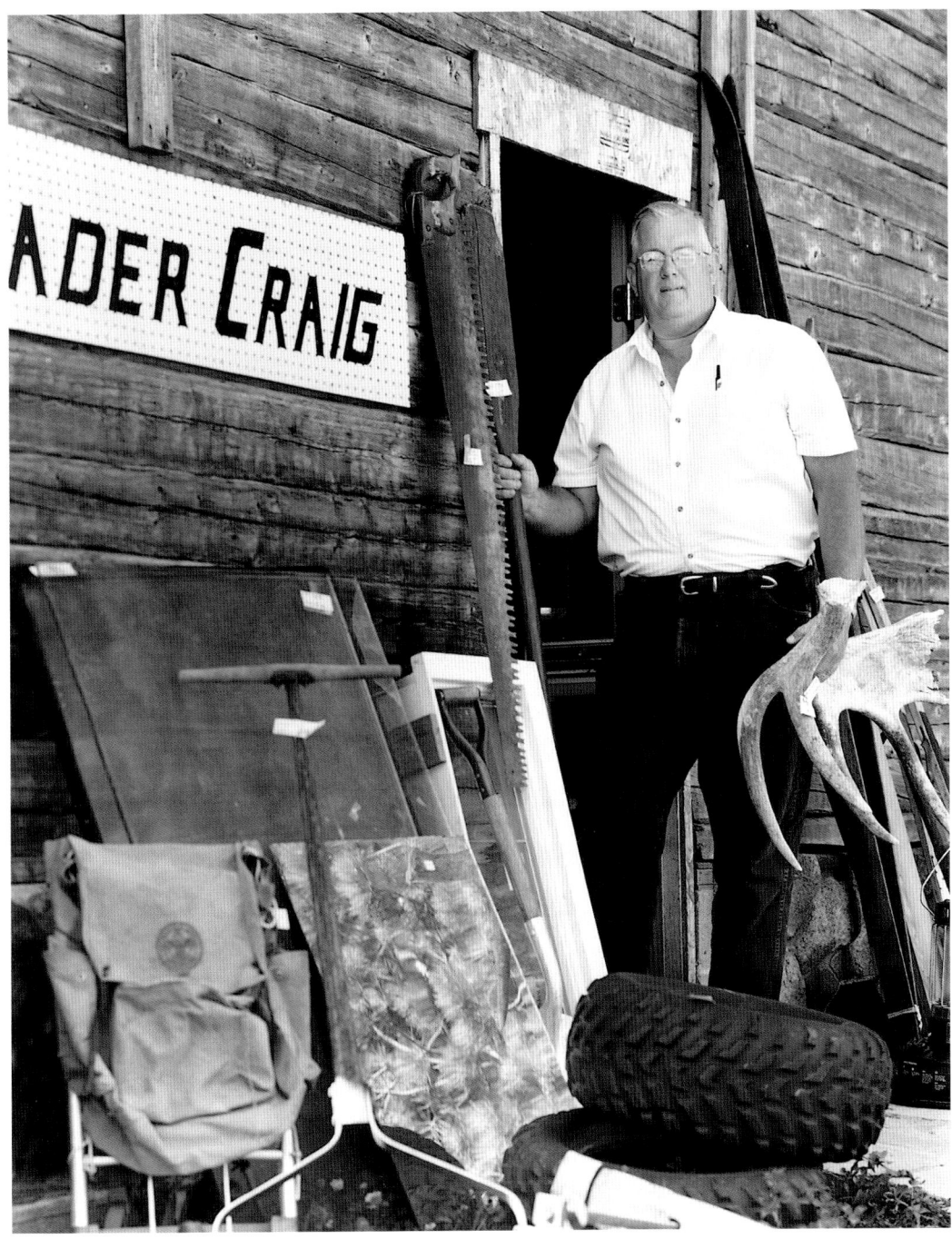

PLATE 35. "Trader Craig" Loughery, radio host and auctioneer

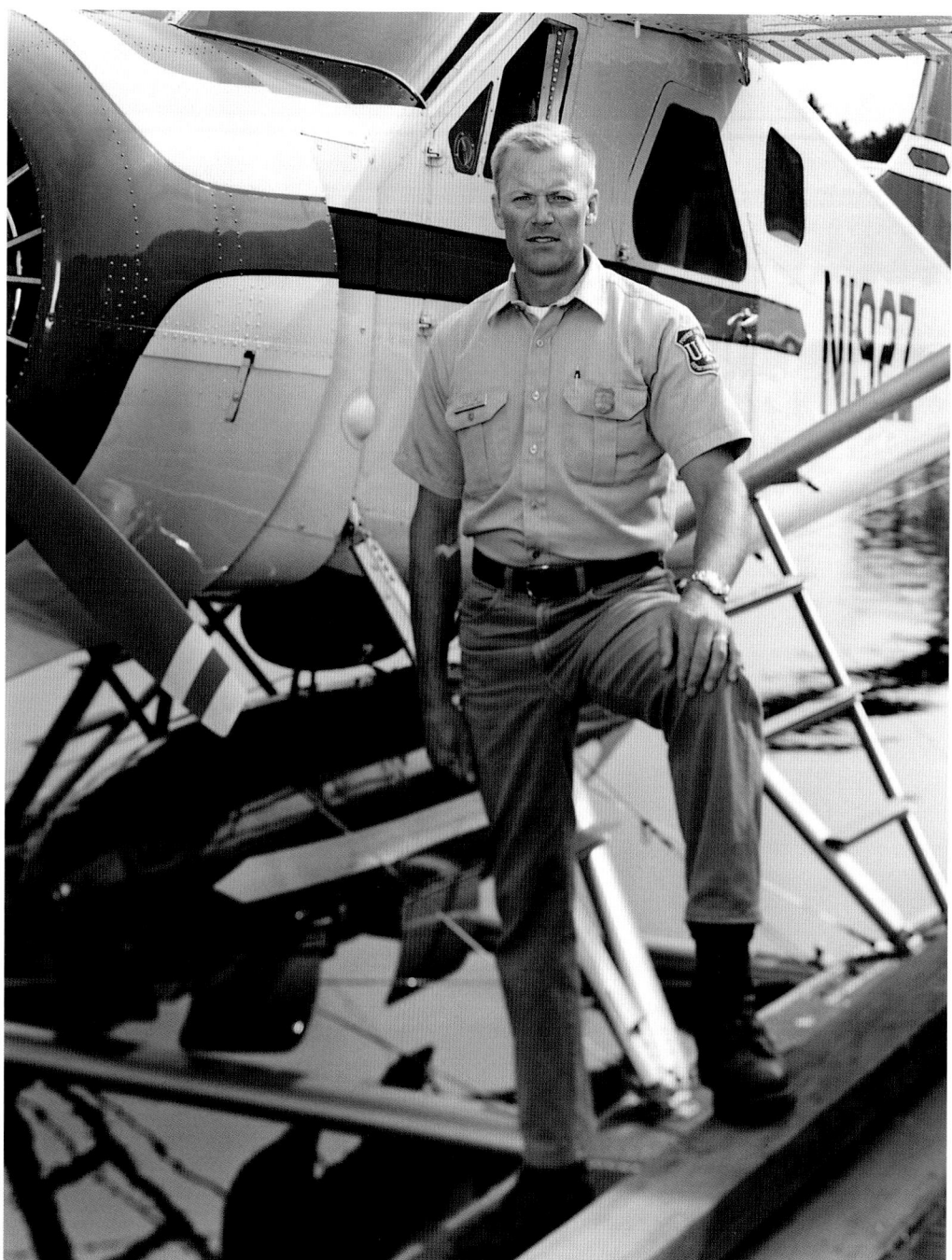

PLATE 36. Pat Loe, seaplane pilot, U.S. Forest Service

The Tinder Box

I know a small island where an ancient grove of white pine still stands. There is no need for wilderness rangers to hack a trail through the brush here. The island is a majestic and spacious glade with a towering canopy above and the sun dappling through the high branches onto a rusty gold floor. It smells as sweet as anything you can imagine. Ancient places like this are the exception in the Northwoods now, not the rule. They remain only because they were abandoned at the end of a long-ago logging season or were simply too remote for the lumberjacks to reach during a half century of aggressive clear-cutting.

Regardless of its age or origin, this forest generates a deep passion among the people of Ely and the more than 200,000 tourists who come to play in the border country every year. No one here is indifferent to the woods. The Ojibwe have always felt that the border lakes embodied a special quality and named the region Quetico for "gentle spirit."

The 1978 passage of the Boundary Waters Canoe Area Wilderness Act was a pivotal moment in a century-old argument over how to manage this special place, so rich in natural resources. The act, signed by President Jimmy Carter, formally designated 1.1 million acres, adjacent to another 1.2 million acres in Canada's Quetico Provincial Park, as a protected wilderness. This protection is total and unprecedented—no logging, no mining, no man-made structures. Motorboats are limited to a very small area, snowmobiles are forbidden, entry permits are required, and campers must pack everything out that they take in. You cannot even take glass bottles or aluminum cans into the Boundary

Waters Canoe Area Wilderness (BWCAW)—the liquor stores on Sheridan Street can set you up with plastic beer containers for your trip.

The BWCAW has the only nonmilitary no-fly zone in North America, so it is rare that the quiet is broken by the whine and sputter of low-flying props. When it does happen, odds are that it is U.S. Forest Service seaplane pilot Pat Loe or one of his colleagues in a gorgeous 1959 DeHavilland Beaver on a mission deemed vital enough to fly below the ban. They may be fish stocking, swooping down to 200 feet above the lakes to drop tiny trout from a hopper in the plane's belly, or bringing relief to an injured camper. On their most challenging days, they engage in "fire suppression," landing briefly to scoop a thousand pounds of water out of a lake in a mere eight seconds. Then they lift off with a sharp roll, resisting the drag of the water tube by sloping at a precarious angle off the left float, rising up and away from their gleaming reflection, a startle of silver and red in this green, green world.

Despite its size and beauty, there are those in Ely who have never stepped foot in the Boundary Waters—many of them on principle. "It looks the same there as it does here. What's the difference? The line is arbitrary," says one longtime resident. Others in Ely have prospered providing gear and services to the thousands of paddlers who pass through town. Some have risked friendships and livelihoods to preserve the Boundary Waters as pure wilderness, while others have risked just as much to prevent the rigid restrictions. Organizations with large memberships exist on both sides of the issue: the Friends of Boundary Waters Wilderness advocate adding even more acreage to the wilderness area, while Conservationists with Common Sense look to reduce restrictions and allow for broader use.

On Ely's eastern edge, Vermilion Community College offers degrees across the spectrum. You can gain a certificate in "wilderness management" or "parks and recreation" or, if you'd prefer, "professional timber harvesting." No matter your choice, it must be said again that everyone here loves the forest. Ann Chapek says she is working on her associate's degree to be a forestry ranger because "I was always big into animals. I knew I wanted to take care of the wilderness."

But what is this wilderness, really? America's insatiable appetite for lumber initially swept past northern Minnesota, the harsh landscape too challenging to exploit. But it swung back around to the Arrowhead region when the mines at Soudan and Tower finally provided the road and rail infrastructure to support the felling of a forest. The supply of white pine had been depleted elsewhere, and so Robert Whiteside became rich selling huge tracts of the Northwoods to lumber barons like Weyerhaeuser. In those days, the forest's produce was measured in "board feet." A mill was set up at Fall Lake, and the town of Winton grew up around it. An unimaginable 2.5 billion board feet of lumber was produced in the forty years between 1880 and 1920.

As this clear-cut progressed, new ideas were being formed in Washington. Presidents Cleveland and McKinley passed protective measures in the name of the latest concept in forestry science—*conservation*. The U.S. Forest Service came into being in the late 1800s, and huge reserves of forest were set aside as public land, but the Forest Service maintained the right to open sections of forest to timber and mineral sales.

And then Theodore Roosevelt changed our thinking about public lands. He insisted we see them not just for their economic value but for their role in the quality of American life. Peace of mind, rejuvenation, recreation could coexist with a sustained yield.

And recreate we did. The Superior National Forest was a major tourist attraction immediately upon its founding in 1909. Early in the century it was designated as a "roadless area," but over time the logging continued, and the Forest Service, with the help of the Civilian Conservation Corps, built more and more roads. The idea of "board feet" became a thing of the past as the pine crop was exhausted and the lumber industry switched to harvesting "pulpwood" for papermaking. By the late 1960s, the frustration of the conservationists was at an all-time high as the newer logging techniques became much more damaging to the environment—huge tractors and steel-treaded bulldozers were tearing up the landscape.

In a firestorm of controversy and open hostility, the people of the Arrowhead region fought on both sides of the wilderness issue. Ultimately, those led by the likes of Bud Heinselman and Sigurd Olson succeeded in gaining the passage of the BWCA Wilderness Act.

The Kainz family, long-standing lumber businessmen in the area, bought the very last available timber before the restriction permanently closed down logging in the BWCAW. Today, third-generation logger Bruce Kainz gains logging rights from private landowners outside of the Boundary Waters, especially the mining companies who strive to extract every natural resource at their disposal. Unlike his predecessors in the legendary logging camps, Bruce works almost entirely alone. He employs an amazing machine that grasps the tree at hand, clips it easily at its base, lifts and strips it of bark in one motion, and loads it directly onto a truck. All this in a matter of minutes. Mostly, Bruce chops birch, which, thanks to its pleasing taste, will end up as toothpicks and tongue depressors.

The government condemned and purchased private property in the protected wilderness, and over time all the homes, lodges, airstrips, logging camps, sluiceways, and roads were torn down or grown over. Only a handful of resident Ojibwe were allowed to remain, and thanks to a community-wide petition, the "root beer lady," Dorothy Molter, stayed in her Knife Lake cabin until her death in 1986 marked the end of human habitation in the BWCAW.

Mining and forestry have diminished as economic drivers for the region, and tourism has proved itself a lasting enterprise. But smaller debates continue, as does the hostility. Illegal snowmobile use persists as riders defy the wilderness protections to reach their favorite fishing spots. When caught, many riders are treated as local heroes, and neighbors chip in to pay for their legal fees.

People still complain that it was "outsiders" who forced the BWCAW restrictions upon them. So many of the decisions have been made at the federal level, and even today the pro-BWCAW groups are largely comprised of leadership from downstate. Though the mining and logging conglomerates were the primary target of the wilderness protection, for local people who grew up on these lakes, it is difficult to accept that they are no longer allowed the free access they once enjoyed. "As I get older I just can't get in there like I used to," complains one fisherman. "Without a snowmobile or motorboat, there's no way I can physically get far enough east on Ensign Lake to catch those walleye." It is hard not to see more than one point of view on this issue.

With the BWCAW firmly established, the larger concern for this beloved place is its management as a profoundly damaged wilderness. When the early loggers pulled out, they left behind a veritable graveyard of a forest. The Civilian Conservation Corps (CCC) replanted the forests all over America, and many of Ely's older folks were among those who worked in the CCC camps in the area, planting quick-growing aspen, balsam, and poplar. Meanwhile, the Forest Service adopted a wilderness management approach that boiled down to "hands-off unless there's a fire." As Teddy Roosevelt said, "Leave it as it is. The ages have been at work on it and man can only mar it." The problem was that man, too, had already been at work on the BWCAW in a big way.

Fire suppression became the overriding premise of the forestry plan, a tactic that is now widely recognized as not only unnatural but dangerous. Forests need fire. It paves the way for reseeding of trees like the jack pine and clears brushy growth on a regular basis to limit its overabundance. Without regular small fires, the forest becomes increasingly at risk for larger, devastating burns. Yet the Forest Service was slow to accept the need for controlled fire management. One logger said to me, "It's a disaster. A waste."

And then came the "blowdown." On July 4, 1999, following a series of summer thunderstorms, a bizarre and dreadful wind called a *derecho* brewed high over the Black Hills of South Dakota and then came crashing down on the Boundary Waters with hurricane force. It lasted only twelve seconds, but it knocked down an estimated forty million trees across nearly half a million acres. Photographer Jim Brandenburg captured the devastated reaction of everyone in the area when he wrote after the storm, "Around my home, acres were denuded, and my family and I stood in shock like those we've all seen on the television after their community has been leveled by a tornado."

If the BWCAW was a fire hazard before the blowdown, it became a true tinder box afterward. Most of the trees were sheared at midpoint, their tops bent over, enabling them to dry rapidly into a highly combustible mass. The fuel density in the forest is now astounding and terrifying. Any fire has the potential to take out hundreds of thousands of acres at record speed. The Forest Service is undertaking heightened efforts to remove the felled timber and implement controlled burns. But until now, the attempt to preserve the wilderness has most certainly contributed to its increased vulnerability. Our love of this forest has been stifling.

The scale of the issue only seems to grow over time. Scientists have modeled the impact of climate change on the Boundary Waters, and we may find ourselves with a prairie instead of a forest in the not too distant future. Attorney Chuck Dayton, whose leadership was instrumental in the early days of establishing the BWCAW, has turned his attention to this larger view. "Global warming is overwhelming. That's what I'm spending my time on now."

Meanwhile, on the edges of the Boundary Waters, private citizens quietly work to restore the forests around Ely to their original grandeur. For decades Dan Schmiechen and his family have annually planted white pines on their island in Burntside Lake. Doc Udovich, an accordion-playing dentist with a large plot of land on White Iron Lake, says, "I gotta have woods and water around. I try to plant about a thousand trees every year. The trouble is I plant the Norway pine, and a week later a rabbit comes by and nips the bud off the top—loses two years of growth in one second. And the deer just eat up the white pine." It seems no matter what we do and how much we care for the forest, it is difficult to make up for all the damage that has been done.

When the soldier in Hans Christian Andersen's tale climbed into the heart of a tree, he emerged with plenty of treasure and also a tinder box. The border country has proved to be similar. This forest, both old and new, has offered up a multitude of treasures, both spiritual and worldly. And it has yielded a tinder box, larger and more volatile than we could ever have imagined.

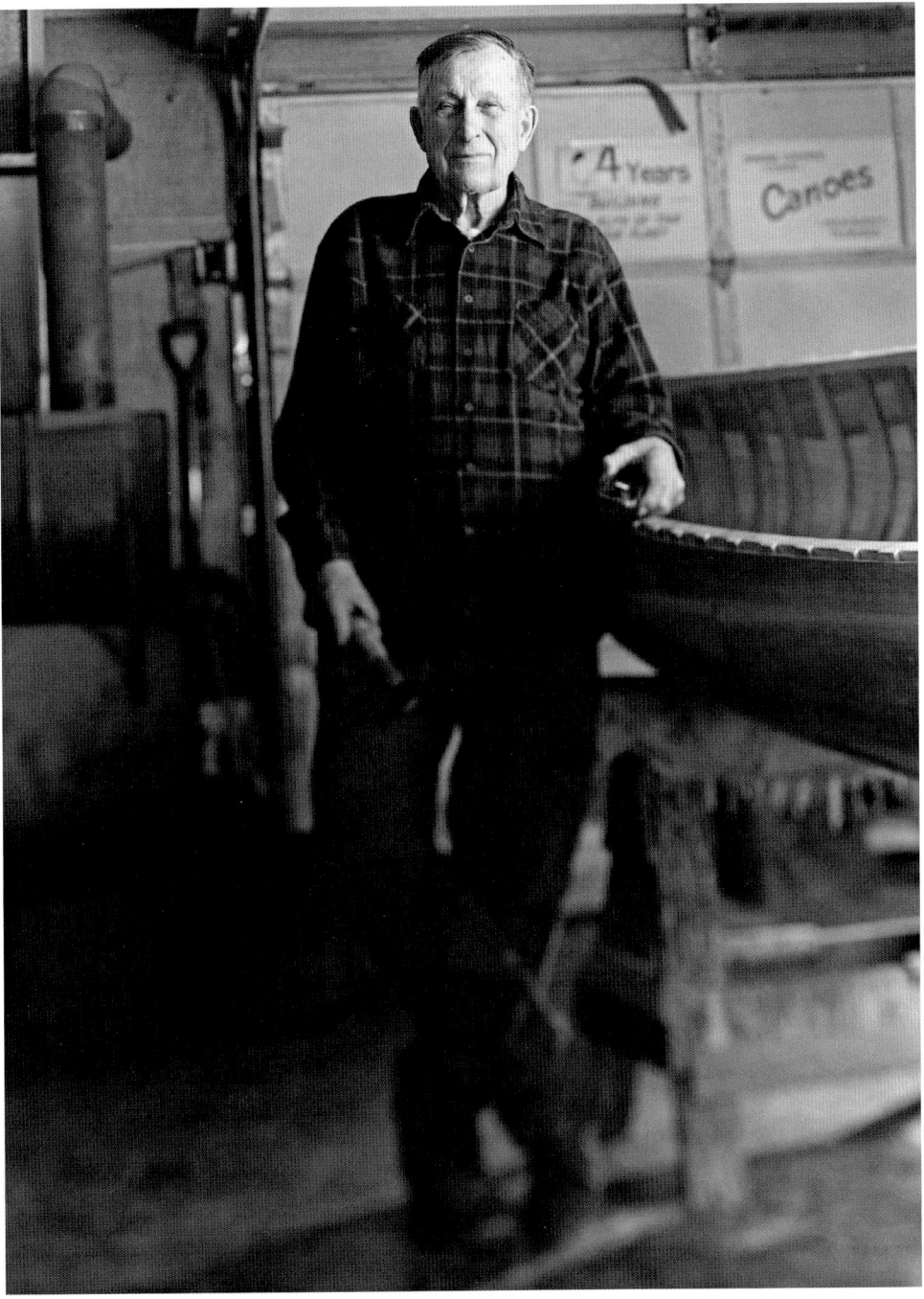

PLATE 37. Joe Seliga, canoe builder

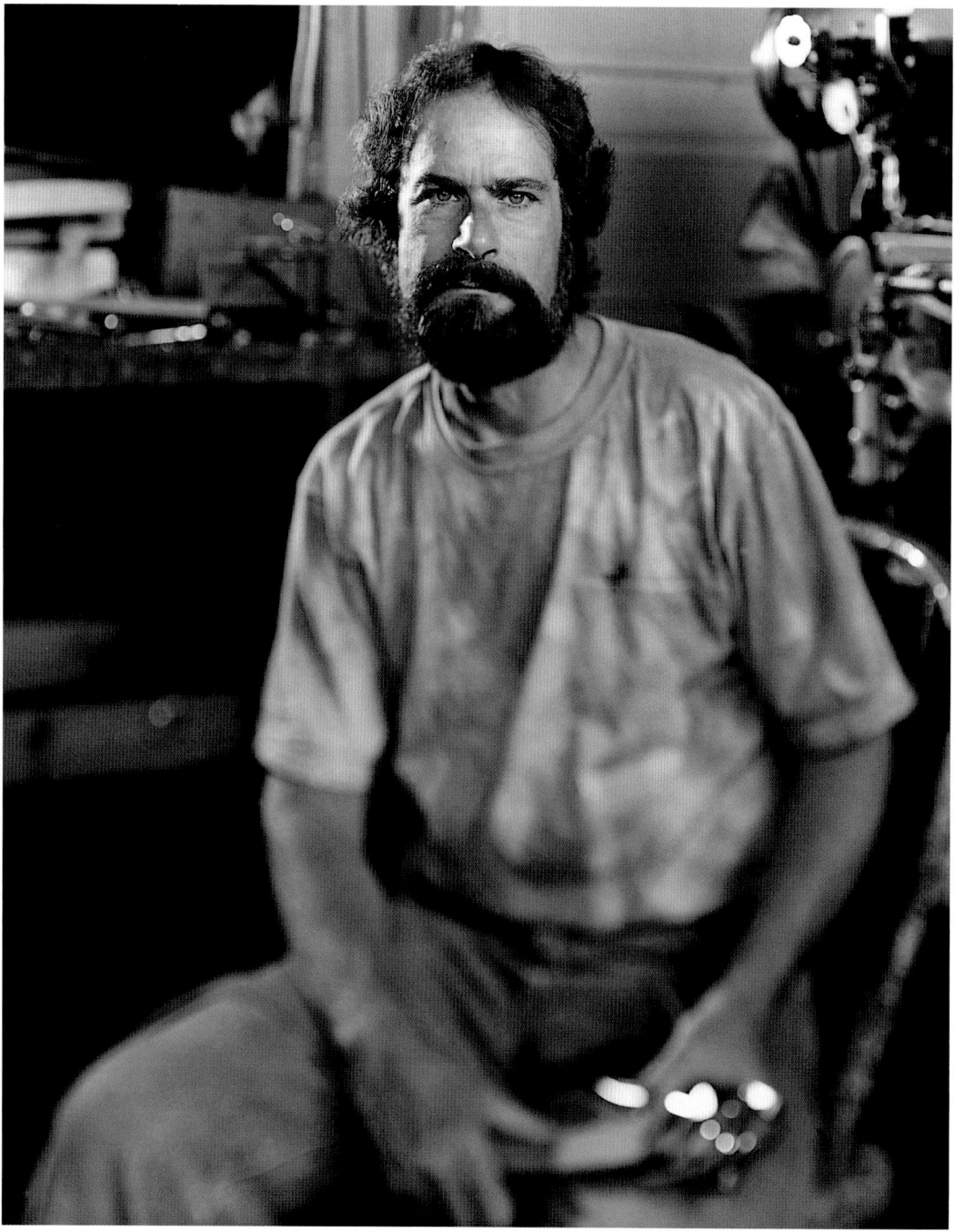

PLATE 38. Henry Held, Henry's Shoe Repair

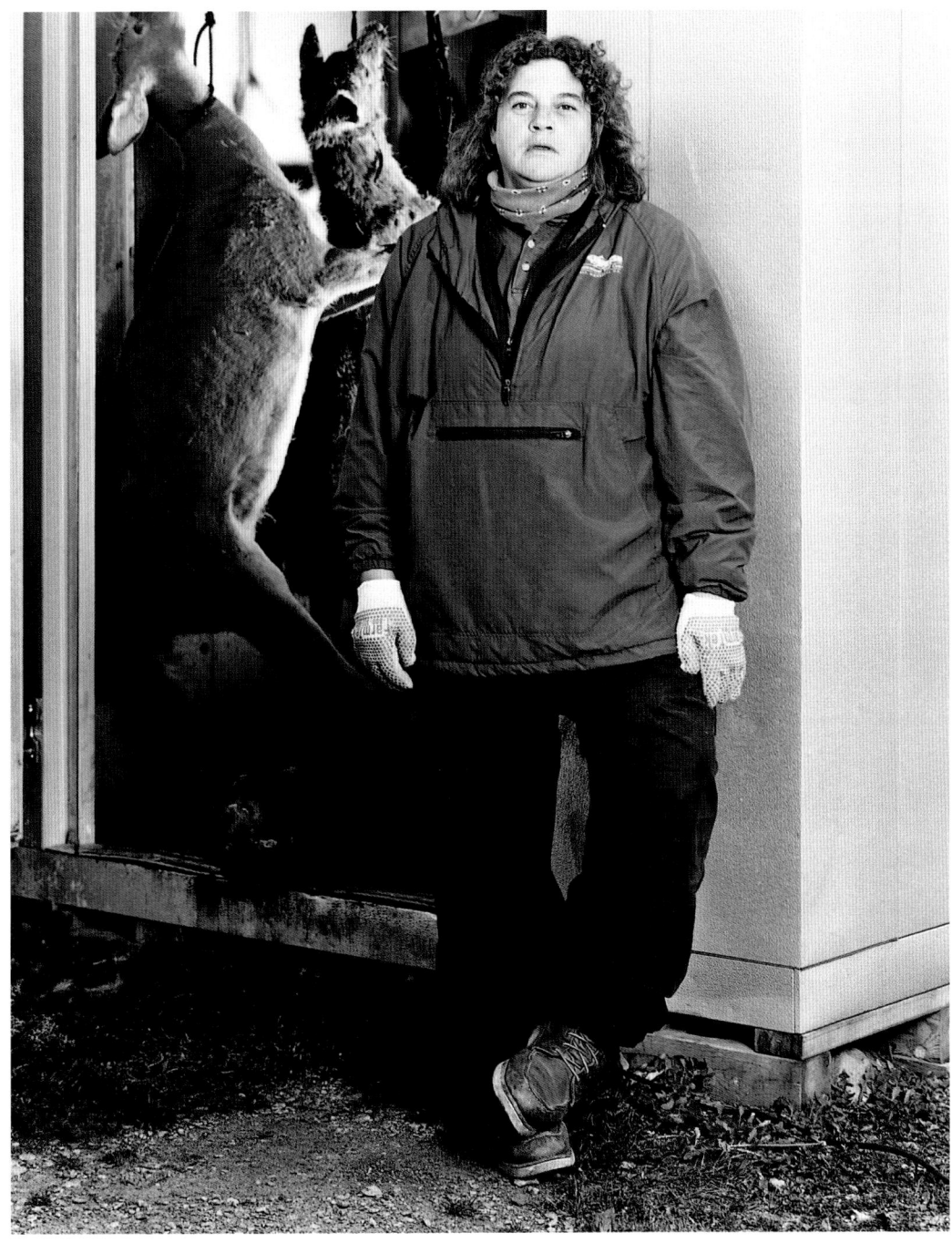

PLATE 39. Lori Schmidt, wolf curator, International Wolf Center

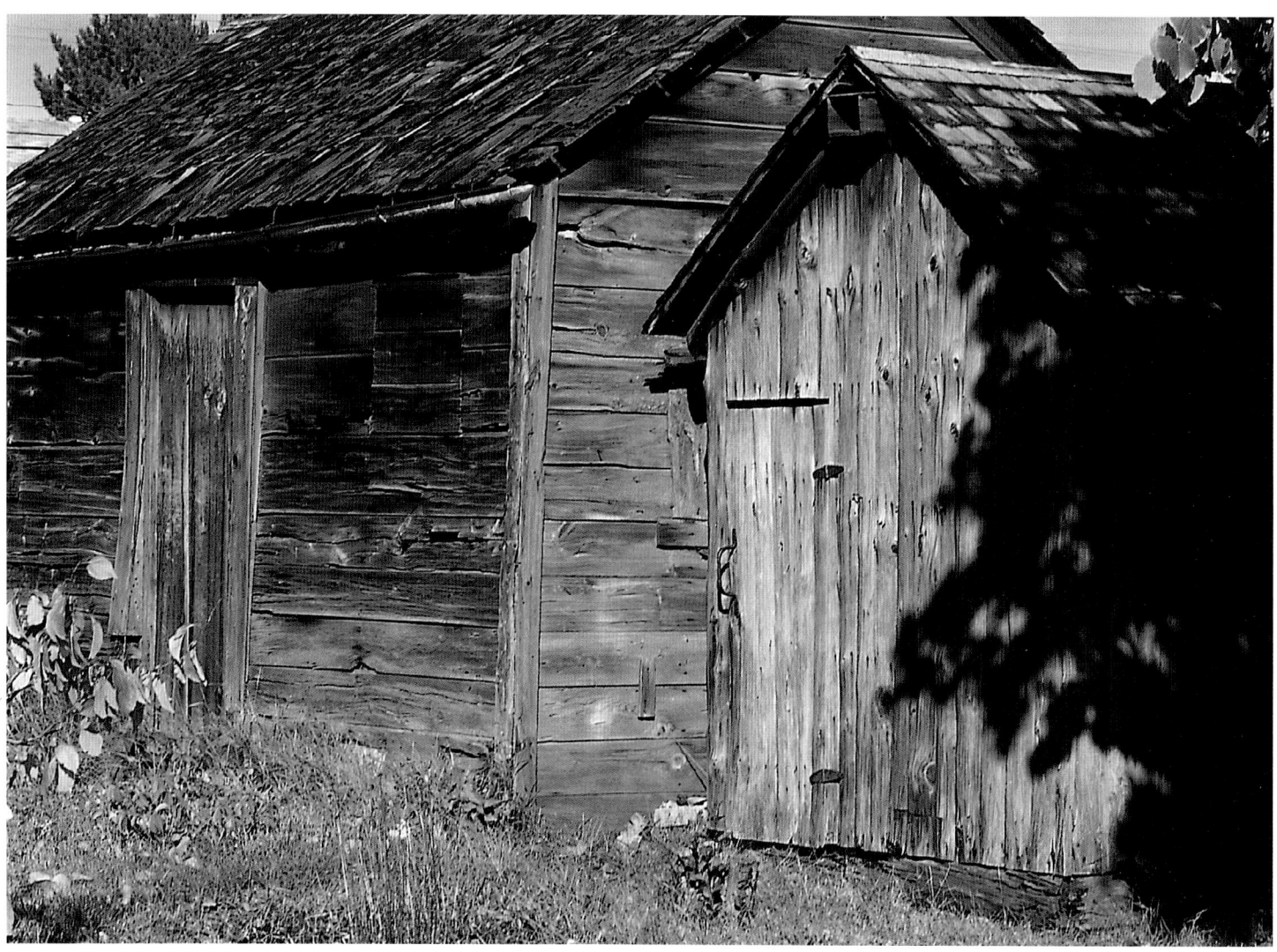

PLATE 40. Sheds, Ely

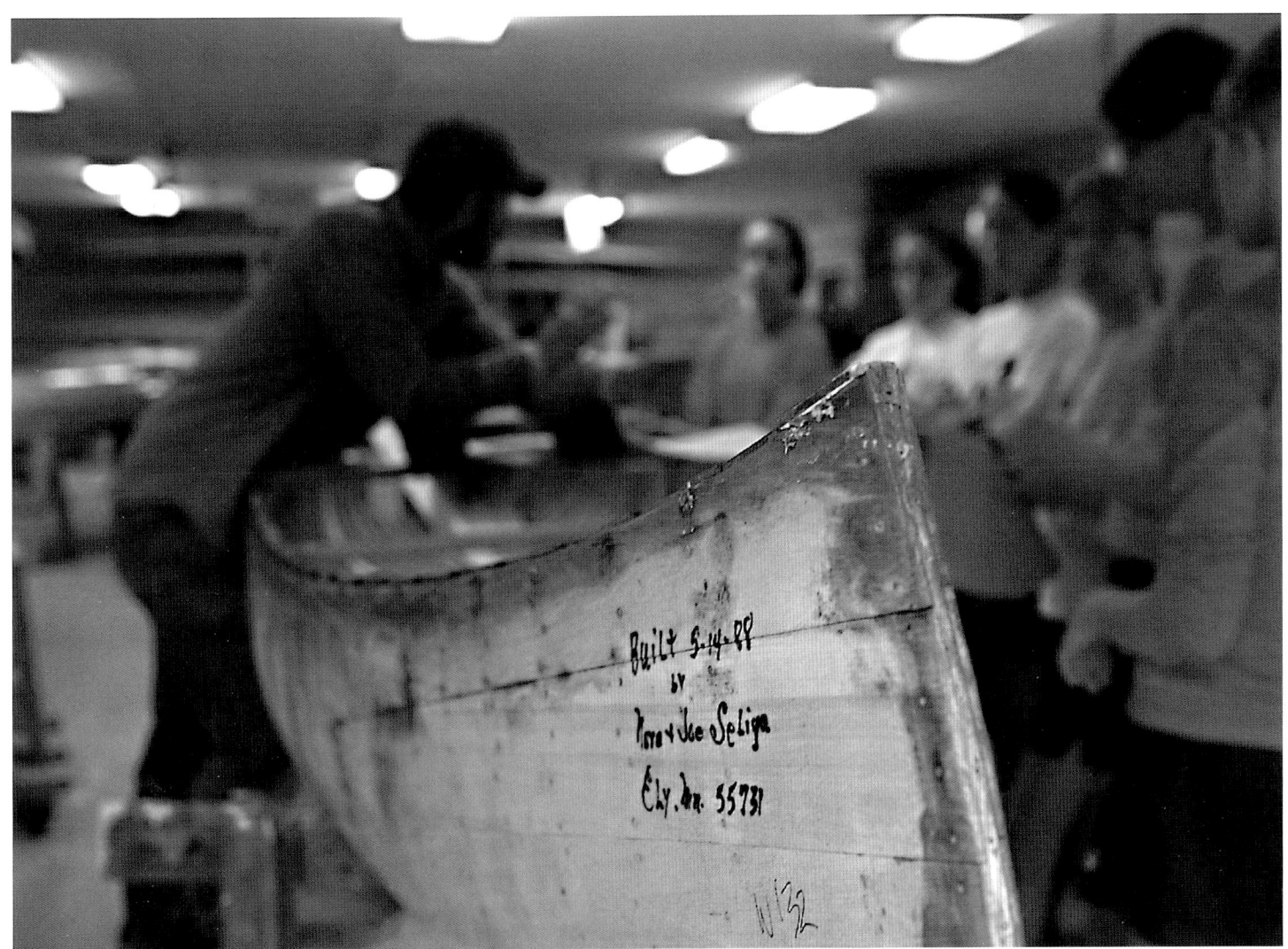

PLATE 41. Seliga canoe, canoe restoration class, Camp Widjiwagan

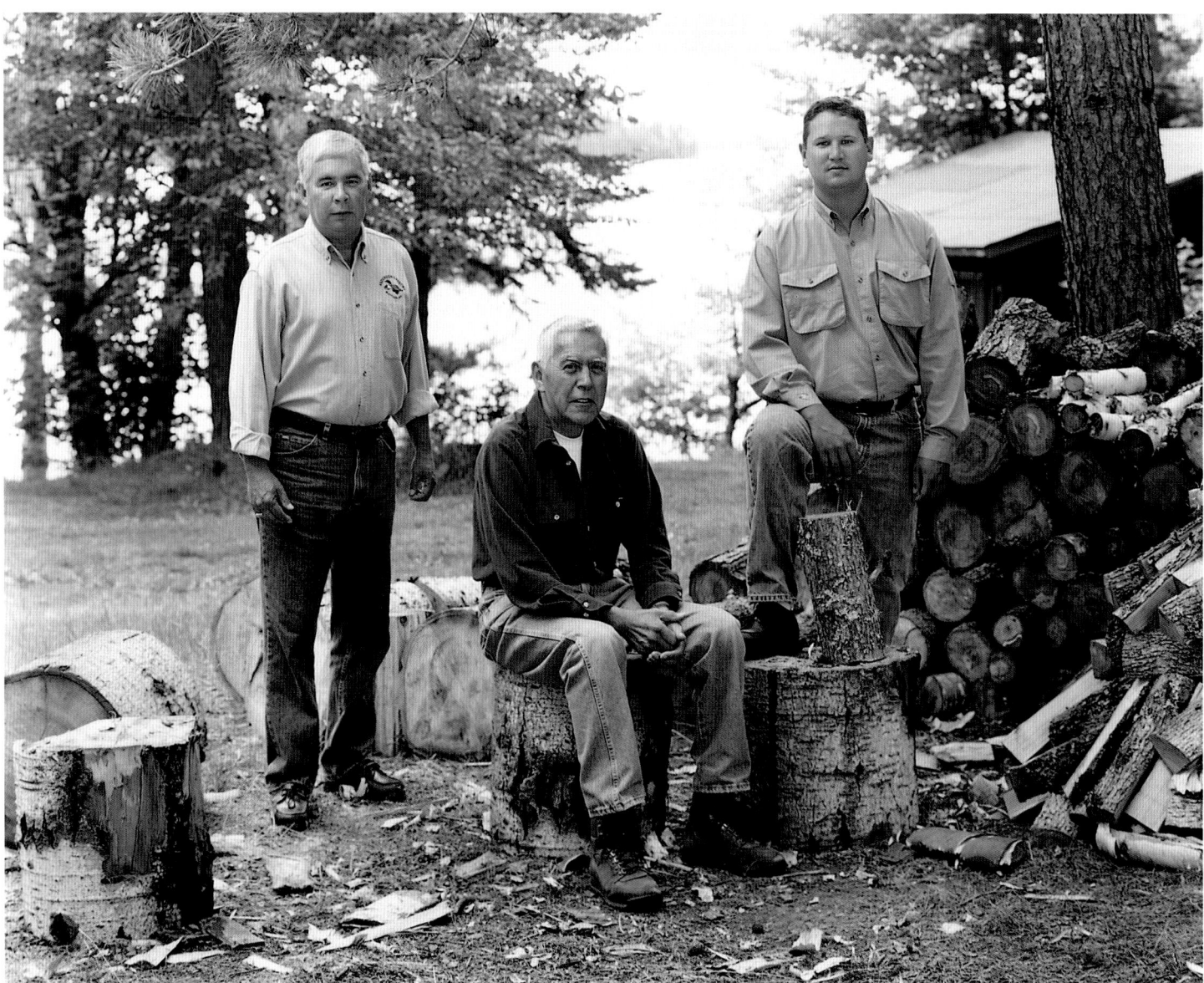

PLATE 42. Three generations of the Anderson family, Anderson's Resort, Burntside Lake

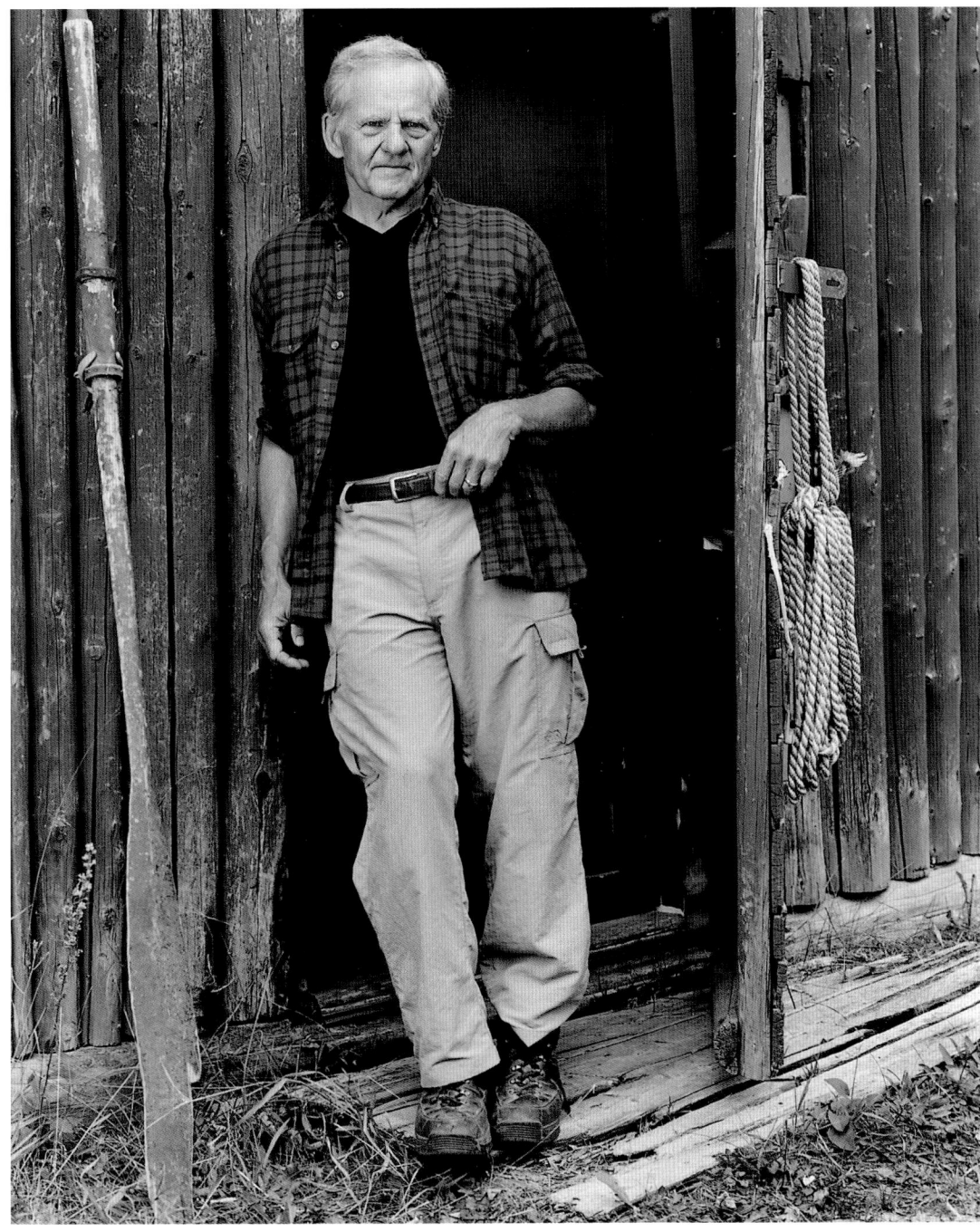

PLATE 43. Chuck Dayton, environmental attorney

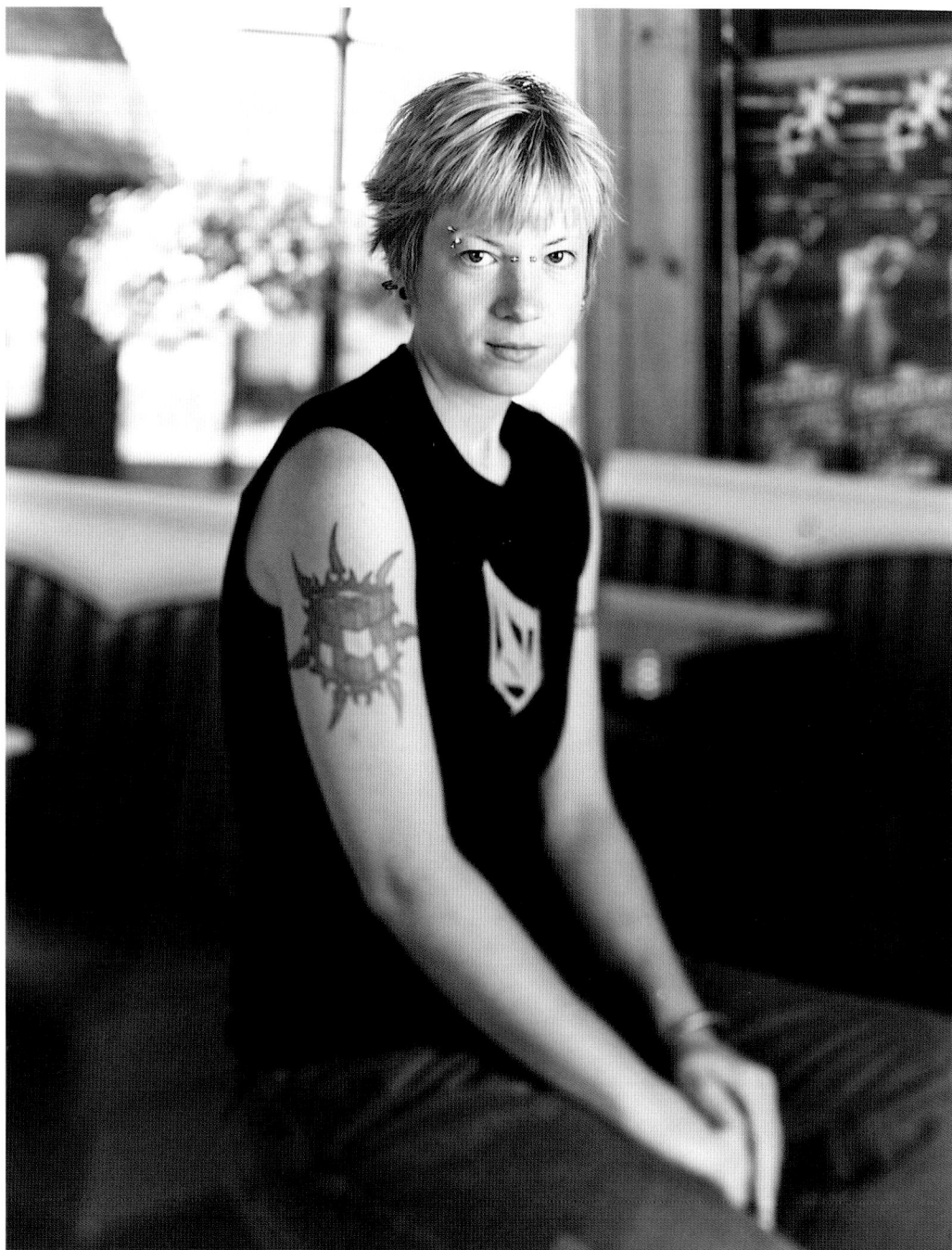

PLATE 44. Ann Chapek, forestry student, Vermilion Community College

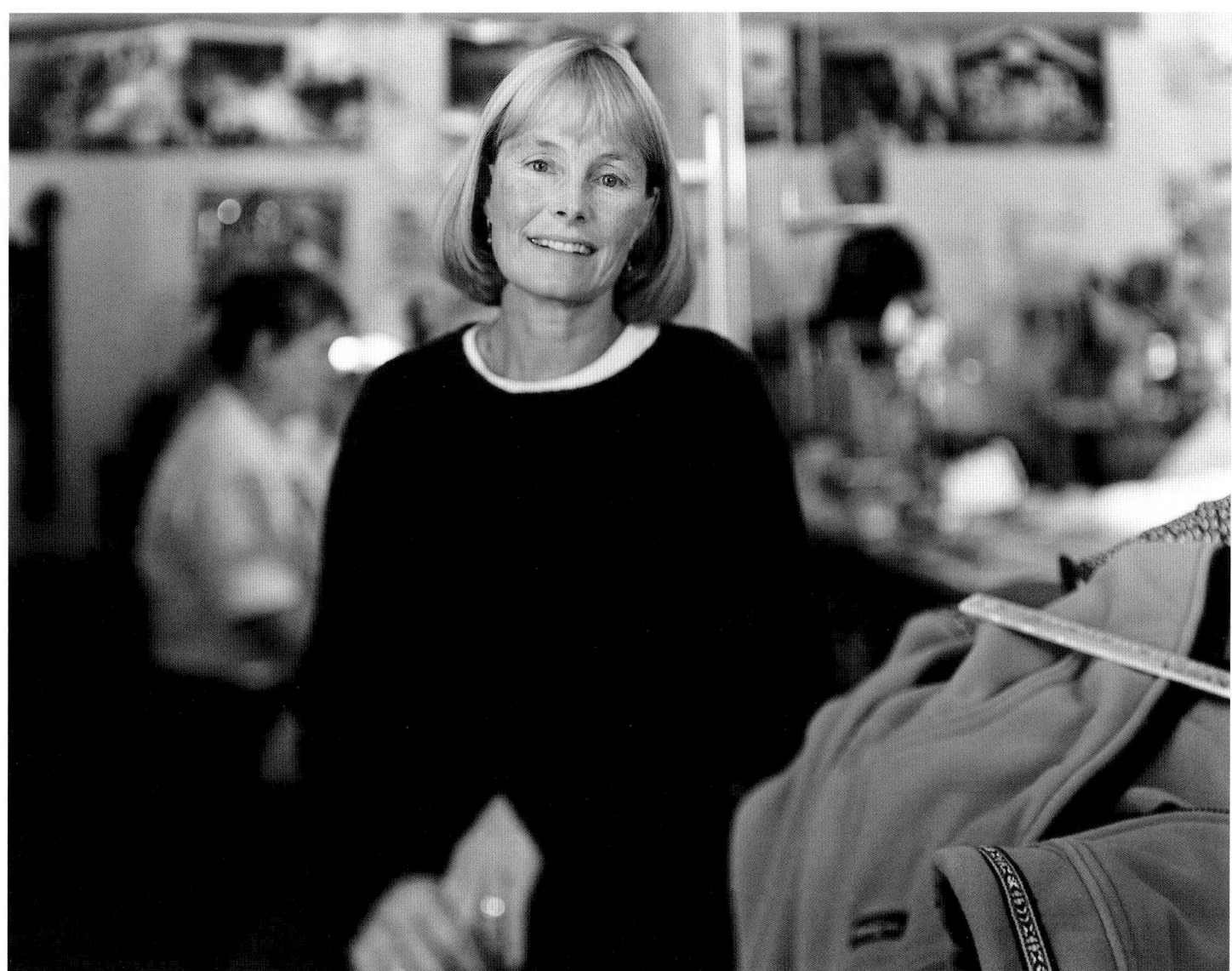

PLATE 45. Susan Schurke, owner, Wintergreen Designs

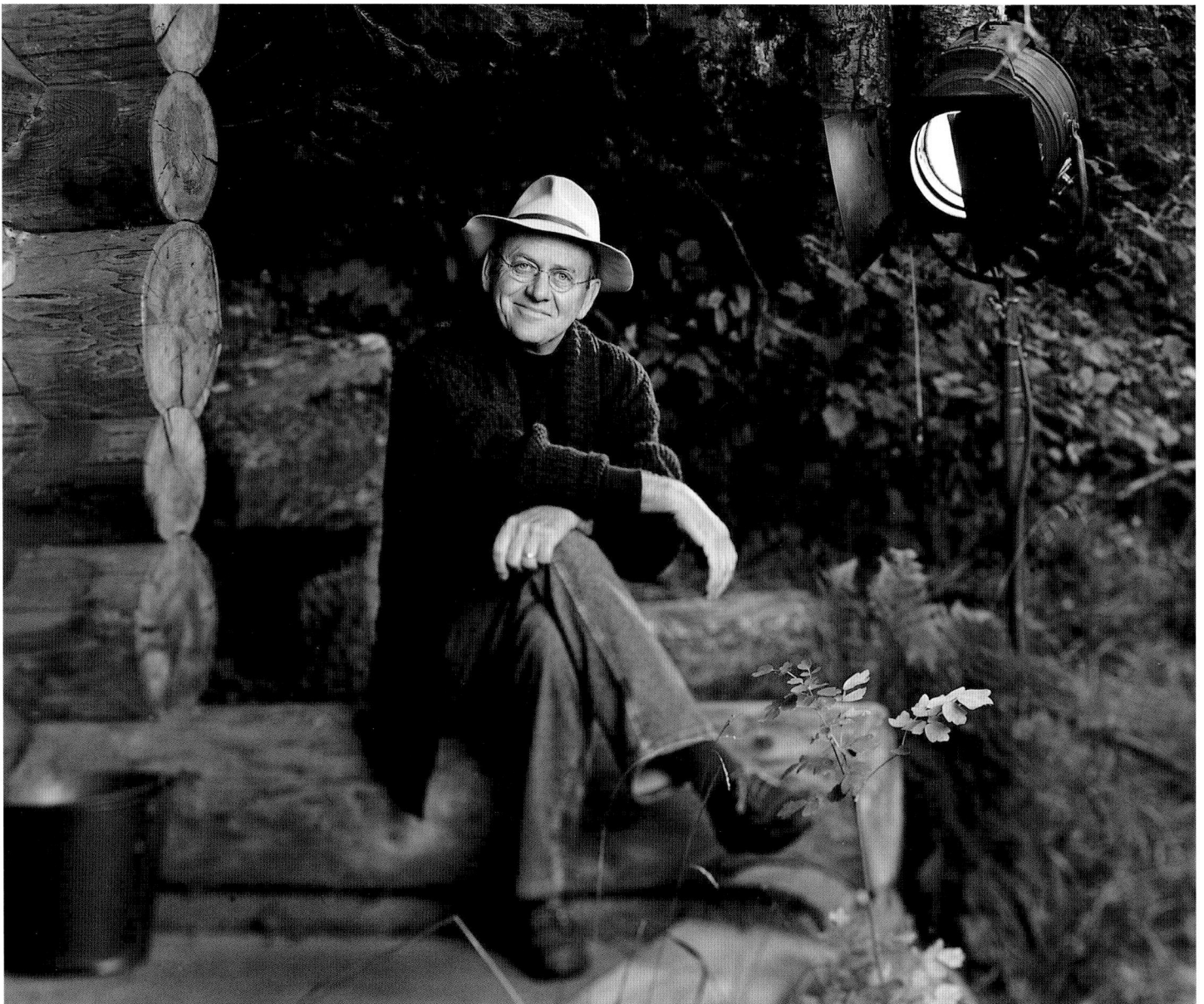

PLATE 46. Jim Brandenburg, photographer and filmmaker

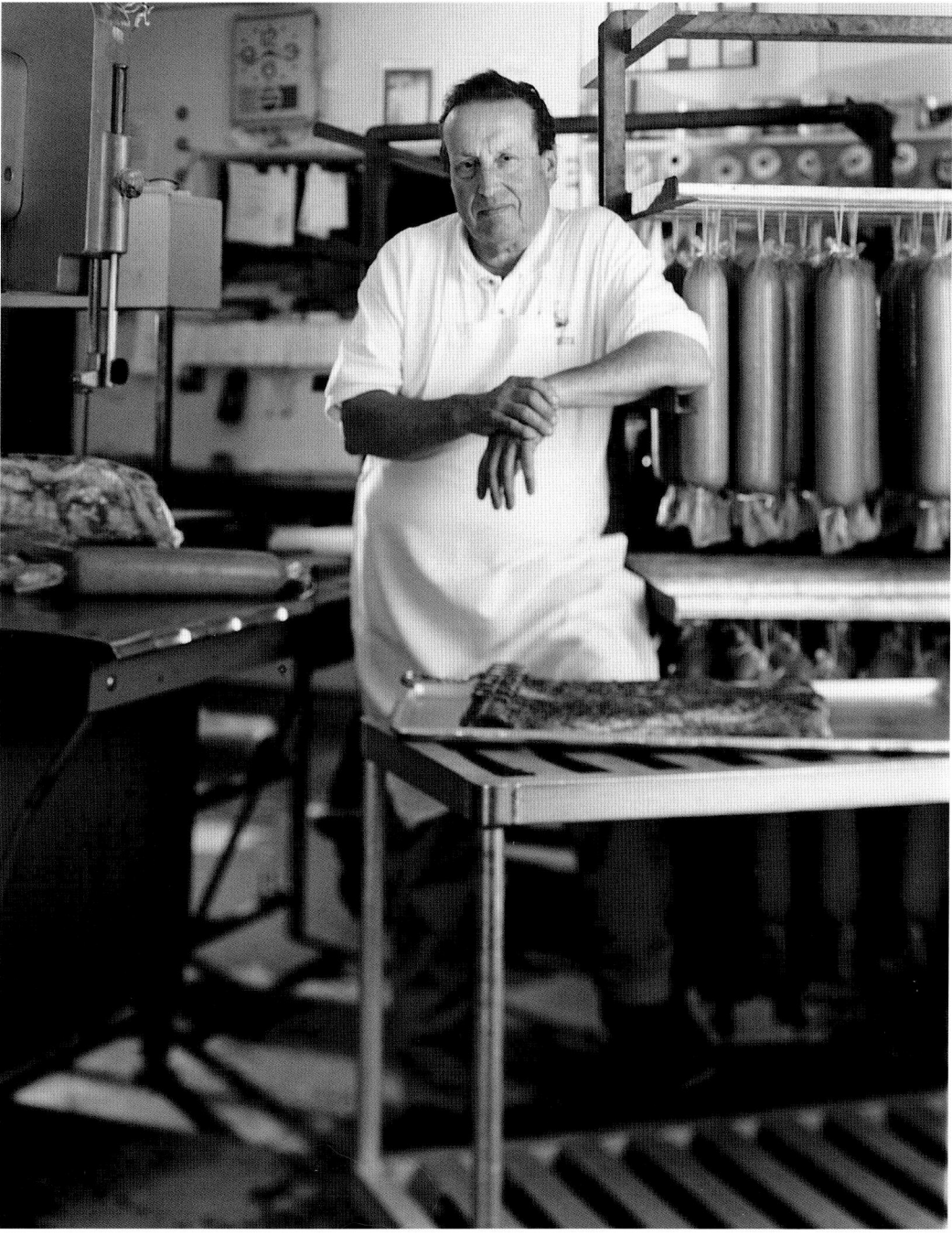

PLATE 47. Pat Zupancich, Zup's Market

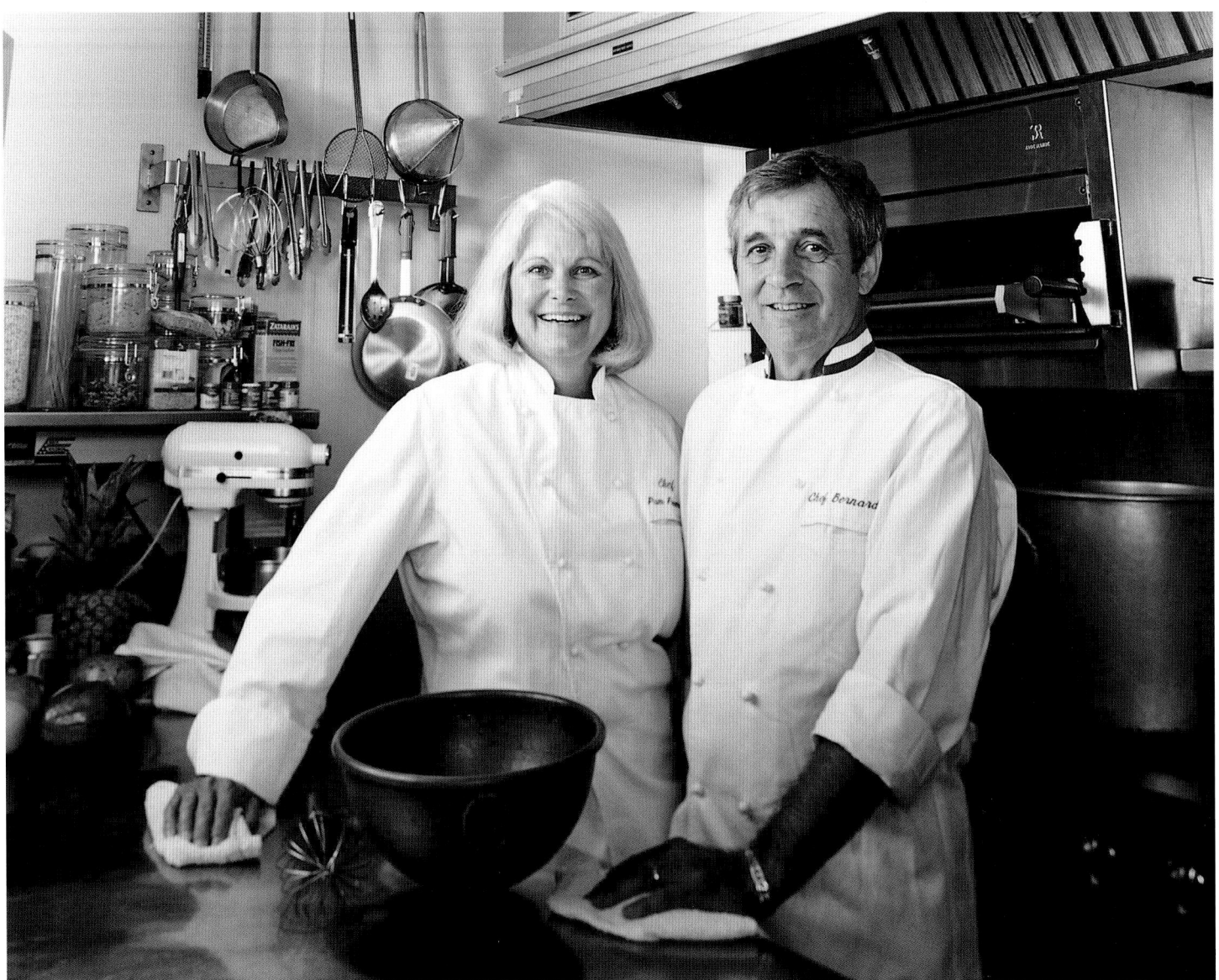

PLATE 48. Pam Freeman and Bernard Herrmann, Mantel House kitchen

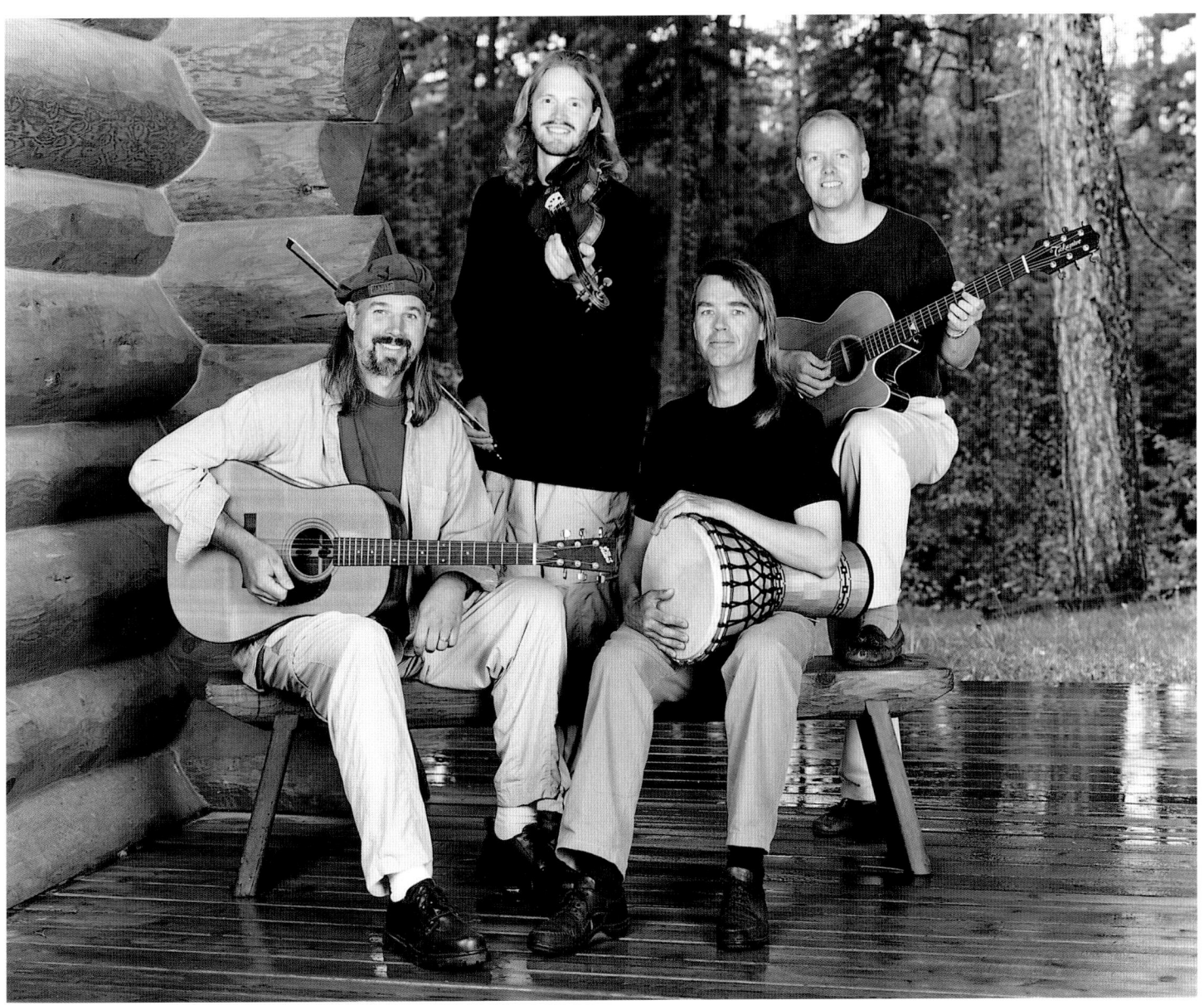

PLATE 49. Pat Surface, Eli Bissonett, Robin Anders, and Rob Mattson, musicians

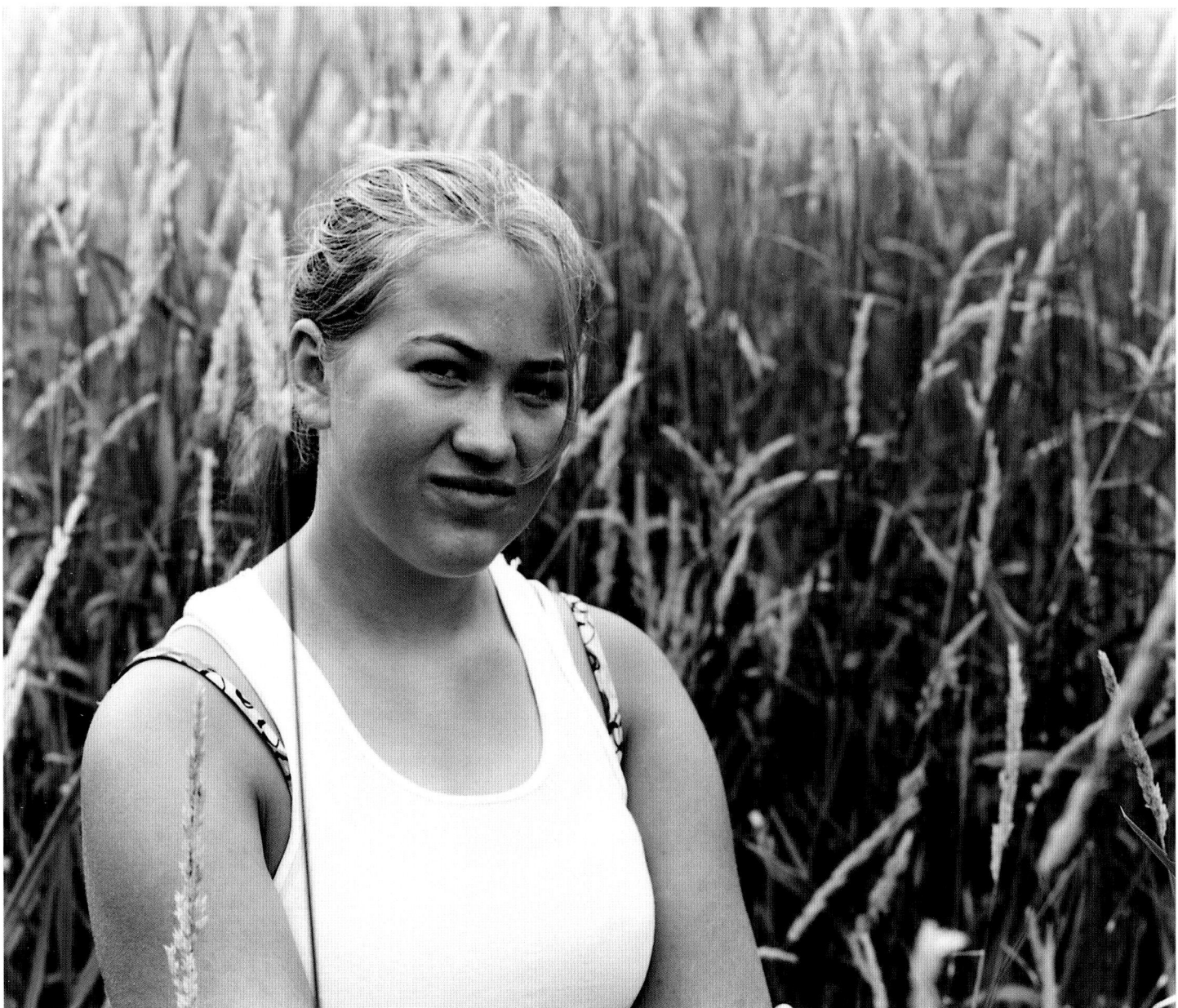

PLATE 50. Kahsha, Ely resident

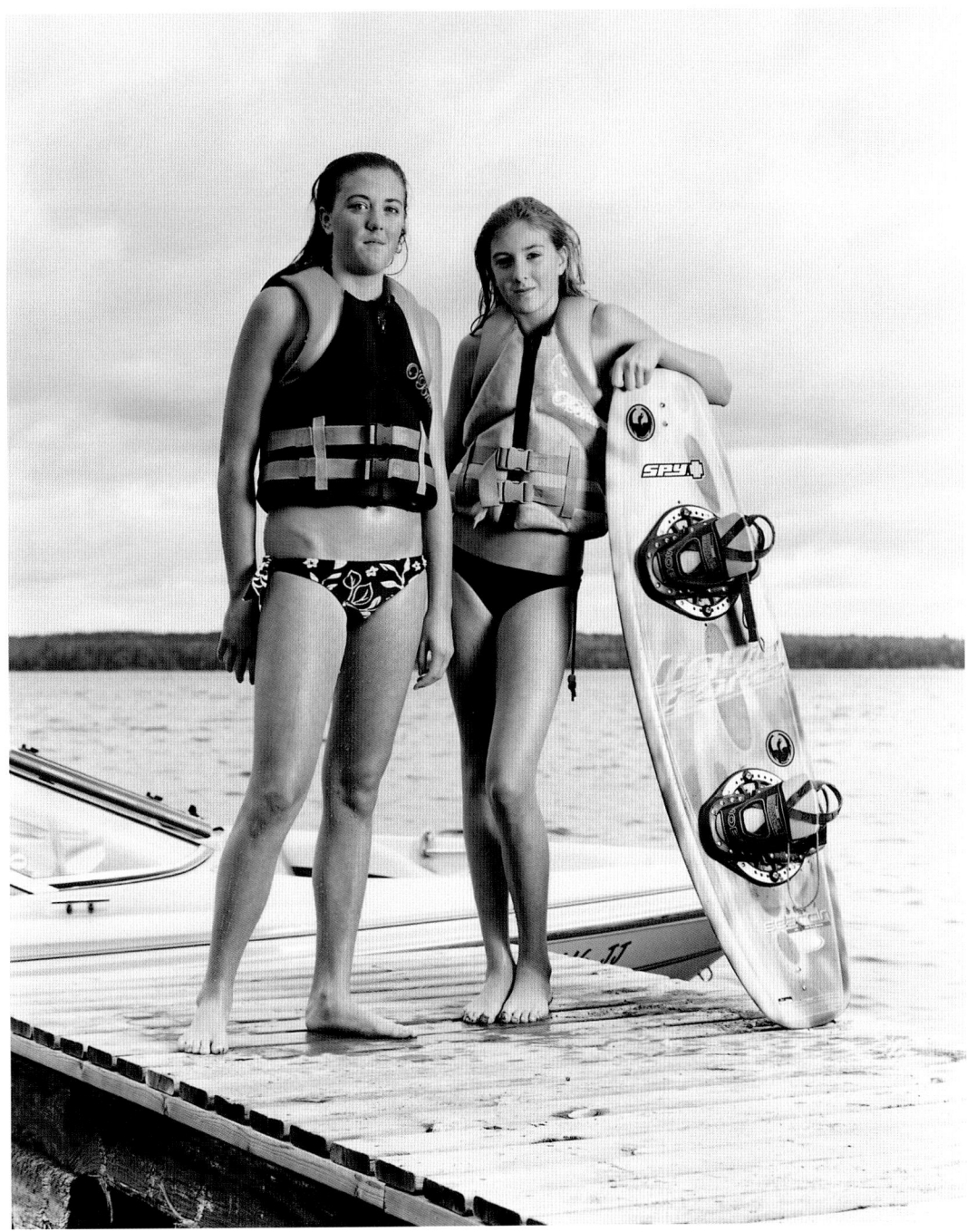

PLATE 51. Cortney and Bailey, Timber Bay Lodge, Babbitt

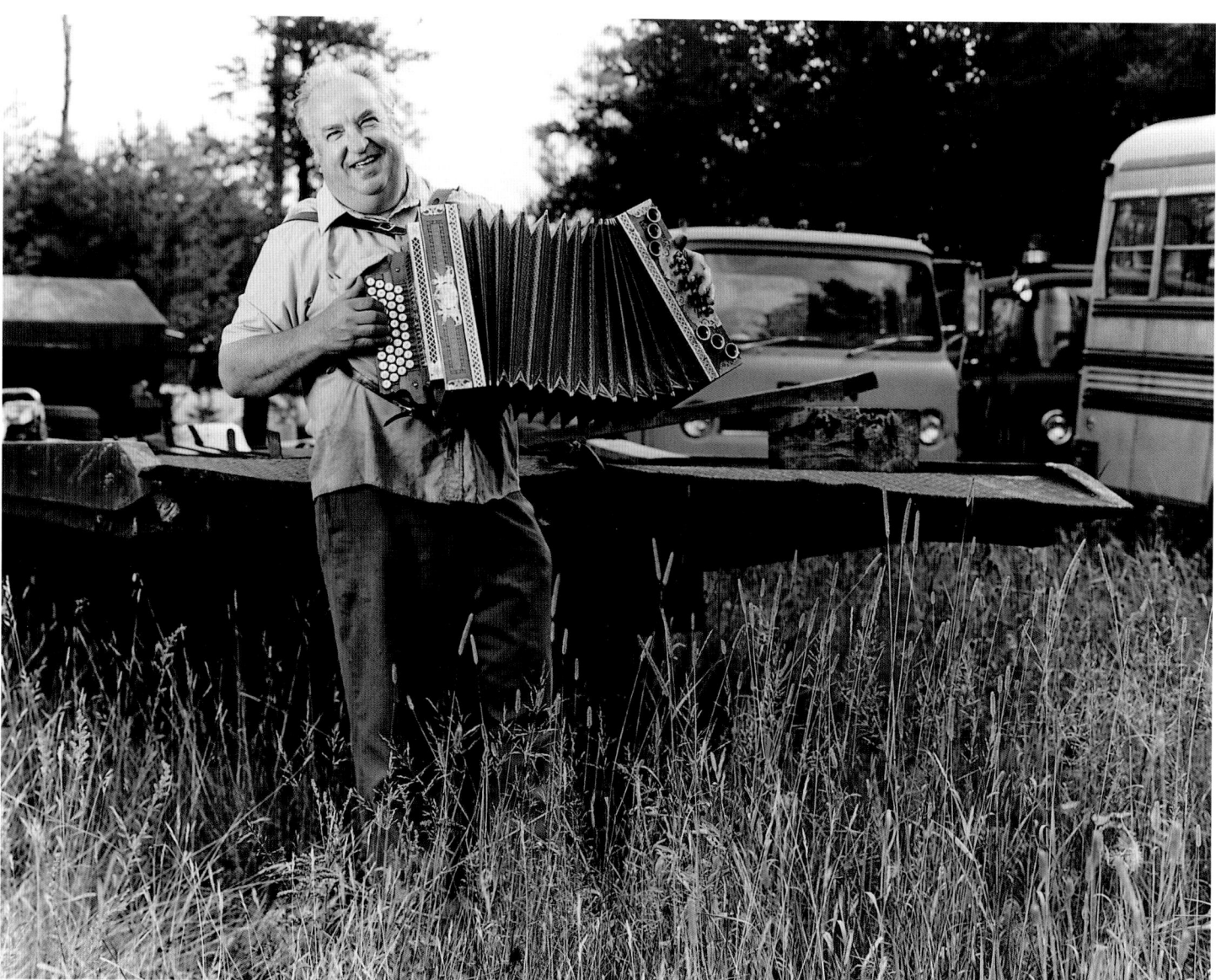

PLATE 52. Dr. Frank Udovich, dentist

WHAT IS in My Heart

It is pouring rain on a lush September afternoon, and Eric Mase is making room for a shipment of wood in his garage-turned-workshop. Tiny square windows cast a misty, fractured light onto a collection of superbly crafted birch-bark baskets in the Ojibwe style. Botanical themes appear in the amber orange of winter bark, intricately etched from beneath a layer of silver summer bark. Perfectly placed spruce-root stitches hold together the white cedar hoops of the baskets. Above our heads, the ribs of a traditional Ojibwe canoe arch across the space like a close-knit canopy of branches. We are surrounded by the woods indoors.

Eric is an artist of extraordinary talent. He uses only organic materials and the time-honored tools and methods of the voyageurs and Native Americans to "help preserve traditional art." He frequently dons the shirt and sash of the *coureur de bois*, or "runner of the woods," to demonstrate and interpret the adventurous life and artistic skills of the French voyageurs, who traveled this remote country for two hundred years.

Eric's craft is well-suited to the Northwoods. Not less so is his character. The frontier nature of Ely's people means that they take every endeavor to its extreme—in a really low-key way. For the most part you will not find boasters or braggarts. What you will find instead are modest people who find myriad outlets for their passions in some truly ingenious ways. These are people with strong aspirations and many talents who have found in Ely a community that allows for a uniqueness of expression. "I never fit into city life," says Eric who moved here from Chicago. "And I'm glad."

Take, for example, Dale "Limey" Tweit, a transplant from London with a knack for blacksmithing and a one-of-a-kind aesthetic. With an inspiration as clear as Kevin Costner's in *Field of Dreams*, Limey traded his Harley Davidson Sturgis for an old junkyard in the woods and transformed it into a miniature golf course. Follow the sign that says "Golfing for World Peace" into Limey's place, shell out five bucks, and you will get a round of bumpy miniature golf, a lovely walk in clover-studded woods, a lollipop, and an ice-cold Coke. Everything here is organic, recycled, and a little wild. Expect to meet a few mosquitoes and perhaps a lynx or hawk along the course. And rest assured that the raspberries you are eating next to the seventeenth hole are pesticide free. "I've got people who come here who don't even play mini-golf," says Limey. "They come and sit in a chair that I've got here in the woods, and my dog'll sit with 'em, no charge."

If this appeals to you, then so too will a drive by Rooster Lekatz's place. His front yard is filled with hand-sawn whirligigs—Uncle Sam, burros with baskets, a row of tulips, and more—all chained together to hinder thieves. Or you might like the fully functional cannon in Seraphine Rolando's front yard that he fires off every Independence Day. He has been working on welding a life-sized pair of steel moose antlers, just for fun.

The pace of life here seems to afford people the chance to pursue their visions, both grand and small. Carol Stouffer, with a quietness grounded in faith and determination, maintains an heirloom garden along the southern wall of her hand-built cabin, committed to preserving things that are worth preserving. Meanwhile, on the shores of a remote lake, a massive conference center emerges from polar explorer Will Steger's expedition camp. The magnificent structure of timber, glass, granite, and ancient Ely greenstone is a looming work in progress that Steger is gradually building by hand. It will be a "think tank" where he hopes to foster greater international discourse and action on environmental issues. It is the culmination of his life's work as an explorer and as the educator he always knew he would be.

For some, there is an optimistic spirit here that allows them to become the person they want to be, or even perhaps a person they never imagined. Anne Swenson brought her family to town in the 1970s from the Chicago area. She started writing a column for the *Ely Echo*, and before she knew it, she had bought the paper and was running it from the ground up, even operating the press herself. She now has an editor but continues as owner and publisher and columnist. "Putting together a newspaper is like putting together a puzzle, and since it's weekly, I get to continually repeat the process. I love what I do. I'm just the luckiest person on earth."

Anne dedicates a significant portion of her energies to supporting Ely's thriving arts scene, particularly through Greenstone Public Art, an organization that encourages local artists while enhancing the life of the community through the beautification of public areas. One can argue that long winters make for fine art, and Ely is a case in point. Arts both ancient and new are sustained in small basements and over garages across town and into the woods. Ely is fast becoming well-known as a regional arts center. It is impossible not to trip over high-quality creations here, from the gorgeous images in the Brandenburg Gallery on Sheridan Street to a memorial exhibit of Bob Cary's ink drawings in an upstairs room at the Northern Grounds Café. The Blueberry Arts Festival and the Ely Winter Festival both attract tens of thousands of tourists to see and buy the work of more than 150 locals. For a town of 3,700, that is pretty impressive.

Even those who prefer to see Ely as canoe country will find the best in artistry here. In a wood-scented barn near Shagawa Lake, Jeanne Bourquin handcrafts between two and eight canoes every year. It is a transformative process, turning the hard edges of white cedar planks into the luscious oiled curves of a canoe's ribs, gunwales, and bow. The wait can be up to eighteen months for one of her original "Otters," a wooden structure as gorgeous as any violin or cello. She will charge you the same whether she builds it by herself or you travel to Ely to help her and learn a little bit of her trade in exchange. I can hardly believe her when she says, "I never really decided to be a canoe builder," but it is true. Her first priority was to paddle; the canoe building is simply an extension of her pursuit of the perfect day on the lake.

Like so many before her, Jeanne has been inspired by the much-loved Joe Seliga, who built more than 650 of his famous wood and canvas canoes in a garage behind his house over the course of nearly seventy years. His wife, Nora, worked by his side for most of that time, and even after she died, Joe would include her name in scrawled ink under each canoe's canvas. When we photographed him at the age of ninety-one, he told us he was no longer taking deposits for his work. "I don't want to make a promise and then not be around to deliver a canoe," he chuckled. I do not know the disposition of his last order when he passed away in 2006, but there are hundreds of fortunate people who benefit every summer from Joe's craftsmanship, including many of the teens at Camp Widjiwagan, where there are no less than forty-five Seliga canoes in service.

Across the lake from Widji, a simple path leads from a dock into a sheltered clearing. There is an old cabin here that has been restored and raised to allow for a garden level below the original structure. It is small and plain but perfectly suited to its place inside the forest from which it was built. Milli Salmela Bissonett pulls us in quickly to keep out the blackflies. The room is near empty. In the absence of furniture, the floor has become the most striking feature—a gleaming expanse of polished wood—followed closely by the vertical ridges of Finnish-style pine walls. Behind a pair of graceful potted grasses, one can barely make out a small sitting area. "I've been working on making my house more empty," explains Milli. "I'm sorry I've complicated my life with stuff. Less is more for sure."

Milli's eye for design is a fixture in Ely. She is a third-generation Finn in the area and spent eight years of her life studying and practicing the decorative arts in Finland. She is passionate about many things—dreaming, nature, her children, the culinary arts, and more. Music is among the most public manifestations of Milli's passions. She was the host for many years of *Morning Moment*, a radio show on WELY that featured world music, incorporating folk, classical, and jazz. Many of her announcements and introductions were made in Finnish, and she relished the time devoted to the show for it dedicated a space in her life for the study of music and language. Like so many in Ely, her love of music is a direct expression of her cultural heritage.

Were it possible, I would like you to hear the sound of Doc Udovich playing a waltz on his Mervar button accordion, an instrument manufactured by Slovenian immigrants in Cleveland. We stand listening in an expansive field overlooking White Iron Lake, surrounded by Doc's collection of big metal things: fire engines, bulldozers, cars, trucks, wagons, school buses, and more. None of them are linked by any particular criteria for acquisition. Some he has bought, but many of them he traded for dental work. "That was good!" yells our son Jack when the accordion squeezes closed for the last time. And it really was. Like food at a picnic, music is best outdoors.

"Music is an inspiring medium that has an incredible spark that blends with all people, all places," says Milli. "I think it's a real magic." Out on the lawn of Wintergreen Designs one warm summer evening, her son Eli and friends create a little magic of their own for a crowd of about a hundred people. Locals and visitors alike gather to hear the soulful strains of Eli's fiddle mingling with the northern twilight. For Milli, this is a moment that captures the very essence of a life well lived—a life made possible in this northern town. "Music, my family, the natural world—weaving them together. This is what is in my heart."

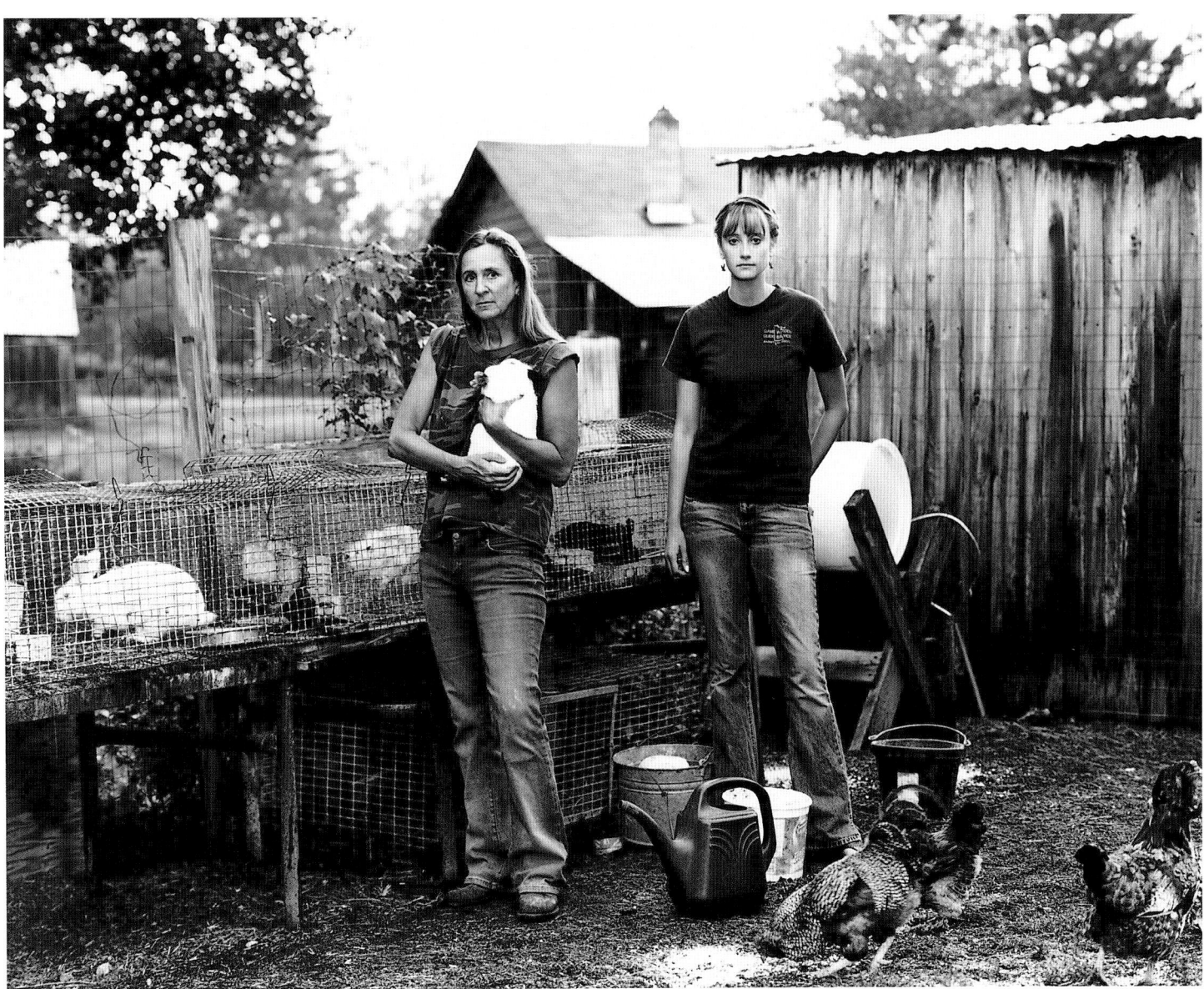

PLATE 53. Wendy and Amber Schlueter, Babbitt

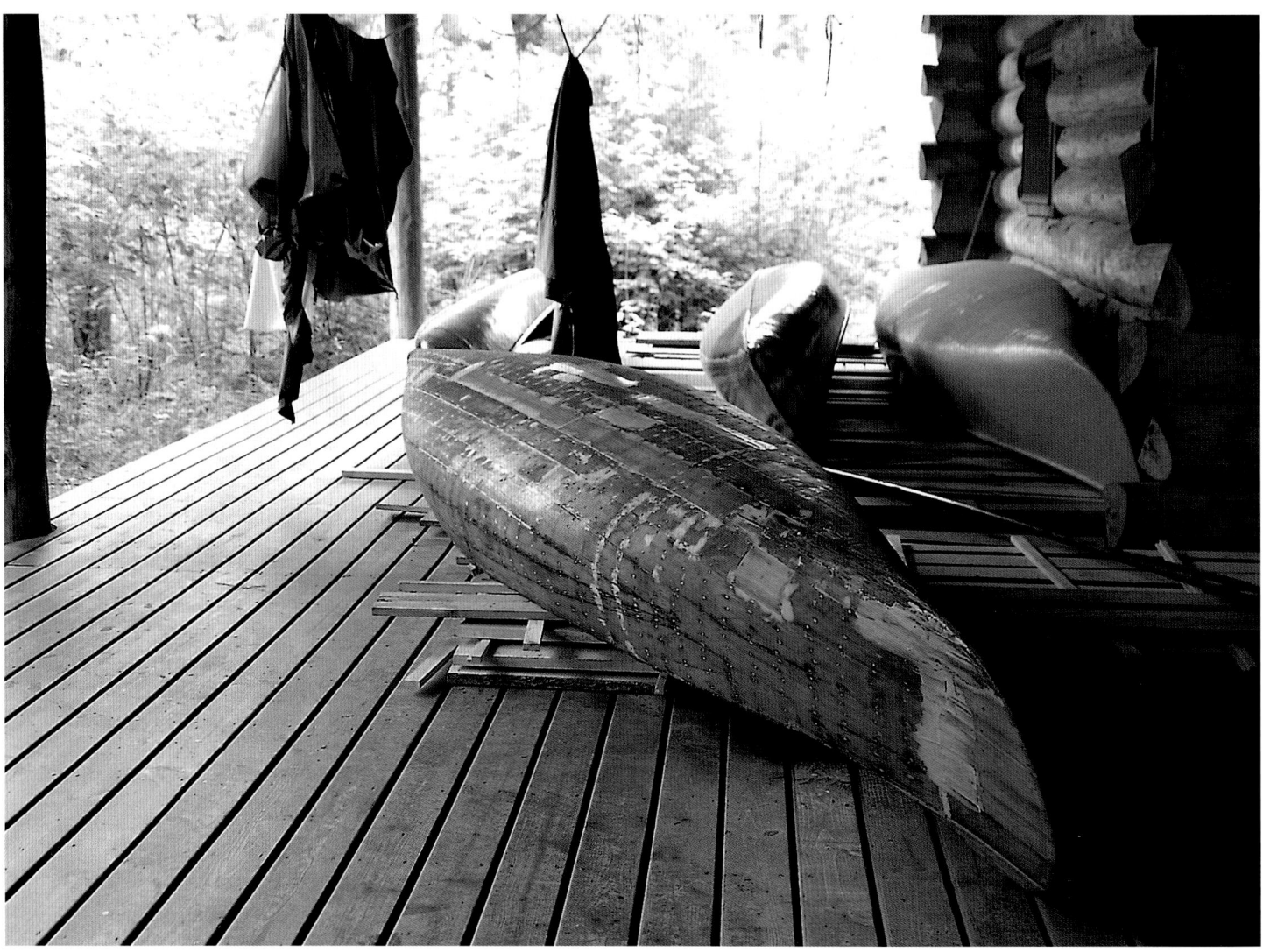

PLATE 54. Camp Widjiwagan, Burntside Lake

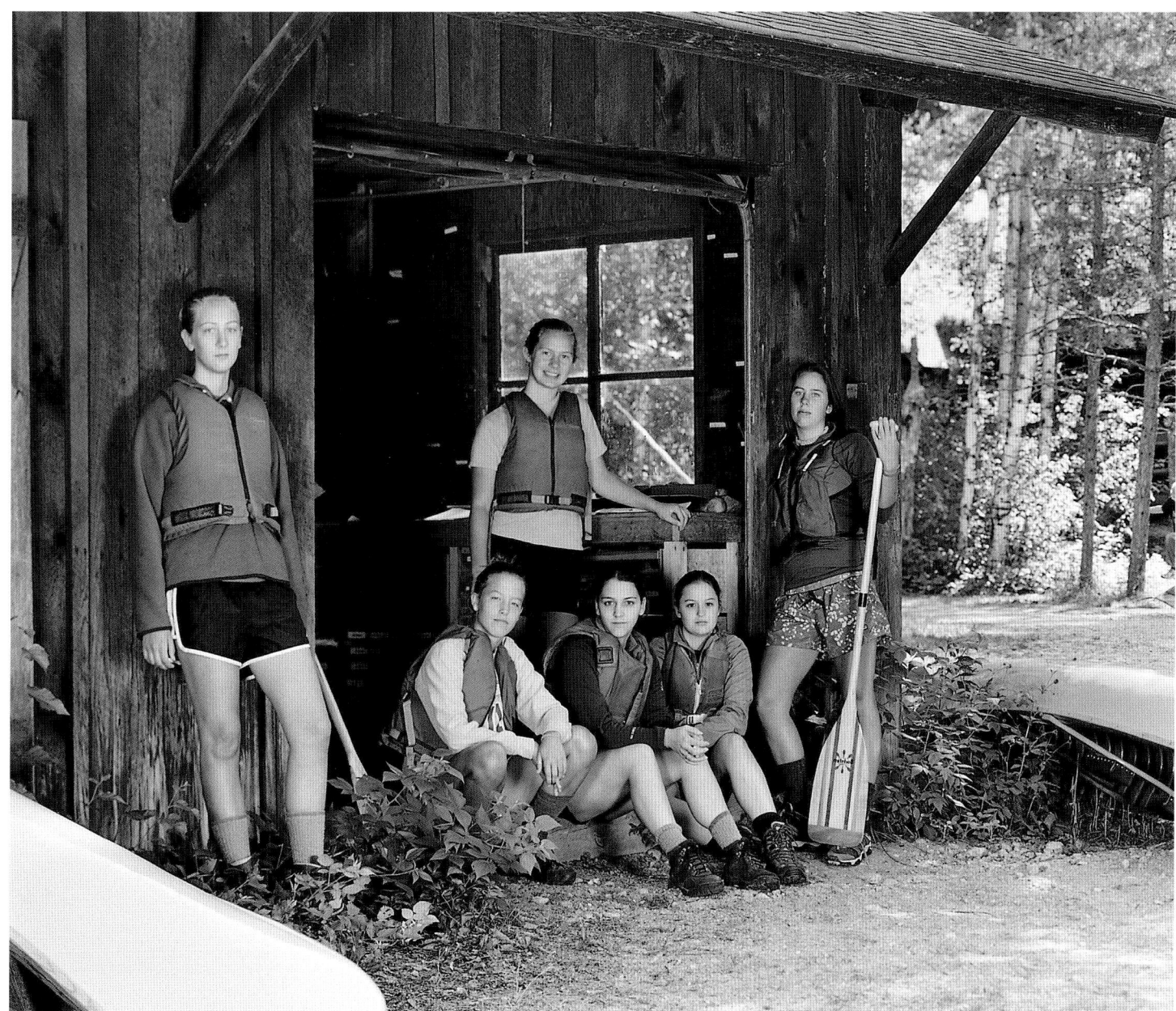

PLATE 55. Camp Widjiwagan

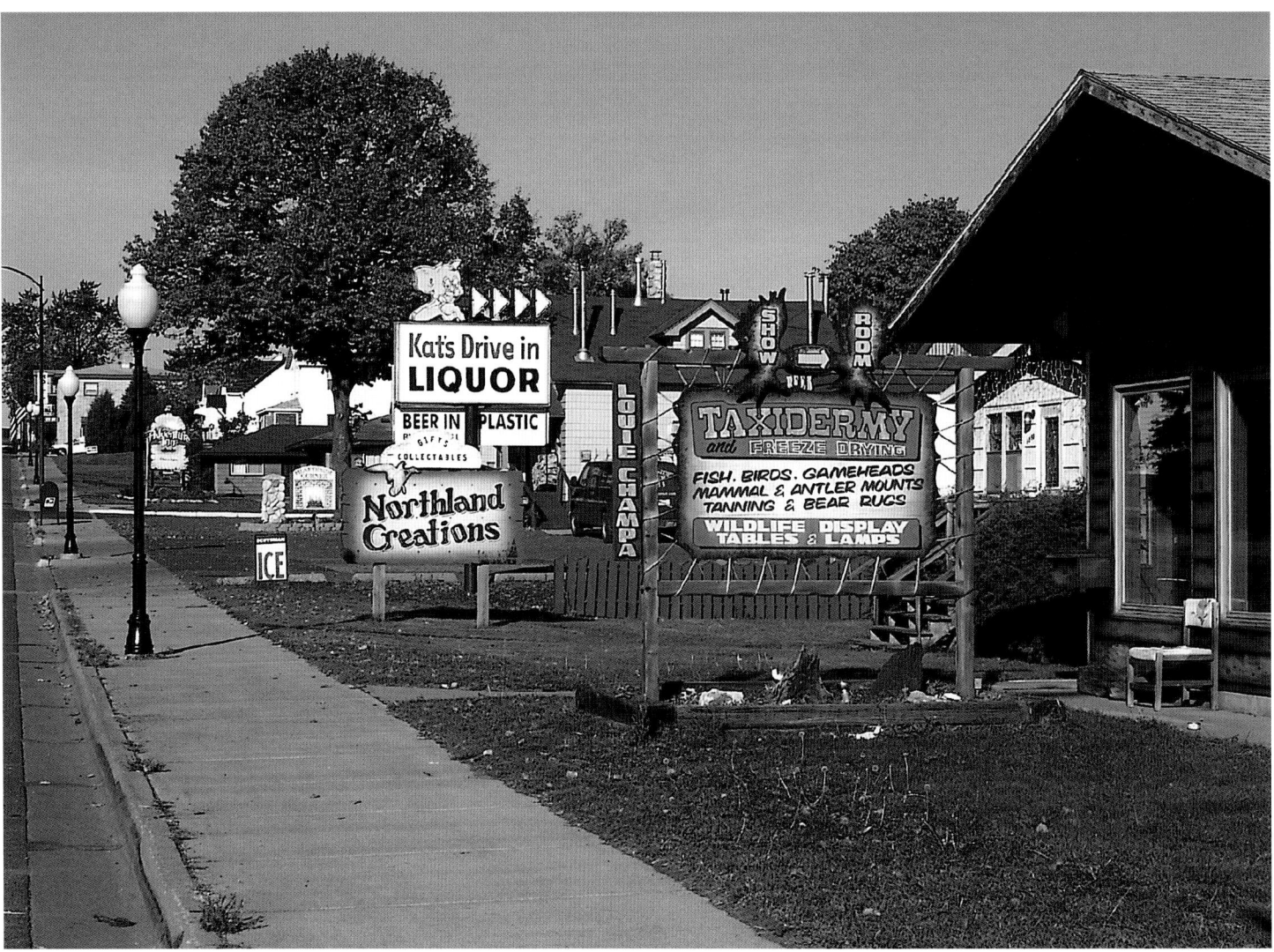

PLATE 56. East Sheridan Street, Ely

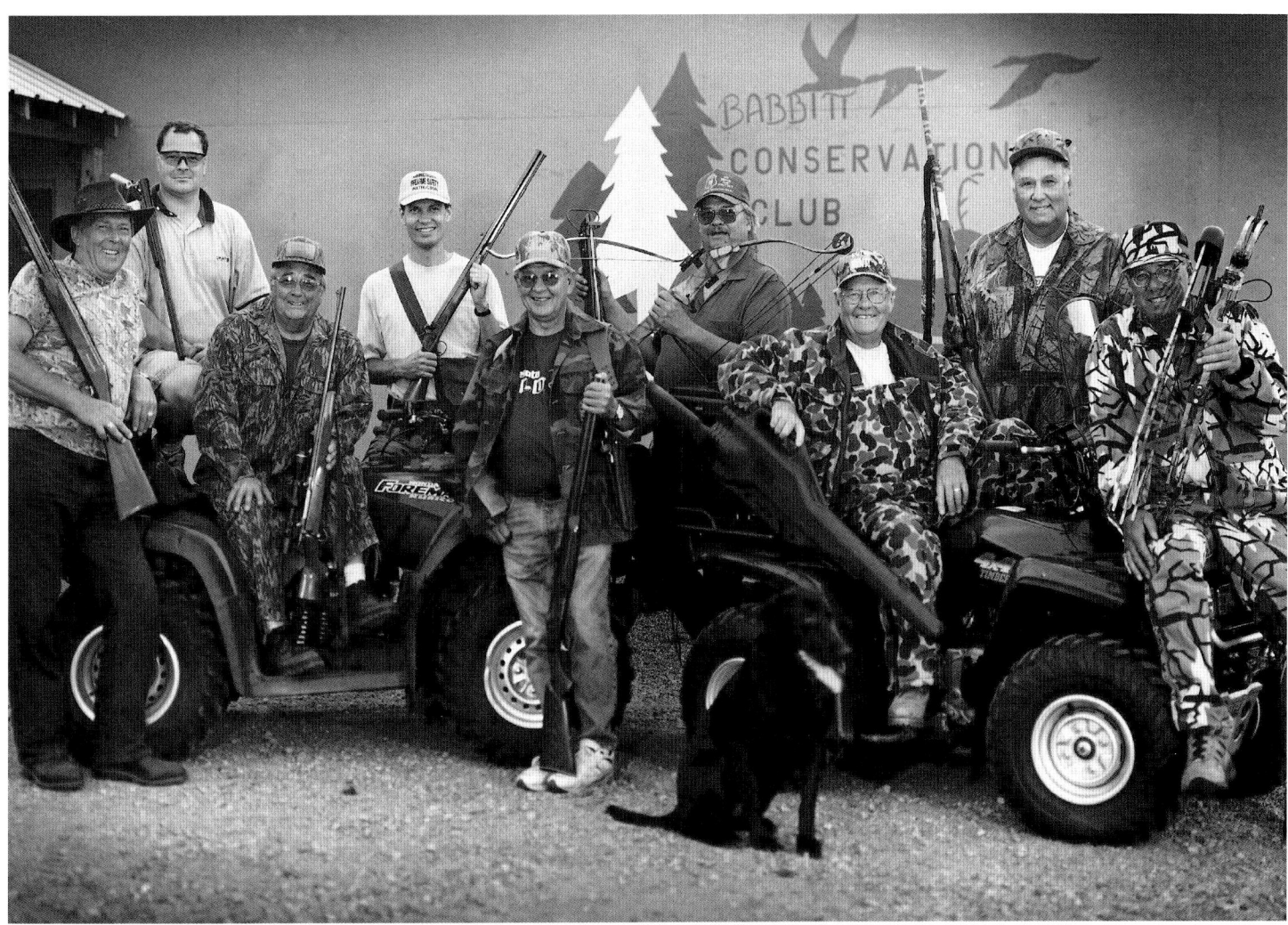

PLATE 57. Babbitt Conservation Club

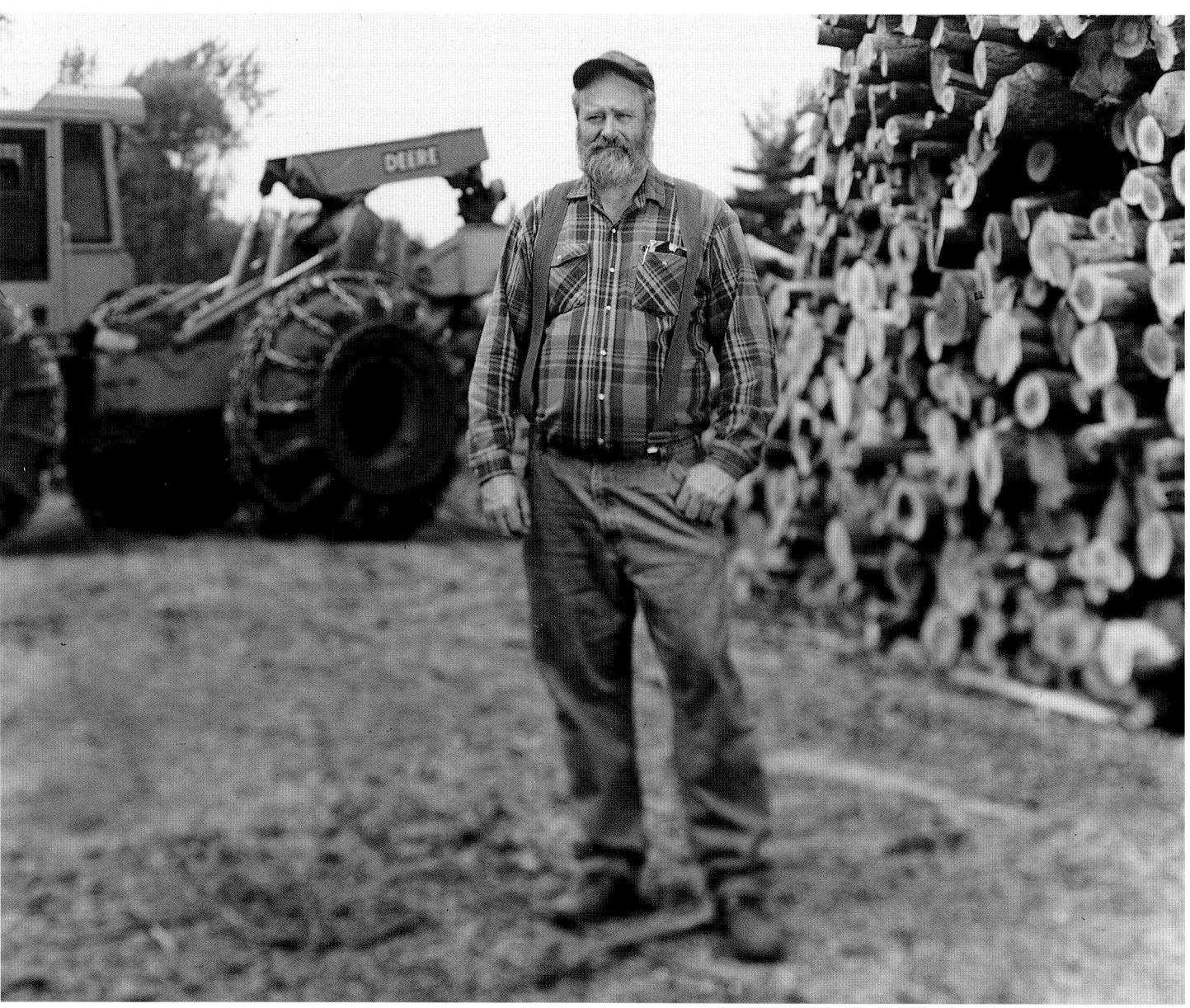

PLATE 58. Bruce Kainz, logger

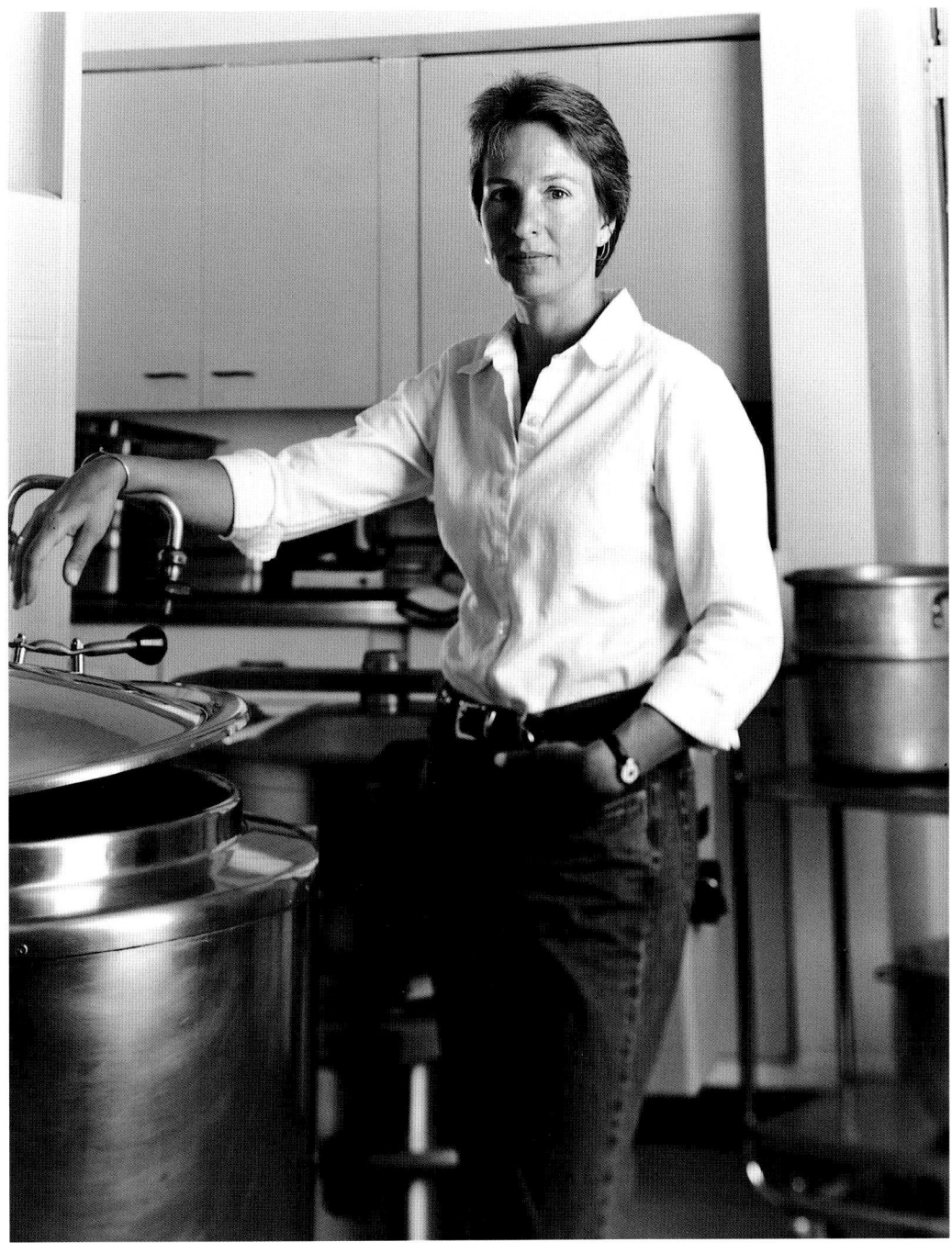

PLATE 59. Robyn Bertelsen, lunch lady, Ely Public Schools

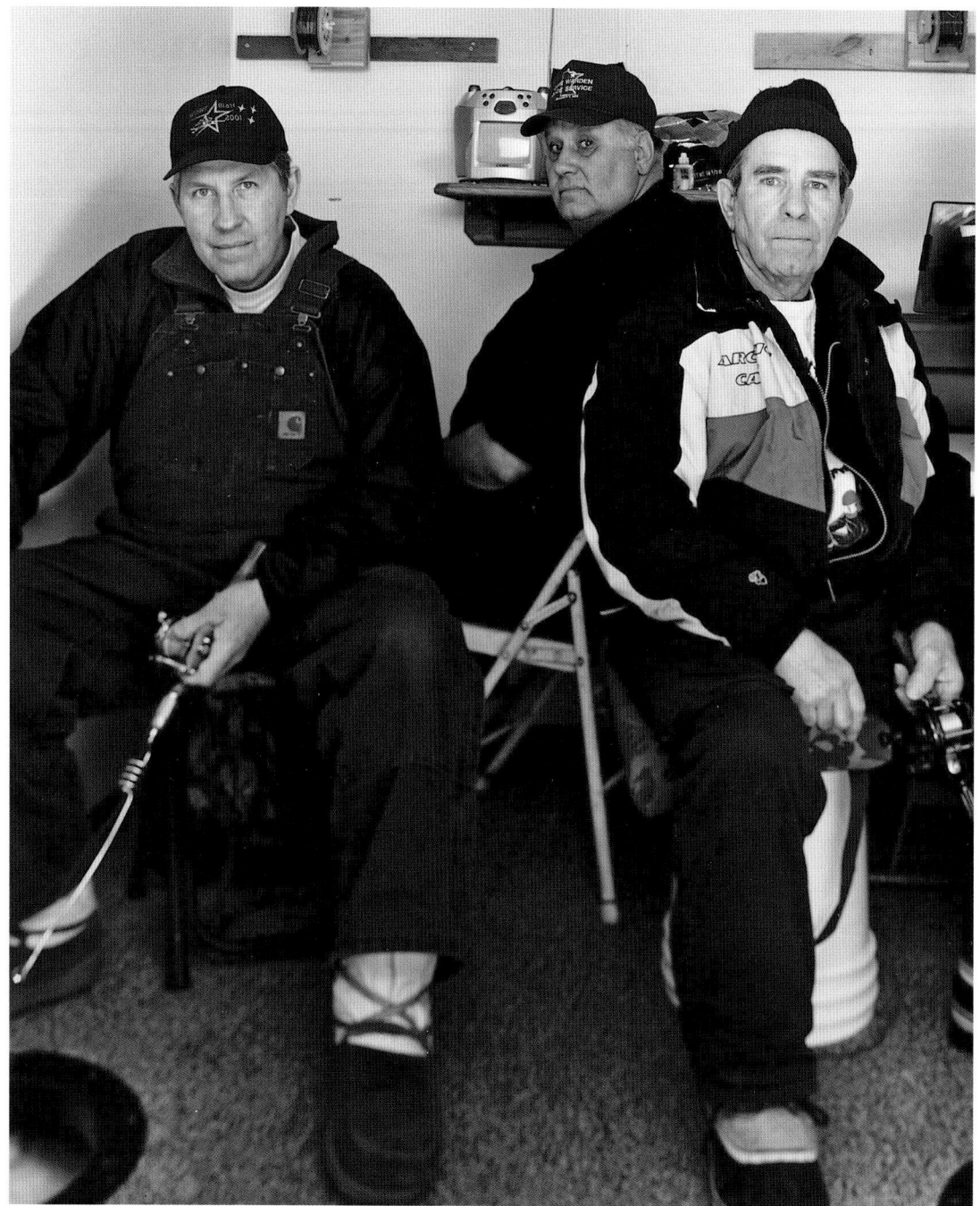
PLATE 60. Dave Serena, Ken Schlueter, Tony Serena, fish house, Snowbank Lake

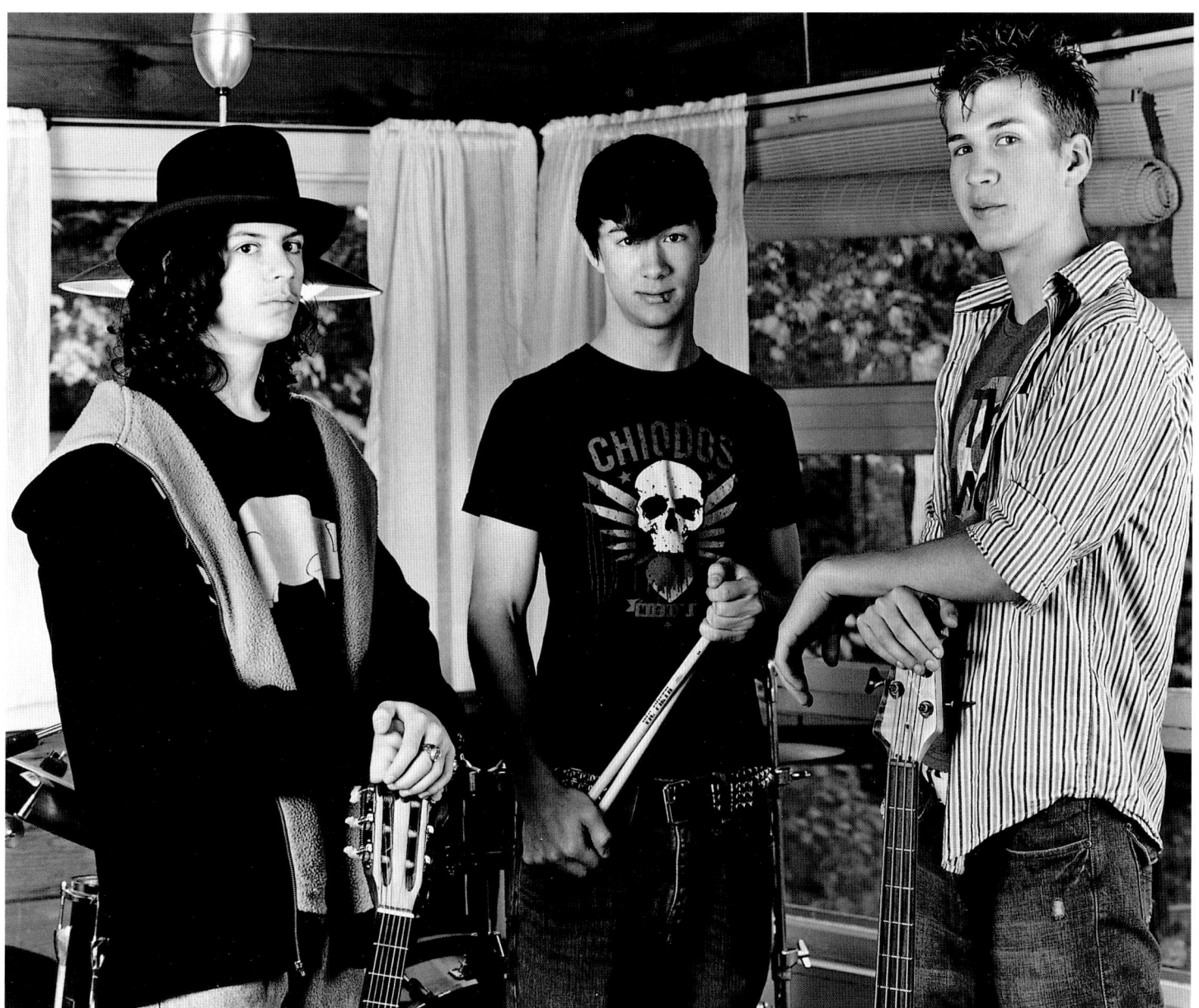

PLATE 61. TB & the Blasters, rock band

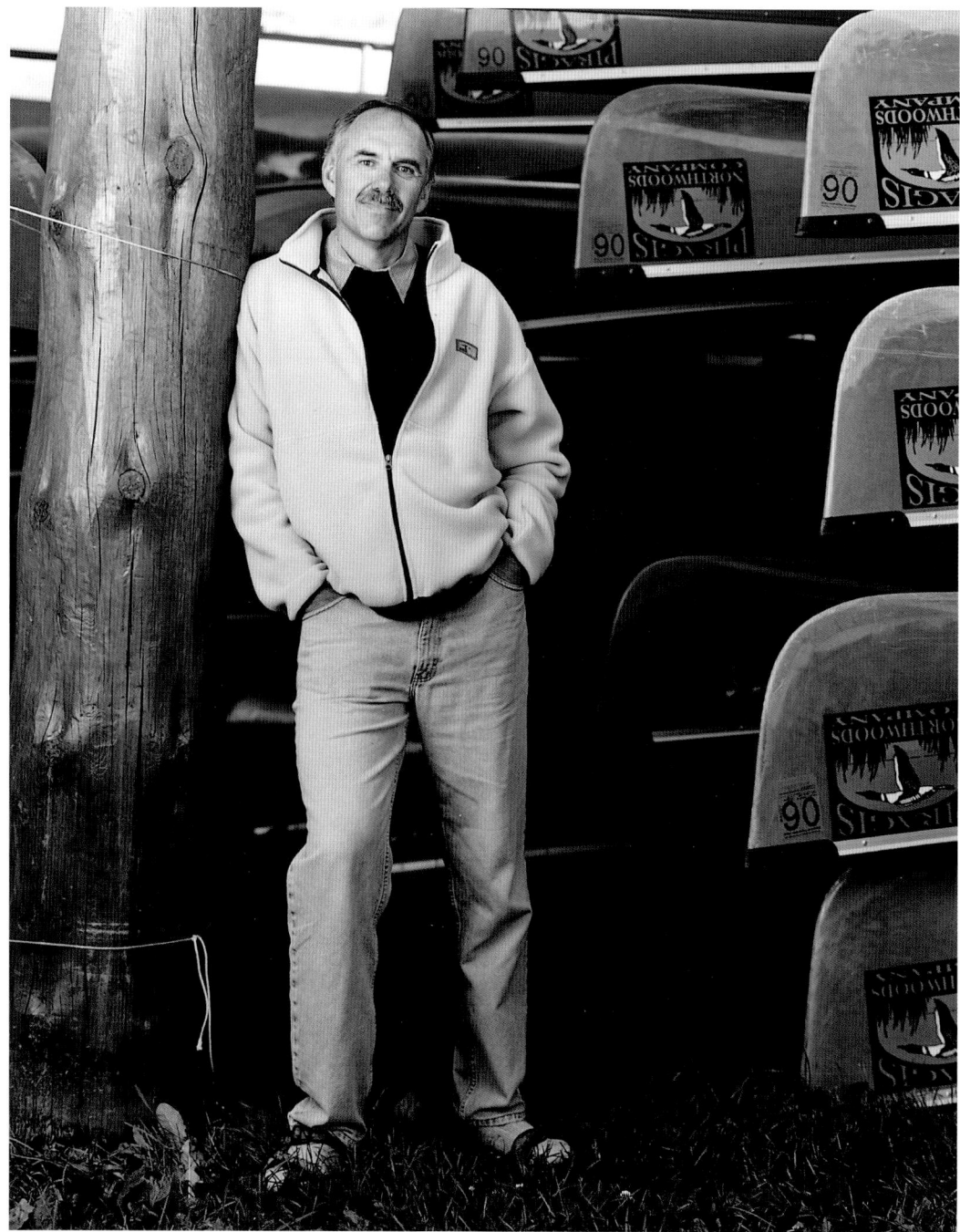

PLATE 62. Steve Piragis, owner, Piragis Northwoods Company

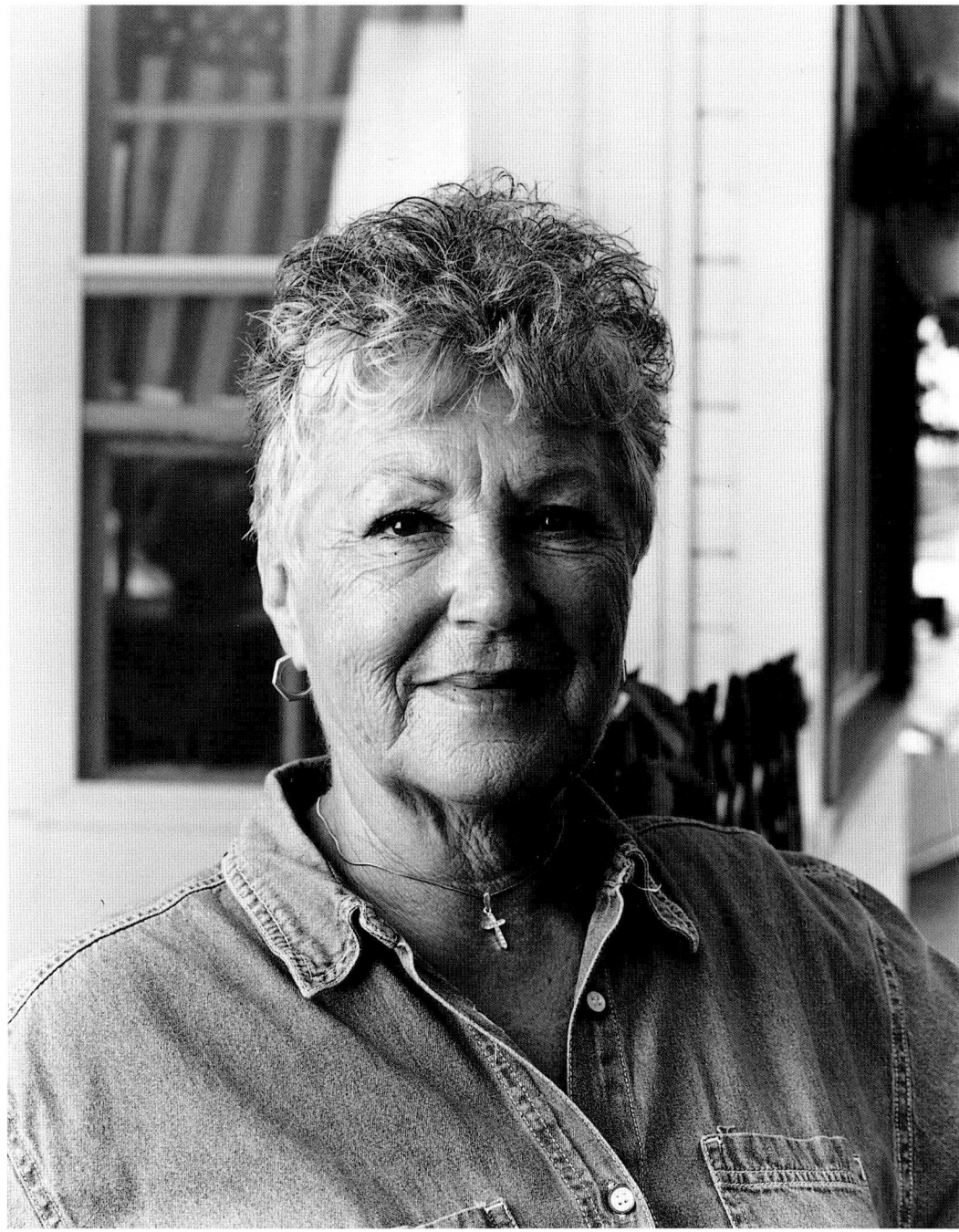

PLATE 63. Frana Cherico, owner, Miners' Inn

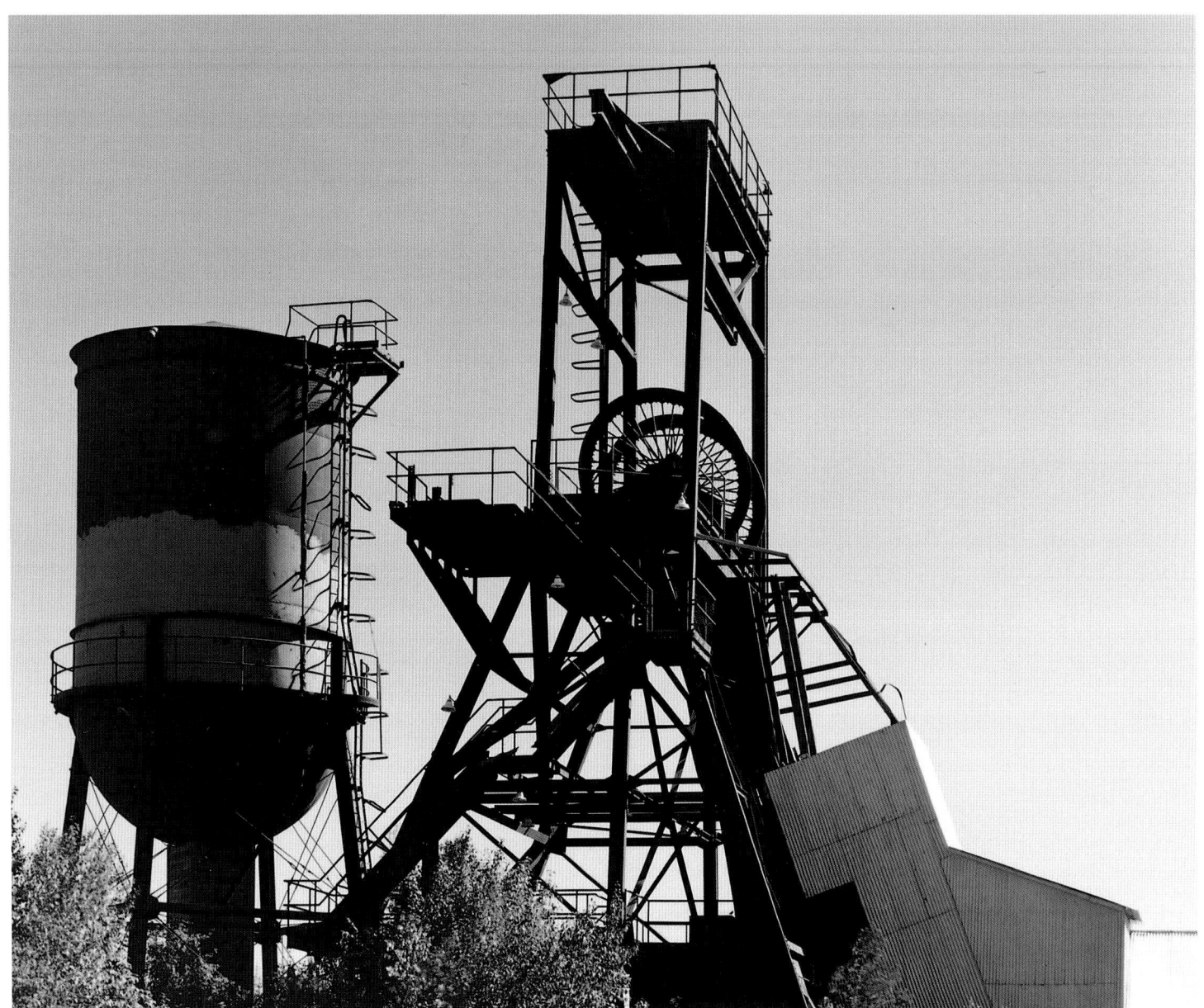

PLATE 64. Headframe of Pioneer Mine, Ely

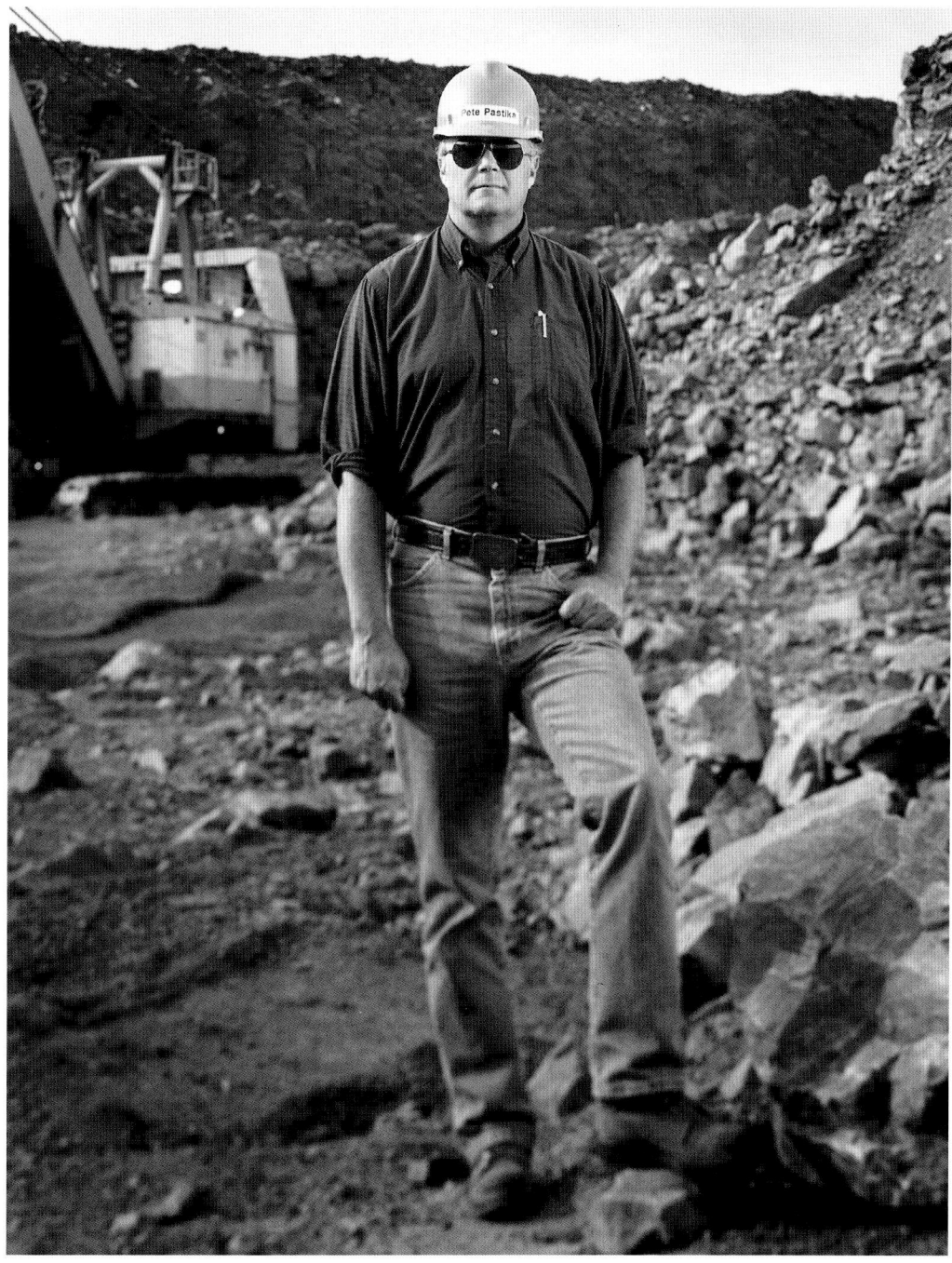

PLATE 65. Pete Pastika, mine engineer, Babbitt

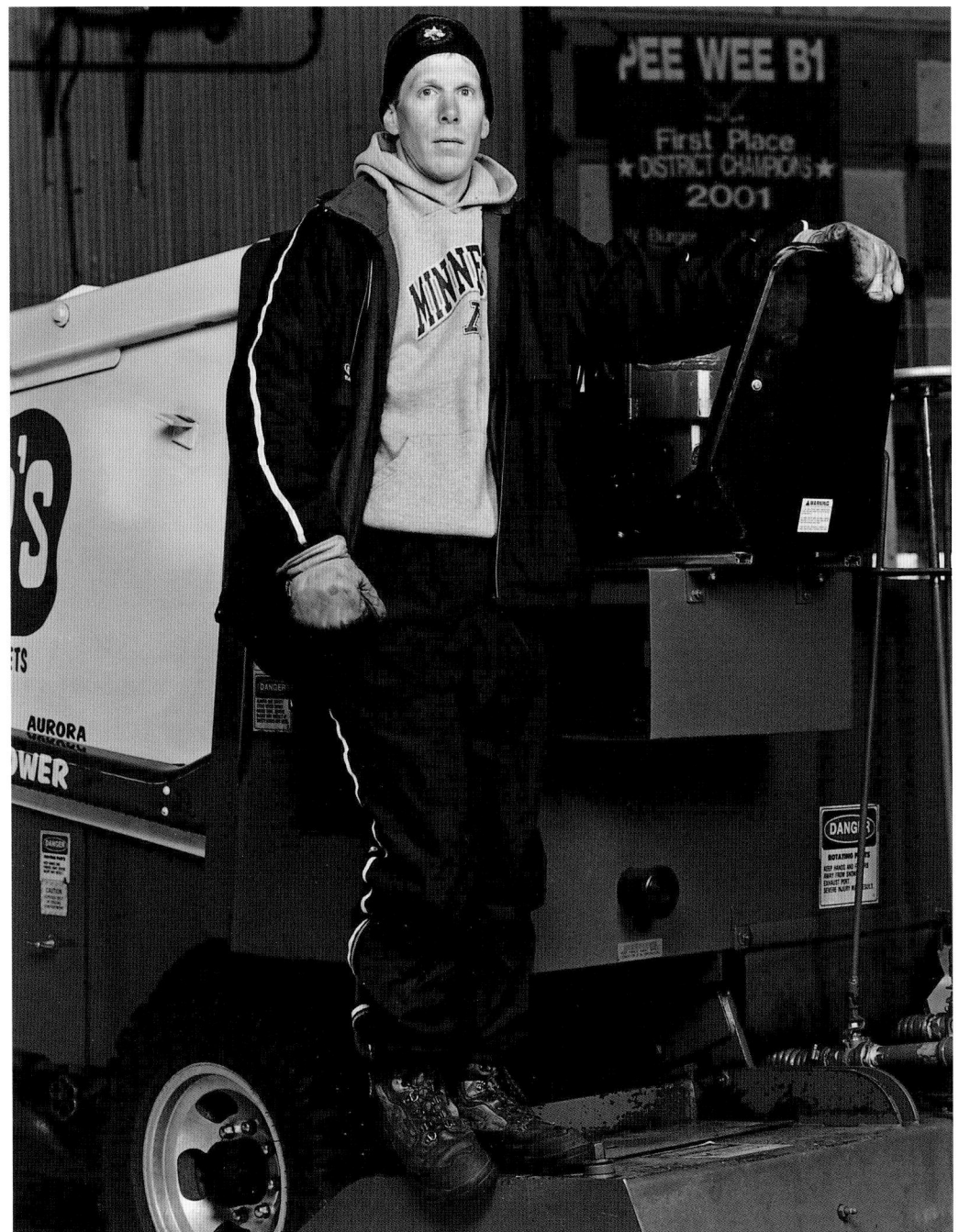

PLATE 66. Dan Olson, Ely Ice Center

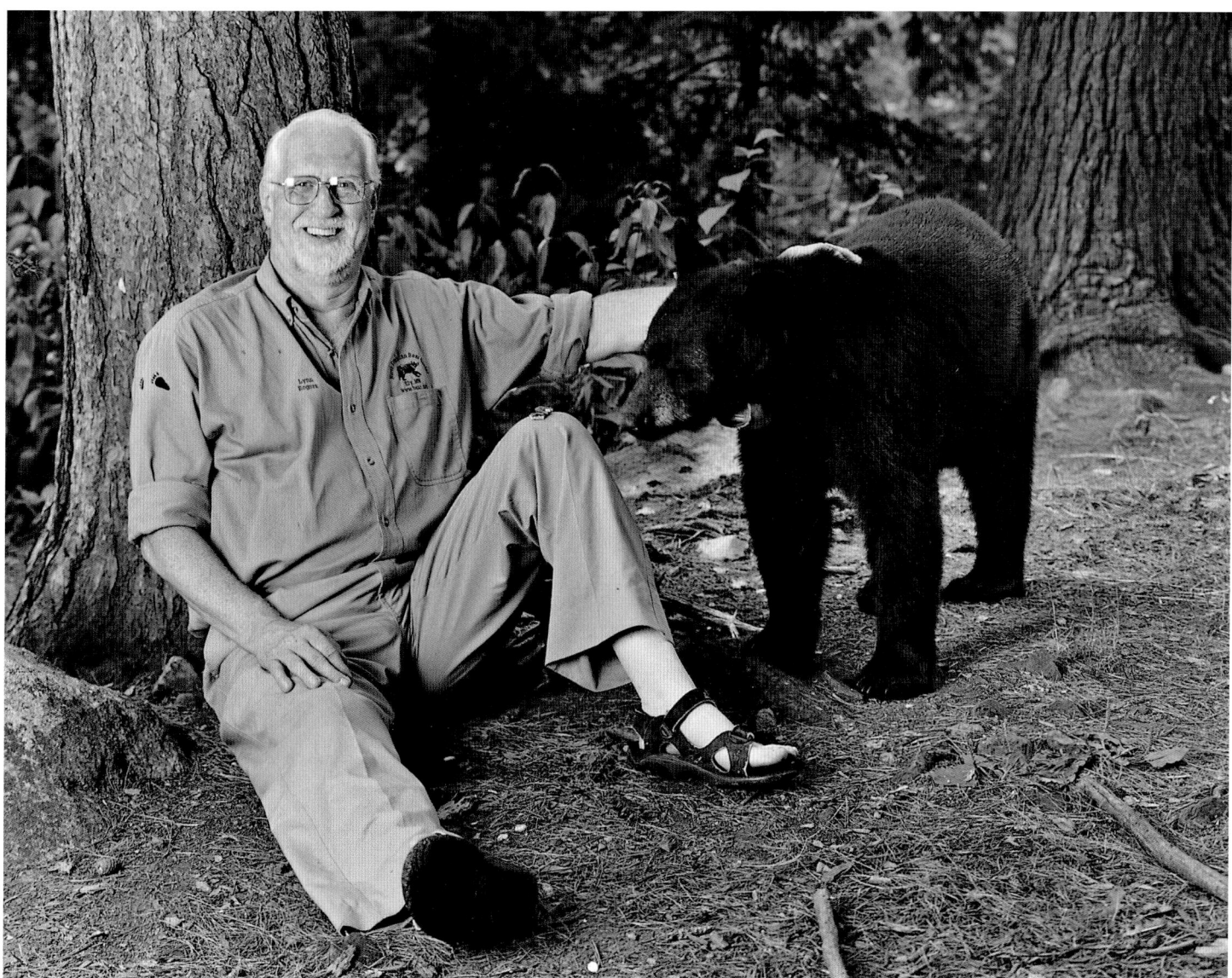

PLATE 67. Dr. Lynn Rogers, North American Bear Center

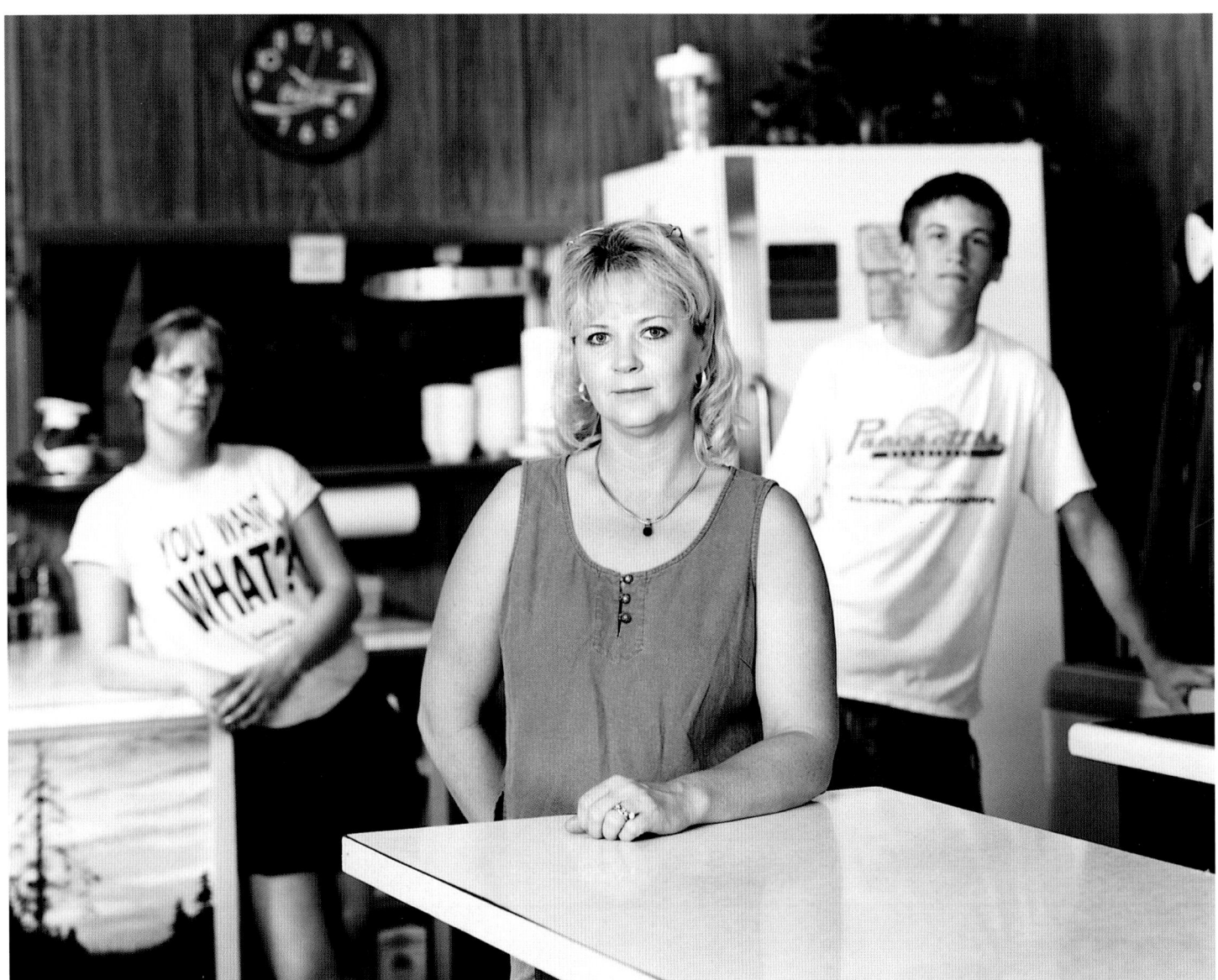

PLATE 68. Bonnie Anderson with Kj and Derek, owner, Britton's Café

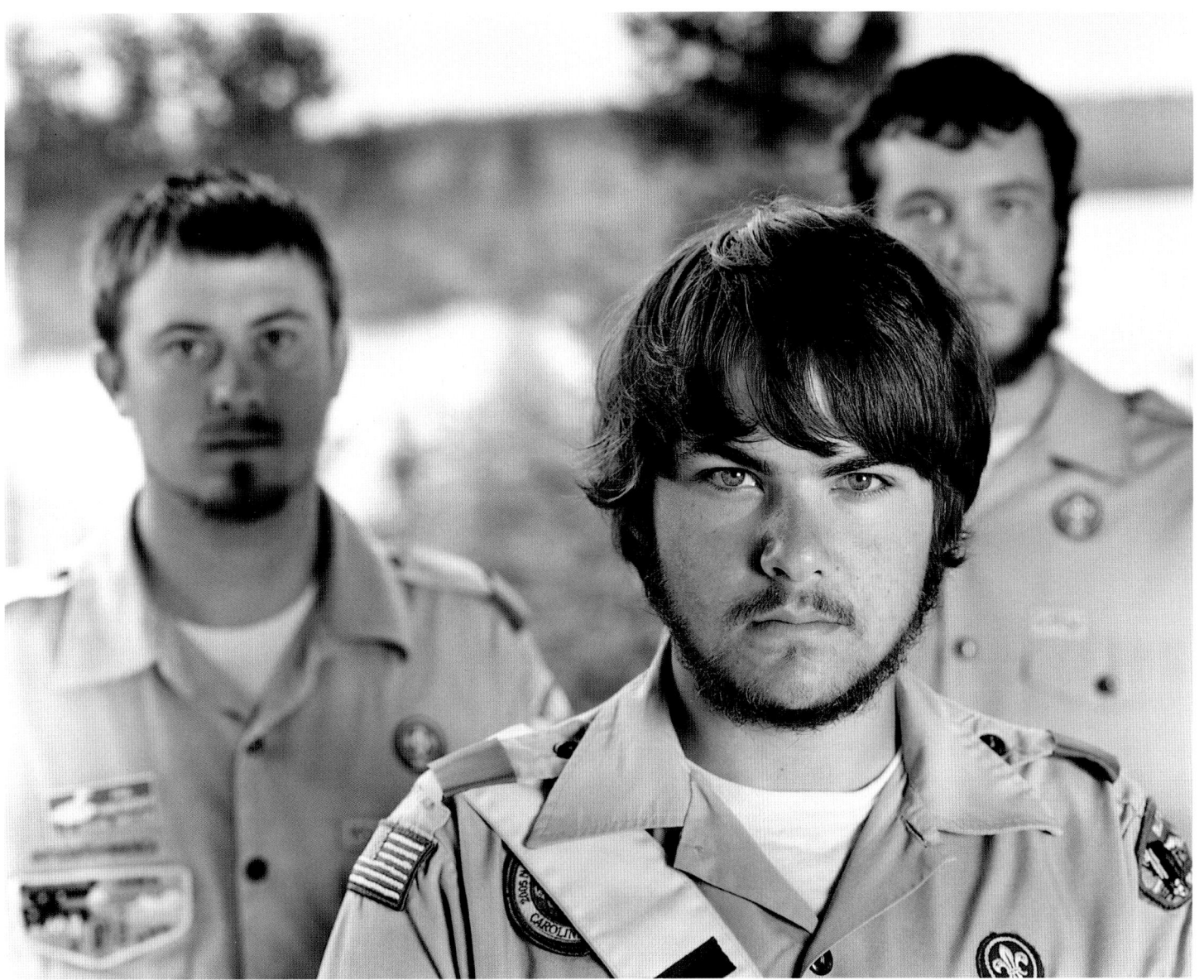

PLATE 69. Ryan, Jeff, and Philip, Charles L. Sommers National High Adventure Base, Boy Scouts of America, Moose Lake

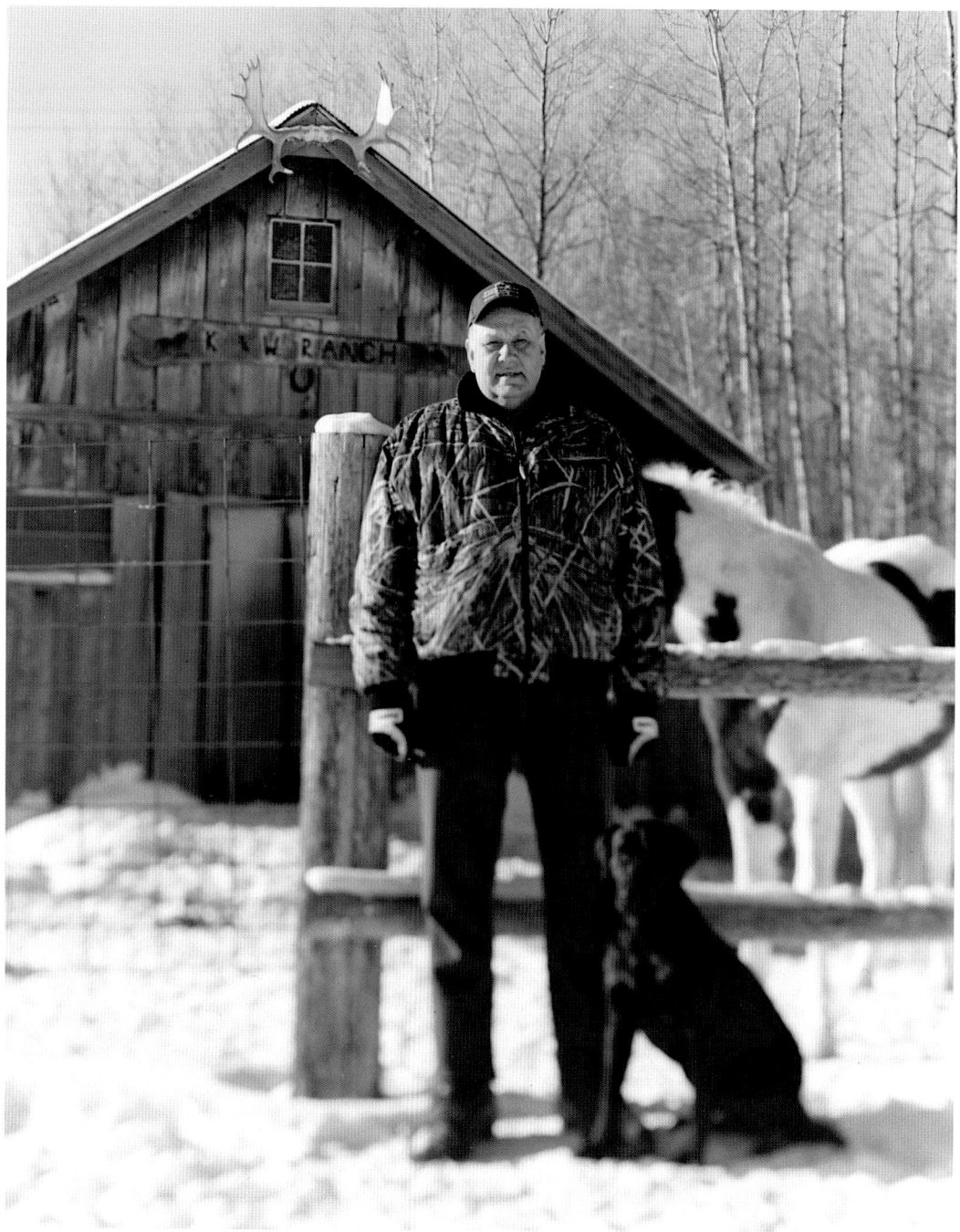

PLATE 70. Ken Schlueter, retired conservation officer, Babbitt

Wild Neighbors

We opened the U.S. Department of Agriculture brochure titled "How to Live with Black Bears" to find an image of a furry black head bobbing in the middle of a lake. The caption read, "black bears can swim to island campsites." Now, *that* is the kind of information a person really needs to know.

After years of honing up on bear lore, hiking with bear bells, and singing songs along the trail so as not to surprise anything big and scary, we eventually came across our first bear on our cousins Nan and Gerry Snyder's back porch. Their *island* back porch, that is. The juvenile bear, perhaps two years old, was fresh and fluffy, having just dried off from his inter-island swim. He reminded us instantly of our German shepherd fresh from the groomer—a little sheepish to be caught so clean but not embarrassed enough to stop him from moving a little closer. We backed into the cabin and enjoyed our bear encounter through a protective pane of glass as he placed his clawed front feet on our door and tried unsuccessfully to get a really good whiff of us. His mouth grasped the rope of the dinner bell hanging by the door, and he pulled hard. Amazingly, the sudden clang did not startle him, but he soon grew bored and loped away, taking a bite out of Gerry's golf cart seat on his way.

Reports of the young bear's escapades spread quickly through the island community on Burntside Lake. Short of a few composting bins, nothing, and certainly nobody, had been harmed by this young animal, probably recently abandoned by his mother and somewhat confused. Most everyone was sad to think that he might be shot during the upcoming bear hunting season. But there were likely those who kept an ear to the ground on the bear's location in preparation for the start of hunting season in late September. And I would be willing to bet someone started baiting for him as soon as the law would permit.

The Minnesota Department of Natural Resources (DNR) estimates that up to 35,000 black bears (*Ursus americanus*) live in Minnesota, many of them in the dense and remote woods of the Arrowhead. Typically maxing out at about three hundred pounds and three feet at the shoulder, the black bear is notoriously timid, unlike its cousin the grizzly bear, who was long ago extirpated from Minnesota. Nevertheless, black bears find themselves interacting with humans fairly regularly and can rapidly become habituated to our presence. In many ways, the black bear exemplifies the ongoing tension between the town of Ely and the surrounding "megafauna," a tension that sparks heated debate among residents, the DNR, and tourists who come to view the wildlife, or kill it.

In dry years, when the berry crop is poor, hungry bears appear throughout Ely, foraging in garbage cans and the city dump. While they may prefer hazelnuts and wild blueberries, "they'll actually eat anything," says retired game warden Ken Schlueter, and they get pretty brave if they need to. One of our friends banged pots and pans together to chase a large bear out of her dog's kennel, where he had found some leftover kibble. And Ken's wife, Wendy, found herself being charged by a bear who had found plenty of delicious fresh-laid eggs in her chicken coop.

Their flexible attitude to dining makes black bears particularly easy to bait, and baited they are—by the thousands. In 2006, almost 15,000 bear hunting permits were issued in northeastern Minnesota. This is a dramatic increase from the 3,300 permits issued in 1983. Of course, not all hunters get their bear, so the actual number of bears killed is only about 3,400 (compared to 1,000 bears in 1983). Despite the increase in bear hunting, Minnesota's bear population has more than doubled in the past twenty years, and the DNR seems to have given up their efforts to relocate nuisance bears, choosing instead to issue permits to kill them.

Now, it may be unsportsmanlike of me to repeat this, but several people have told me that bear hunting is a little like putting your dog's food out on the back porch and shooting him when he comes to eat it. The skill, I suppose, is in knowing where to put the bowl. The baiting process starts about two weeks before the season opens. Hunters drive south to the Twin Cities and do their own version of foraging. Remember, these bears will eat anything, so the hunters pick up jumbo blocks of peanut candy bars, rotting apples, lard that has been used for deep-frying, and the rather ironic favorite—excess scrapings from gummy bear manufacturers. The trick is to find food that stays tasteful and edible regardless of weather, but that maggots do not like.

Any camper can tell you that a black bear will work really, really hard to get at food. I have used plenty of bear boxes while camping, and I can attest to what it takes to keep a bear and his food apart. Furthermore, bear season is timed to coincide with the bears' annual upsurge in consumption as they prepare to enter their dens for the winter. Hunters take advantage of all this and bury the bait under logs too heavy for smaller mammals to move. They know a bear will dig it up, and they can tell a bear has been there by the mess he leaves. Sometimes, a hunter will hang the bait in a tree and be able to tell how tall the bear is by the scratches he leaves in the trunk of the tree and, therefore, if he is worth pursuing. Some bears leave marks as high as six or seven feet off the ground—these are the ones that would most certainly be deemed worthwhile.

The baiting goes on for days or weeks, and very quickly the bear becomes accustomed to his new and rather surprising stash. Then, one day, the hunter waits for the bear and . . . well, you know what happens next. There are some hunters that take the challenge up a notch by using black powder guns, crossbows, or even traditional bows and arrows. Recently, a man near Ely climbed a tree above his bait spot and leaped out to spear the unsuspecting bear!

If you really want to go all out and bag a bear in an original way, you can apply for one of the few permits issued for Area 22—the Boundary Waters Canoe Area Wilderness. According to the DNR, this "provides a unique hunting opportunity to those who have the necessary experience, equipment, and commitment. It is not recommended for novice hunters or novice canoeists." There are many difficulties inherent in hunting big game in a place where no machines of any kind are allowed. It is one thing to get in there and get the bear; it is another thing entirely to get it out of there without it rotting. The blackflies will be laying maggots in it before you can say "yuck." The bottom line is that you have to haul in about a hundred pounds of dry ice, you need a huge canoe, and let's face it, you and your buddy are only bringing out one bear between you. All this and, really, it is not that much fun hunting in an area where the people you will run across are likely to be rather unfriendly. The DNR warns hunters in this area that campers typically do not like to see bear entrails, blood, or carcasses and will probably find people carrying firearms "intimidating."

The debate about who is more intimidating, the bear or the man, is enduring, and there are significant efforts in the Ely area to bridge the gap of misunderstanding between bears and people. Researcher Dr. Lynn Rogers and a committee of Ely residents recently opened the North American Bear

Center as a place of education, research, and rehabilitation. Rehabilitating bears or even collaring them for research is not without controversy. Hunters are legally permitted to shoot collared bears, resulting in many an altercation between researchers and hunters, altercations that sometimes turn nasty. Like many public policy issues in a town this size, one's opinion and one's actions toward the black bear can make you a set of lasting friends or lasting enemies.

We photographed Lynn Rogers at his research institute west of Ely and found ourselves face-to-face with several bears, one of which took a particular liking to our photo equipment. After the bear tired of the tripod, sniffed our jeans, and nibbled on a few dates, we were at ease enough to take a picture. We actually found ourselves disappointed that the bear was not bigger. We have not carried a bear bell since that day.

For every controversy about the black bear, there have been dozens regarding the eastern timber wolf (*Canis lupus*), or gray wolf. Since the U.S. Fish and Wildlife Service designated the wolf as a threatened species thirty years ago, the timber wolf's range in Minnesota has tripled and its population swelled to more than 3,000—by far the largest density of wolves in the United States. Saved from the brink of extinction, the wolf will soon be "delisted" from the federal endangered species list, and its management will transfer to state governments and local Native American tribes. Idaho's already determined an asking price—just $26.50—for a tag to kill one of their 650 resident wolves.

Meanwhile, tourists flock to fawn over the captive pack of wolves at Ely's International Wolf Center, a major attraction at the eastern end of town. Lots of folks know the wolves at the Center by name, and when roadkill is found, someone will usually scrape it up and bring it to wolf curator Lori Schmidt, who says the wolves are deeply resistant to processed food. This is just one of many reminders that these creatures are not just big, gorgeous dogs, although it is tempting to think of them this way as we talk to them through the chain-link fence at the Center, their intelligent eyes gazing back at us.

There are several wild wolf packs in the Ely area, and famed photographer Jim Brandenburg has made some of their members celebrities in the pages of *National Geographic* magazine. In many ways, these wolves symbolize the wildness that surrounds Ely. As Jim says, "It's really the wolves that brought me here. I thought that if it is wild enough to contain the wolves and keep them happy, then maybe I can be happy here too."

Until the 1960s it would have been unimaginable that large segments of the public would be sympathetic to the wolf. For more than a hundred years wolves were bountied for up to $35 a pelt, resulting in their annihilation from the southern part of Minnesota. Now the argument rages about how to manage the wolf as soon as the feds pull out of the issue. A slew of organizations, including the Audubon Society, Defenders of Wildlife, the Sierra Club, the Humane Society, and many others have issued position papers for or against delisting or advocating particular management strategies. Others, such as the Minnesota DNR, are astonishingly vague and take no stance either way. Predictably, the Minnesota State Cattlemen's Association wants the wolf delisted yesterday. Meanwhile, the Indigenous Environmental Network, the Fond du Lac Band of Chippewa, and other Native American organizations cry for their unique perspectives to be heard.

> *Long ago when the earth was new, and Anishinable (the first man of the Chippewa) was walking the earth naming all of creation, lands and waters, he was alone, and the creator placed the wolf to walk with Anishinable and be his friend and brother. The creator told them what happens to one will happen to the other. This has come to pass. We've had our lands taken, we were hunted for our hair, and pushed to near extinction. We are now seeing the wolf returning and gaining strength in those places he was once destroyed. This teaches us that Anishinable will also return and gain strength in those places he was once destroyed. Perhaps the wolf will lead the way to a more natural living and teach the new comers to respect Mother Earth.*
> (Anne Dunn, Chippewa elder)

As the delisting debate rages, it is amazing to note how well the process has worked so far. The wolf was truly saved from obliteration, and public attitudes toward the wolf have softened considerably. The next step is a difficult one, fraught with emotion for all involved. It is, as the saying goes, rather like having a wolf by the ears.

Meanwhile, the monstrously huge moose tromps his way through Ely and its many bogs without much controversy at all. He is a valuable catch—$310 for one of the 279 permits issued each year, and you only get one permit in a lifetime—and any local person knows to steer clear of him. Of all the characteristics you hear about the moose, the most consistent is its unpredictability. At upwards of 900 pounds (that is the equivalent of six or seven adult deer), you do not want to get in the way of a rutting moose, or a mother and her young, or any moose at all, for it might just chase you down. It is amazing really, given that their antlers can be up to six feet across, that they can even run through the woods. Indeed, moose and other large-hoofed animals, like caribou and elk, were far more prevalent in the Ely area before the logging industry decimated the easily passable forest of large white pines and a new, dense forest of brushy aspen and birch took its place.

Moose certainly do not go out of their way to bother humans, but they have a sort of elephantine way of barging through fences, which can be problematic if you are trying to keep anything in or out of your property. It is particularly disastrous if you run into one on the highway, as your front bumper will most likely take its long legs out from under it while its huge, thousand-pound body lands on the roof of your car.

Local merchants Henry Held and Patti Steger and their many loyal customers swear by the lightness and durability of moosehide for mukluks, belts, and Henry's famous chopper mittens, traditional Northwoods work gloves. Henry is quick to bemoan moosehide's lasting qualities as bad for business. "Moosehide," he says, "when tanned like deerskin, is super wear-resistant and always stays supple. When tanned for belts, it has way less stretch than other leathers, and the cellular structure remains intact for more strength and color retention." In other words, the stuff just does not ever need to be replaced. We know this to be true from our own experience with Henry's belts.

Northeastern Minnesota offers a hunter's paradise of black bears, deer, ruffed grouse, moose, mourning doves, waterfowl, small game, and furbearers including beavers, minks, and muskrats. It is the game warden, now called "conservation officer," who is on the front line of every piece of legislation and every aspect of managing this abundant wildlife. When the first game warden was assigned to these parts more than a hundred years ago, the newspaper at the time said, "Sportsmen and hunters must look out or they may get into trouble."

Today's conservation officer—part of Minnesota's "Thin Green Line"—must move easily between the roles of detective, biologist, sharpshooter, and traffic cop, all while topping Andy Griffith's management-by-good-sense style. Babbitt-based Officer Marty Stage points out, "everyone you deal with has a gun." Despite the inherent risks, these jobs are highly coveted, and once in them, people do not leave. After all, as one officer says, "It's like being a cowboy—you get a bunch of guns, a truck, and a range of 600 square miles."

Early one morning, before the sun rose, we lay cozy in our sleeping bags on Whitshell Island listening to the song of wolves howling on the opposite shore. The pups' voices warbled with an almost heartbreaking innocence. The debate over big game in the Arrowhead is noisy. Yet for most of us who live in or visit Ely, we are connected to these creatures in sweet bursts of harmless surprise—witnessing a herd of deer cross a frozen lake single file, spotting three wolf pups on the Fernberg Trail, slowing to let a moose cross the highway near Isabella, or watching a fluffy young bear stumble his way down the bank to swim to the next island in hope of a better compost heap.

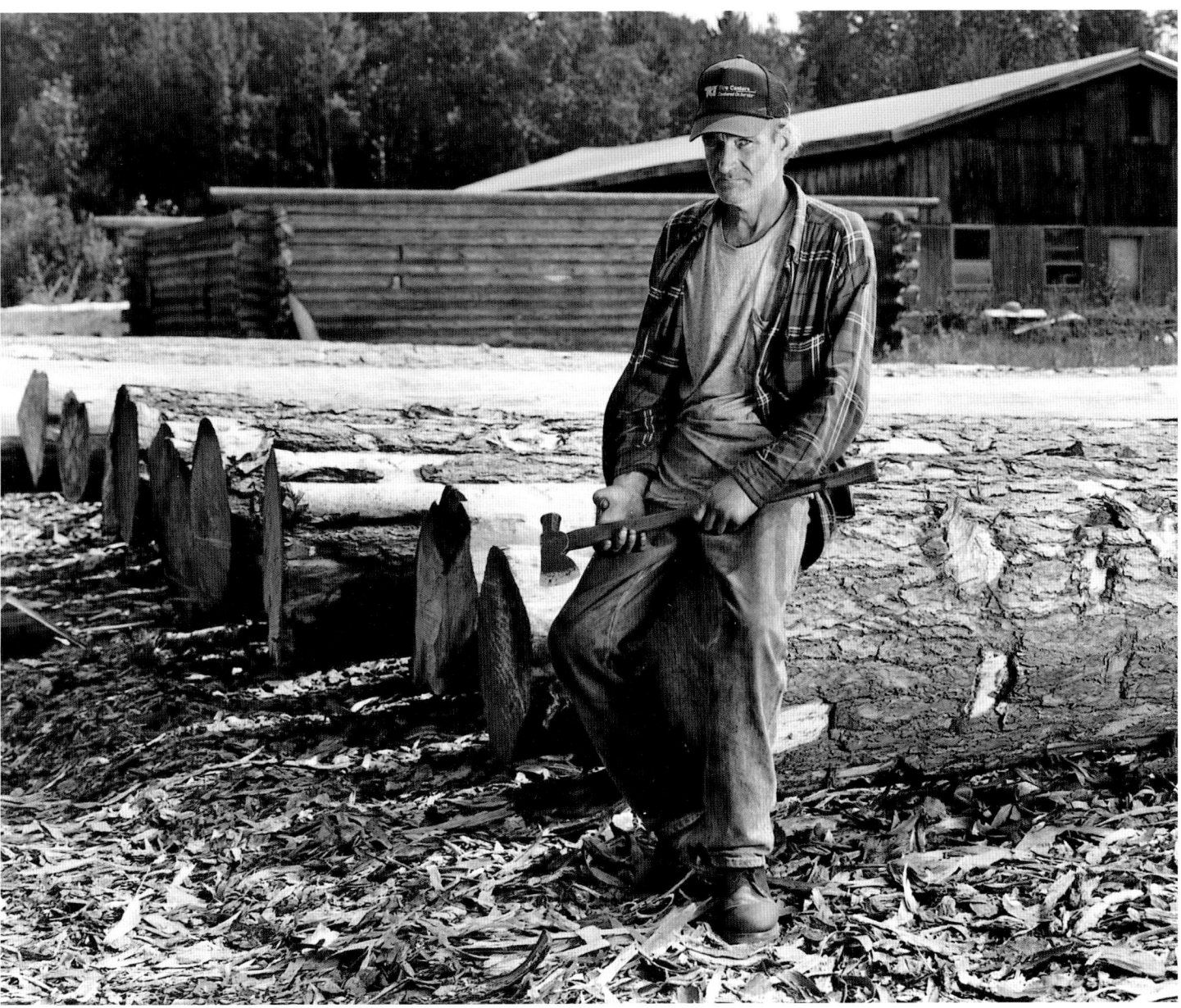

PLATE 71. Brian Kainz, log home builder, Winton

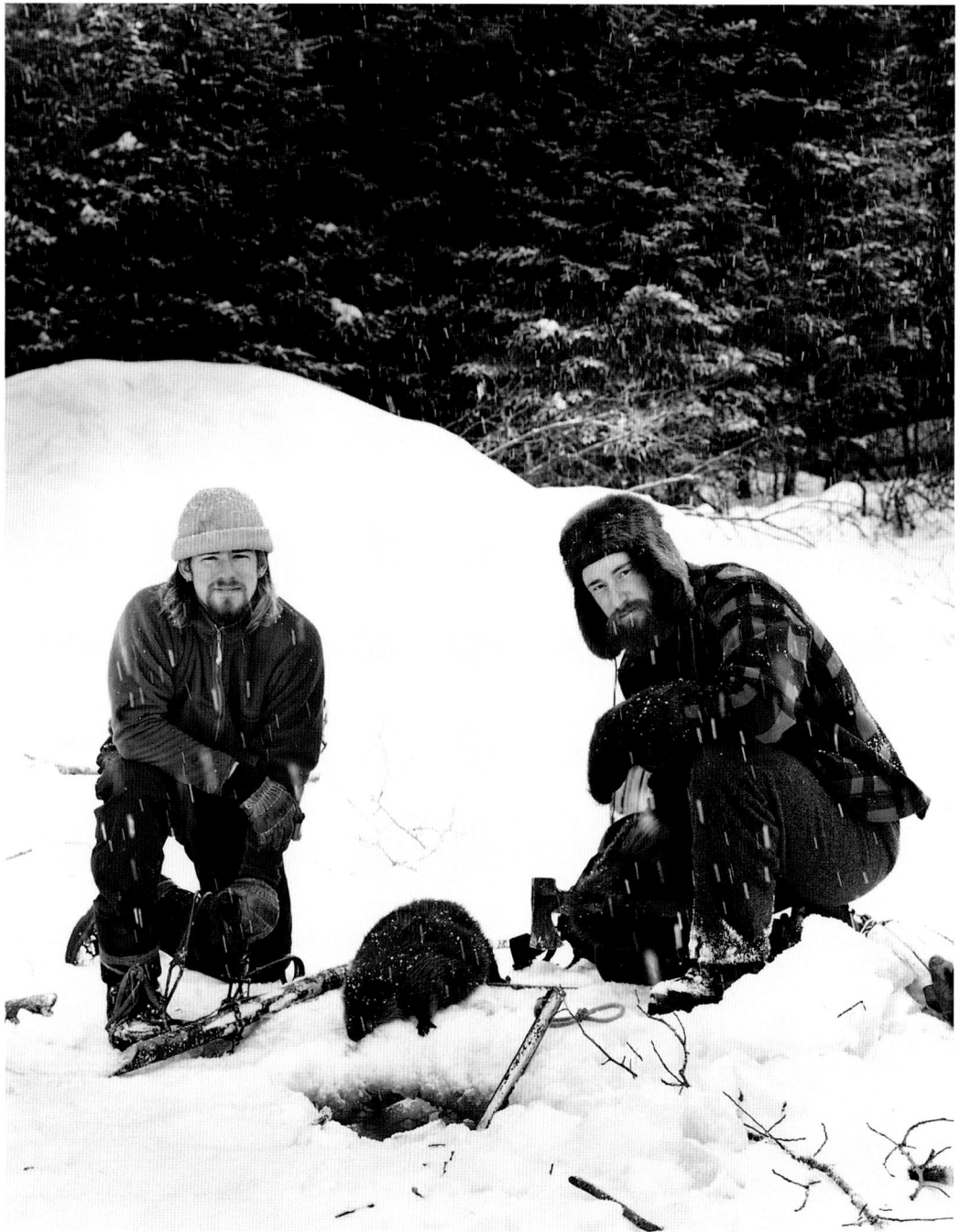

PLATE 72. Chris Maher and Aaron Chick, trappers

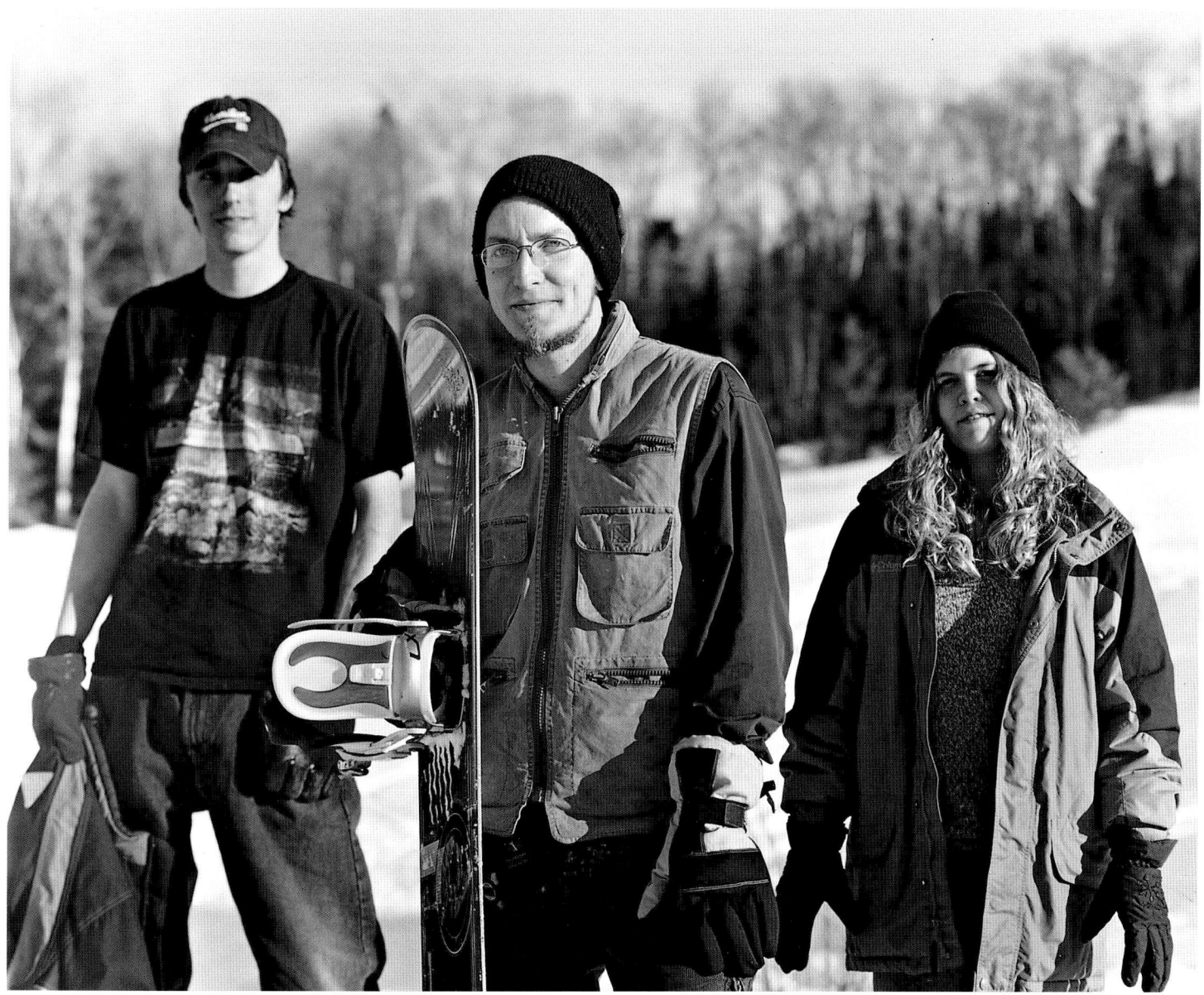

PLATE 73. Jonathan, Damien, and Ashlee, students, Vermilion Community College

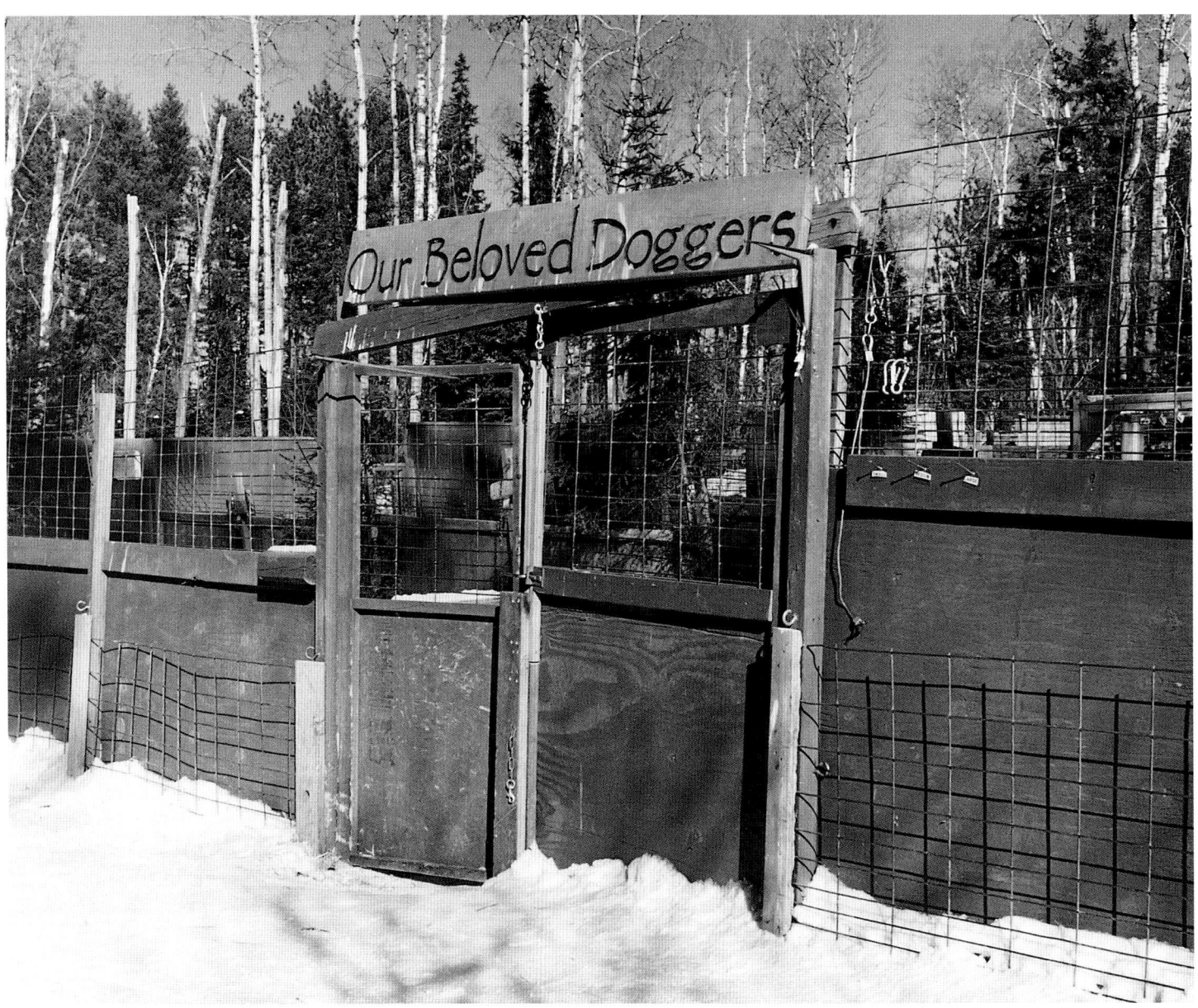

PLATE 74. The "Dog Patch," Wintergreen Dog Sledding Lodge

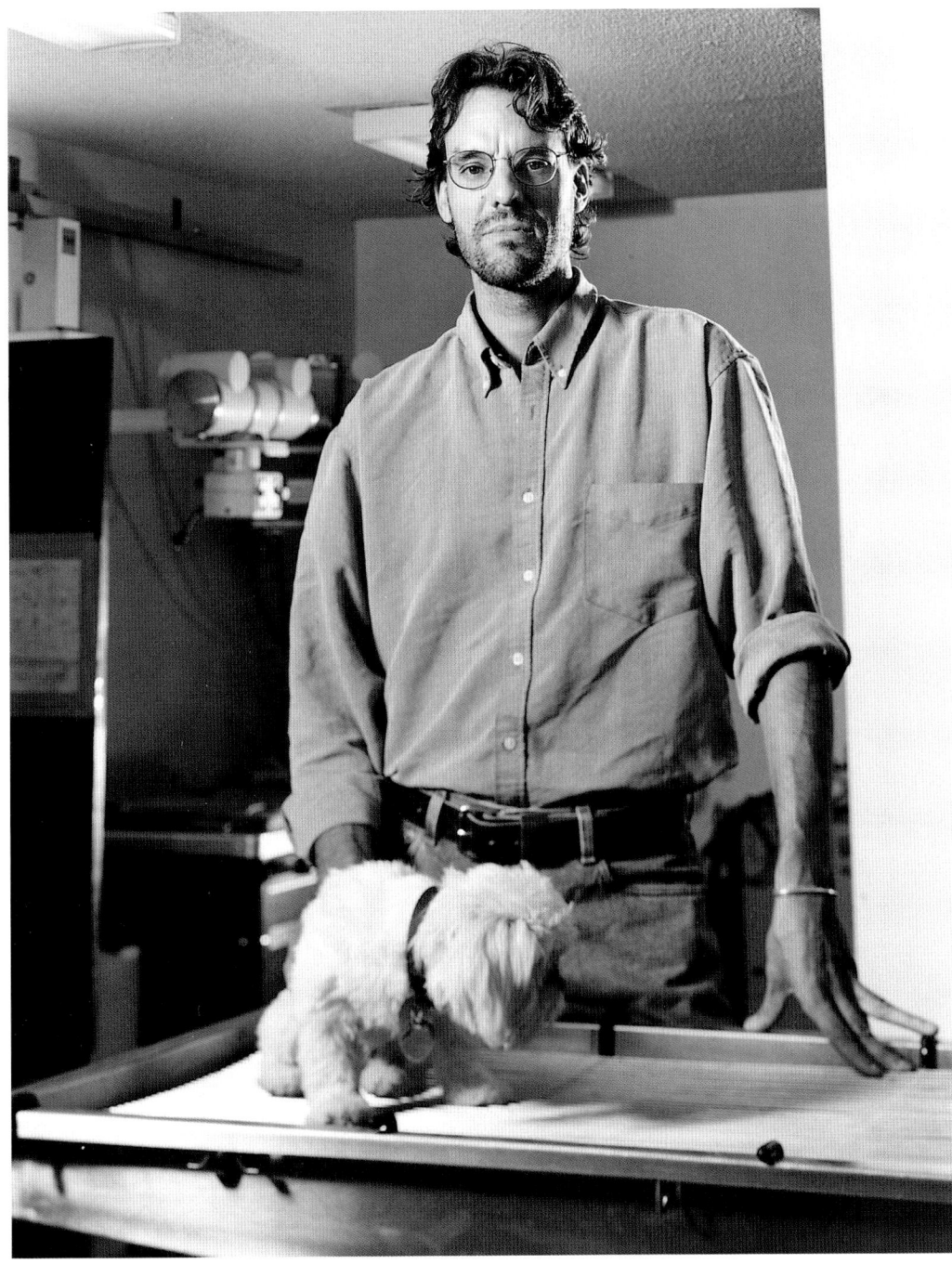

PLATE 75. Chip Hanson, veterinarian

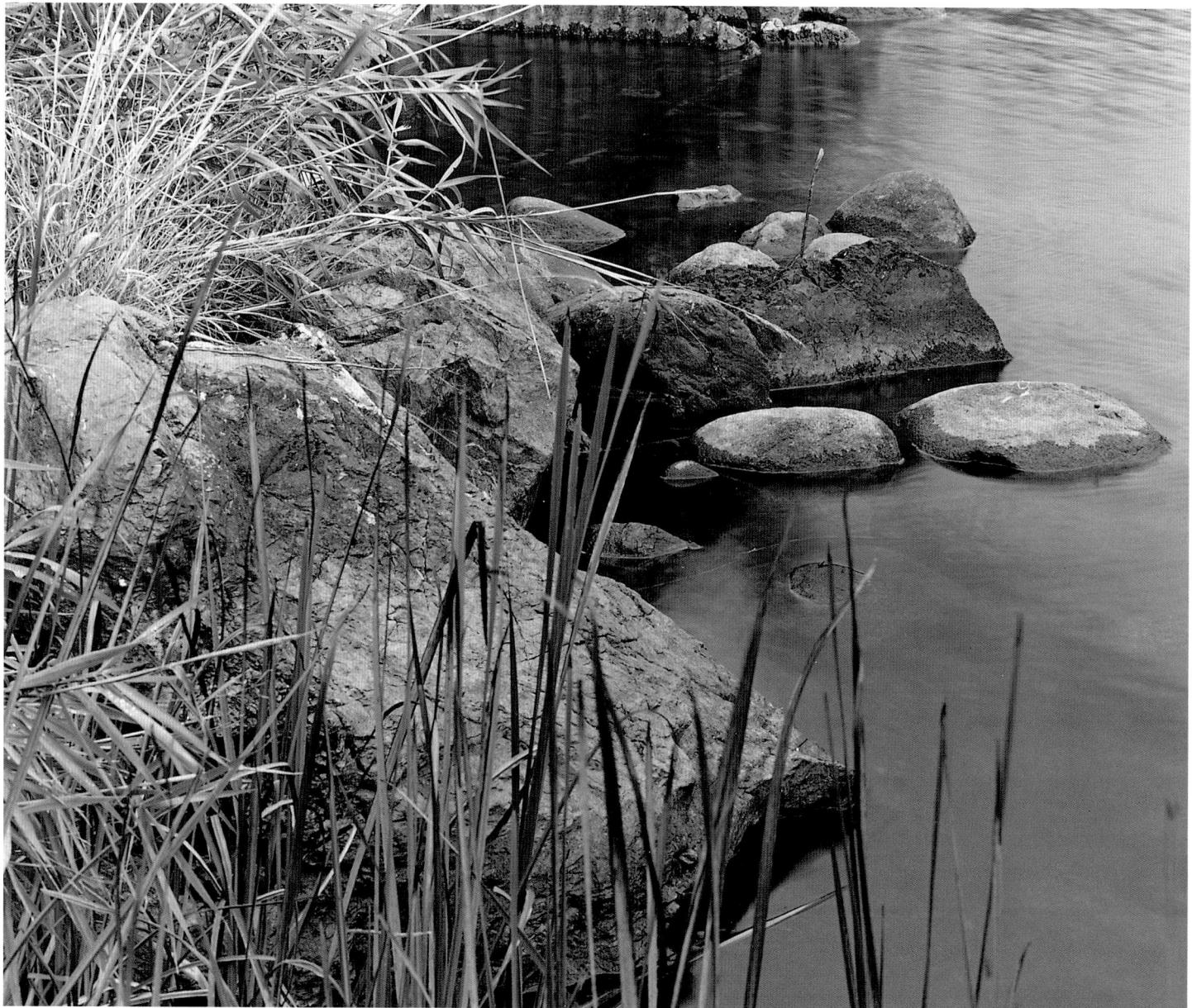

PLATE 76. Shagawa Lake, Ely

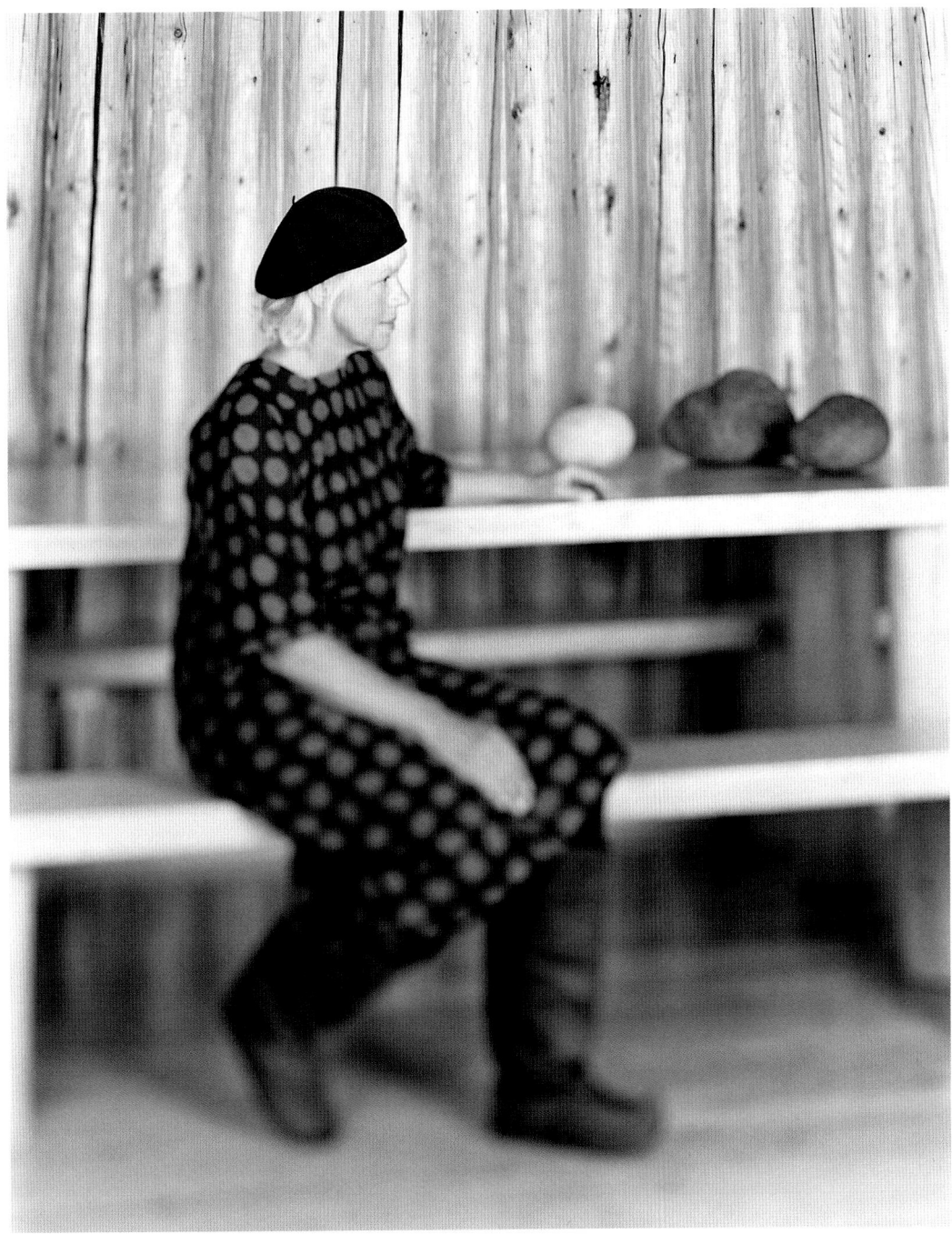

PLATE 77. Milli Salmela Bissonett, Finnish radio host and designer

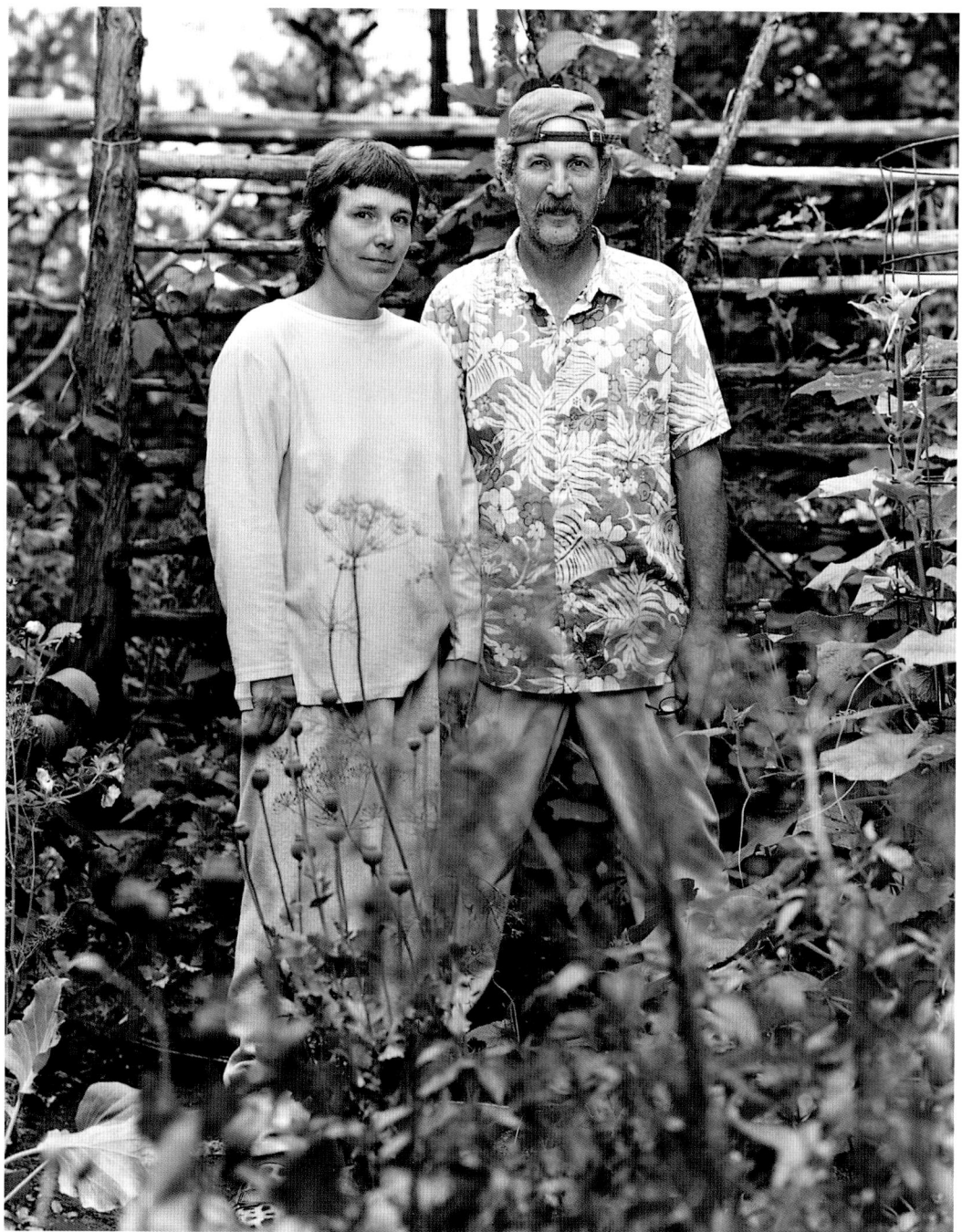

PLATE 78. Bill and Barb Godlin, artisans

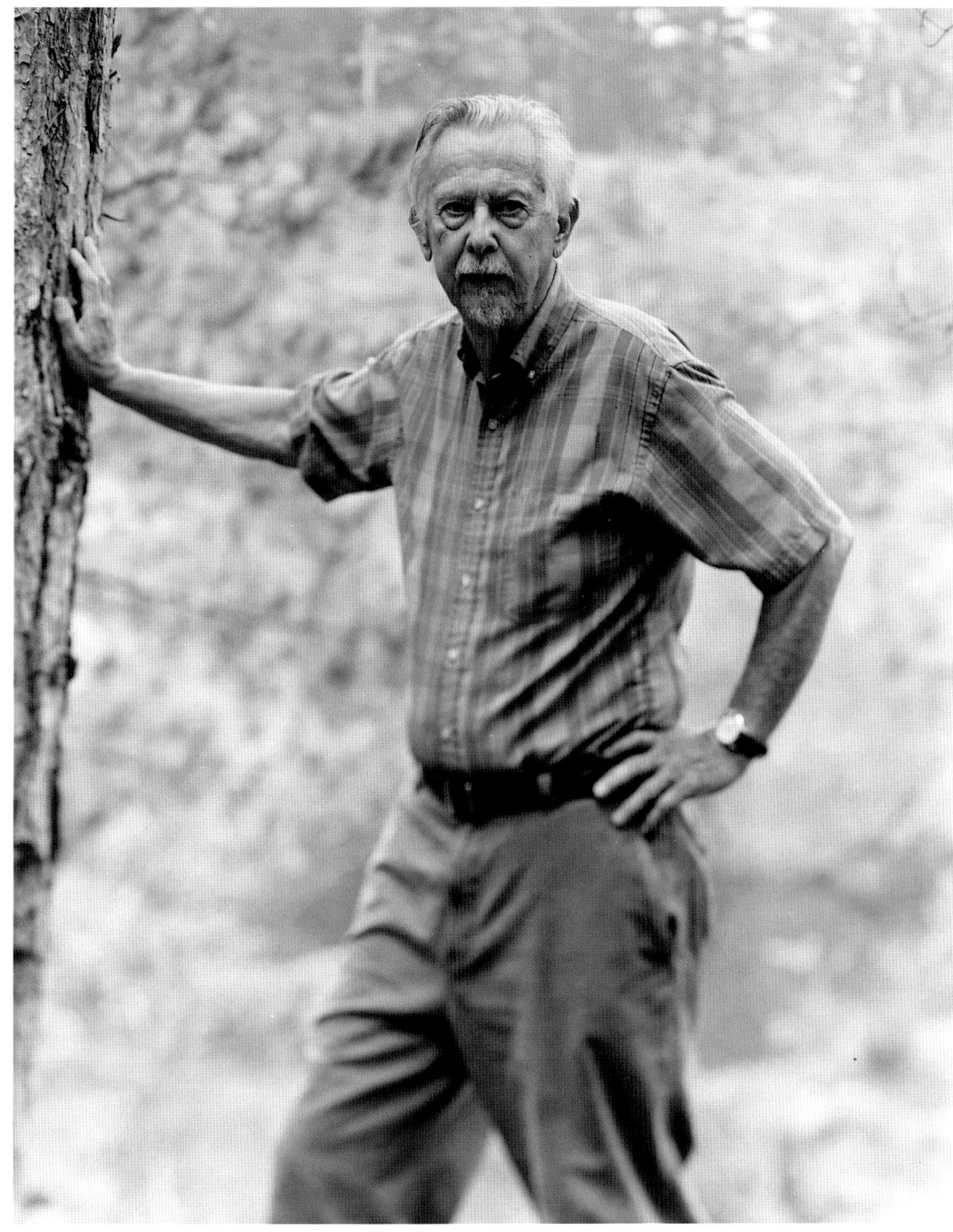

PLATE 79. Marvin Lamppa, Iron Range historian, Babbitt

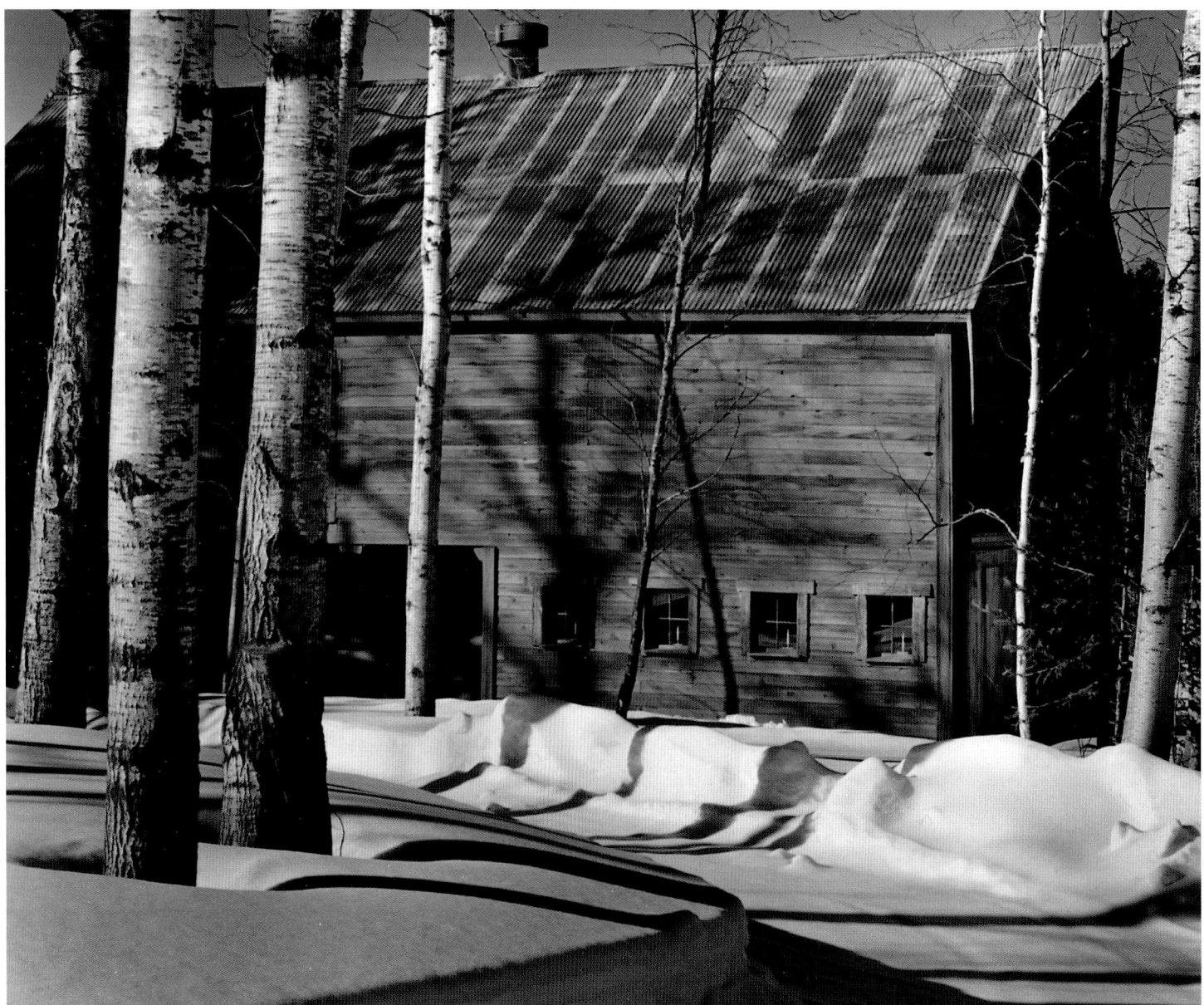

PLATE 80. Barn, Wolf Lake Road

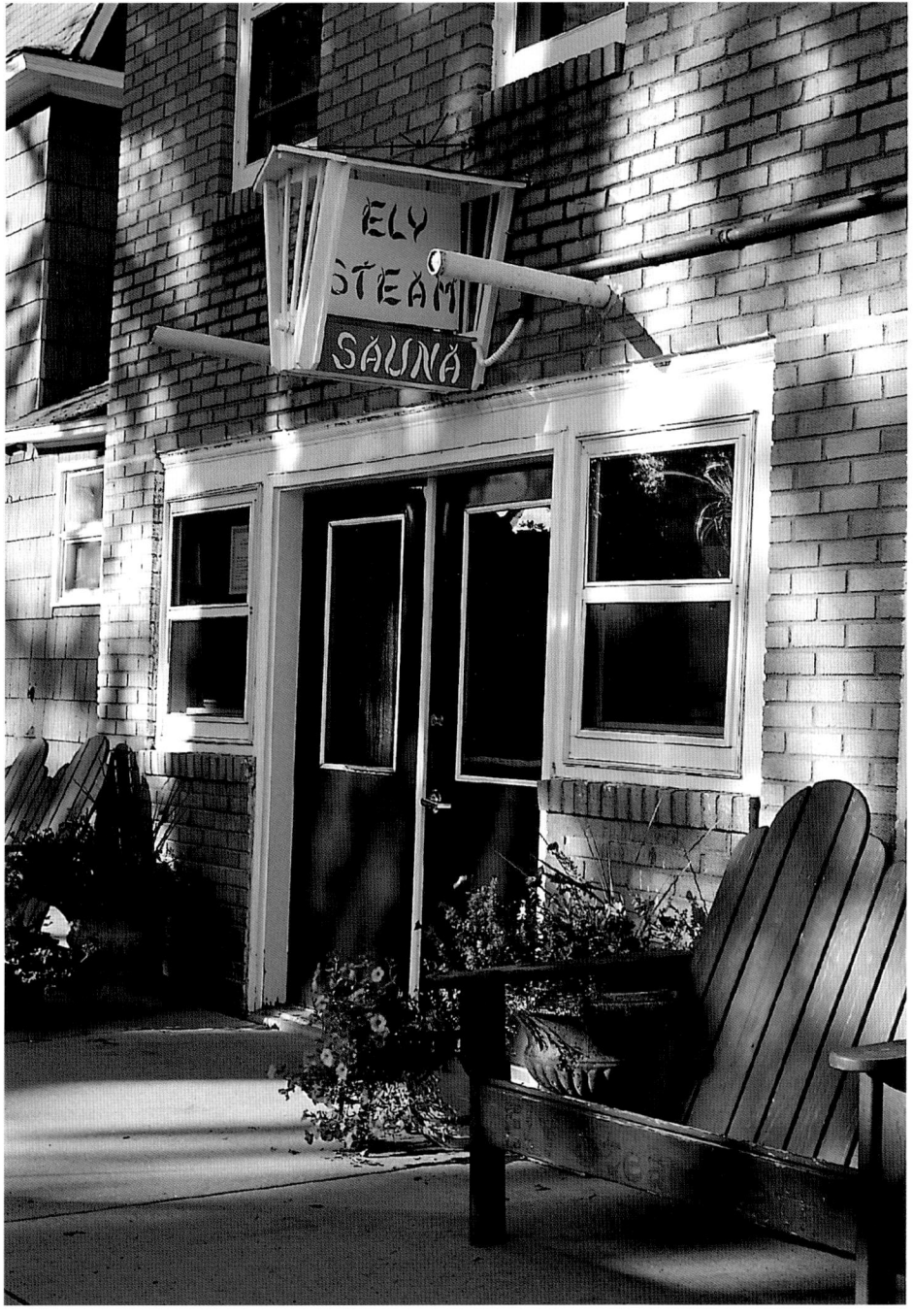

PLATE 81. Ely Steam Sauna

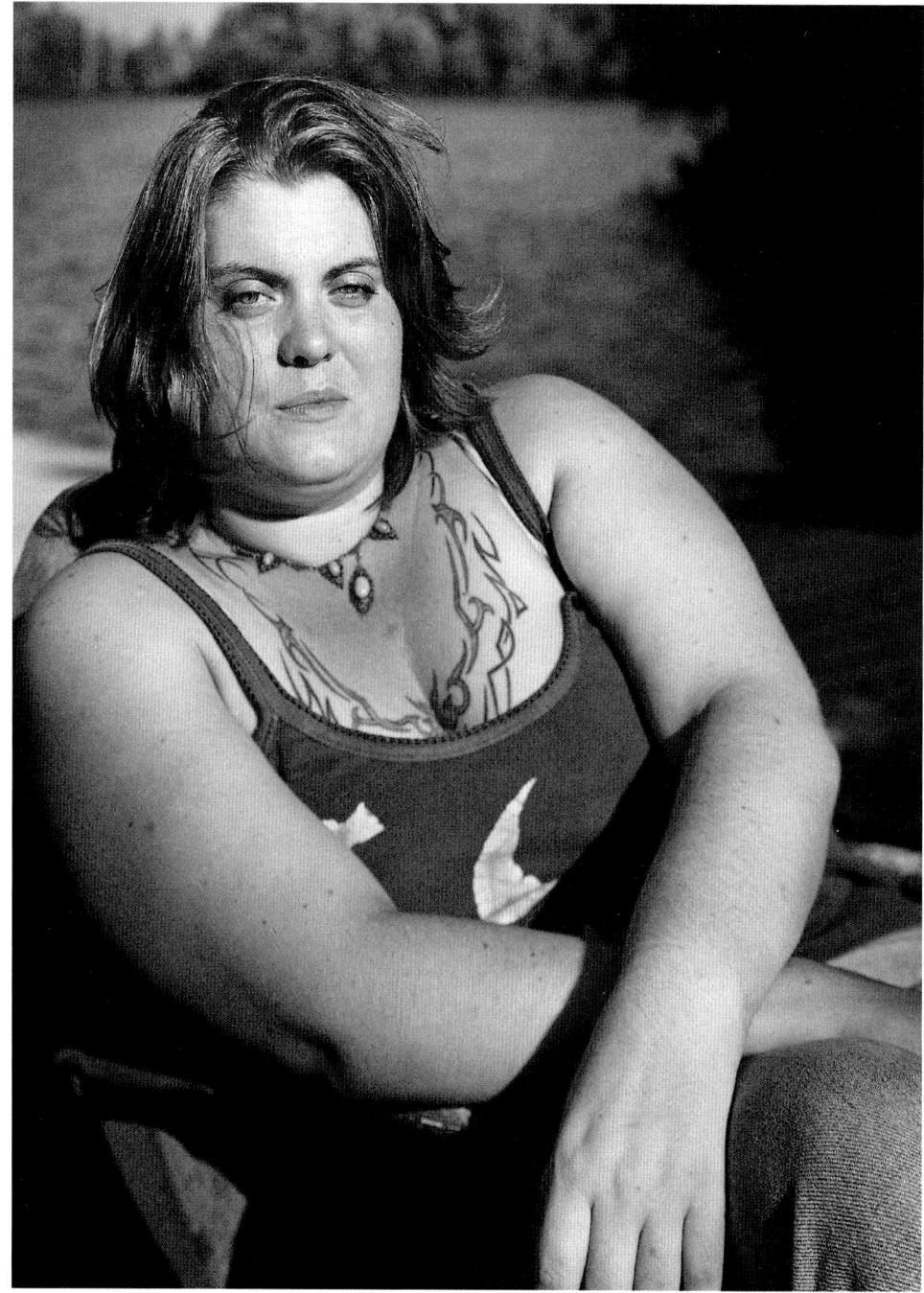

PLATE 82. Ann Thunhorst, Jackpine Lodge

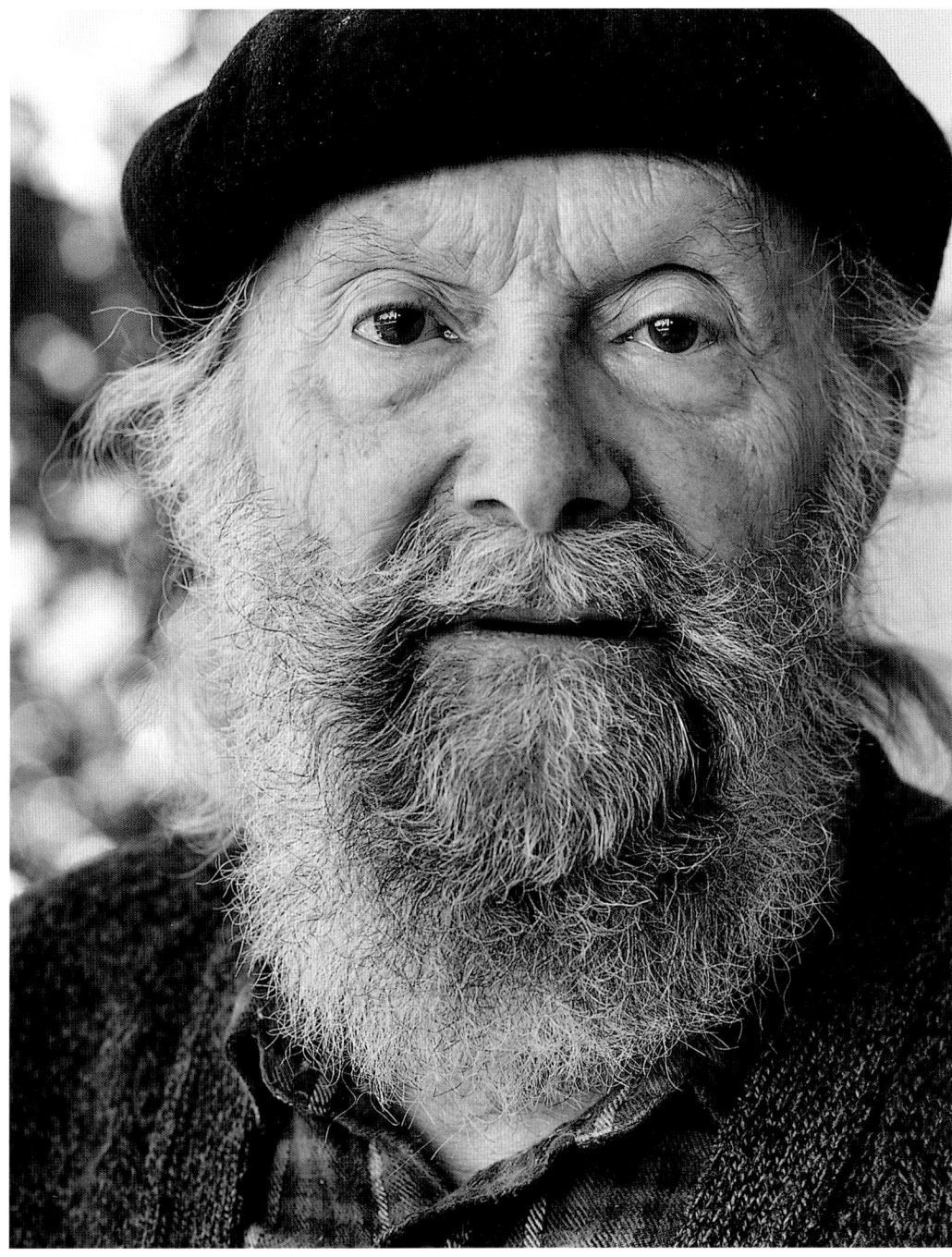

PLATE 83. Oscar Kenig, Ely resident

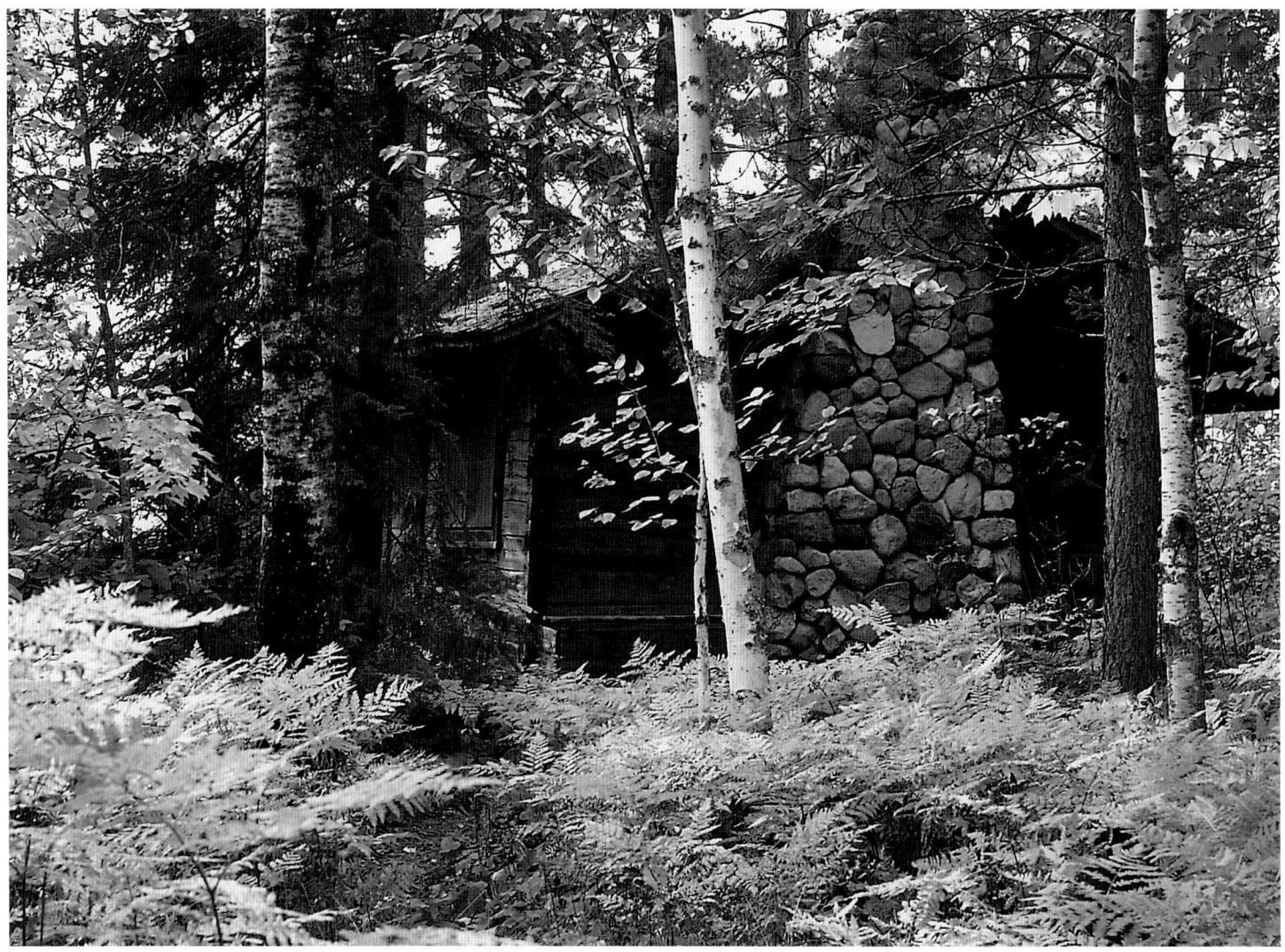

PLATE 84. Sigurd Olson's cabin, Listening Point, Burntside Lake

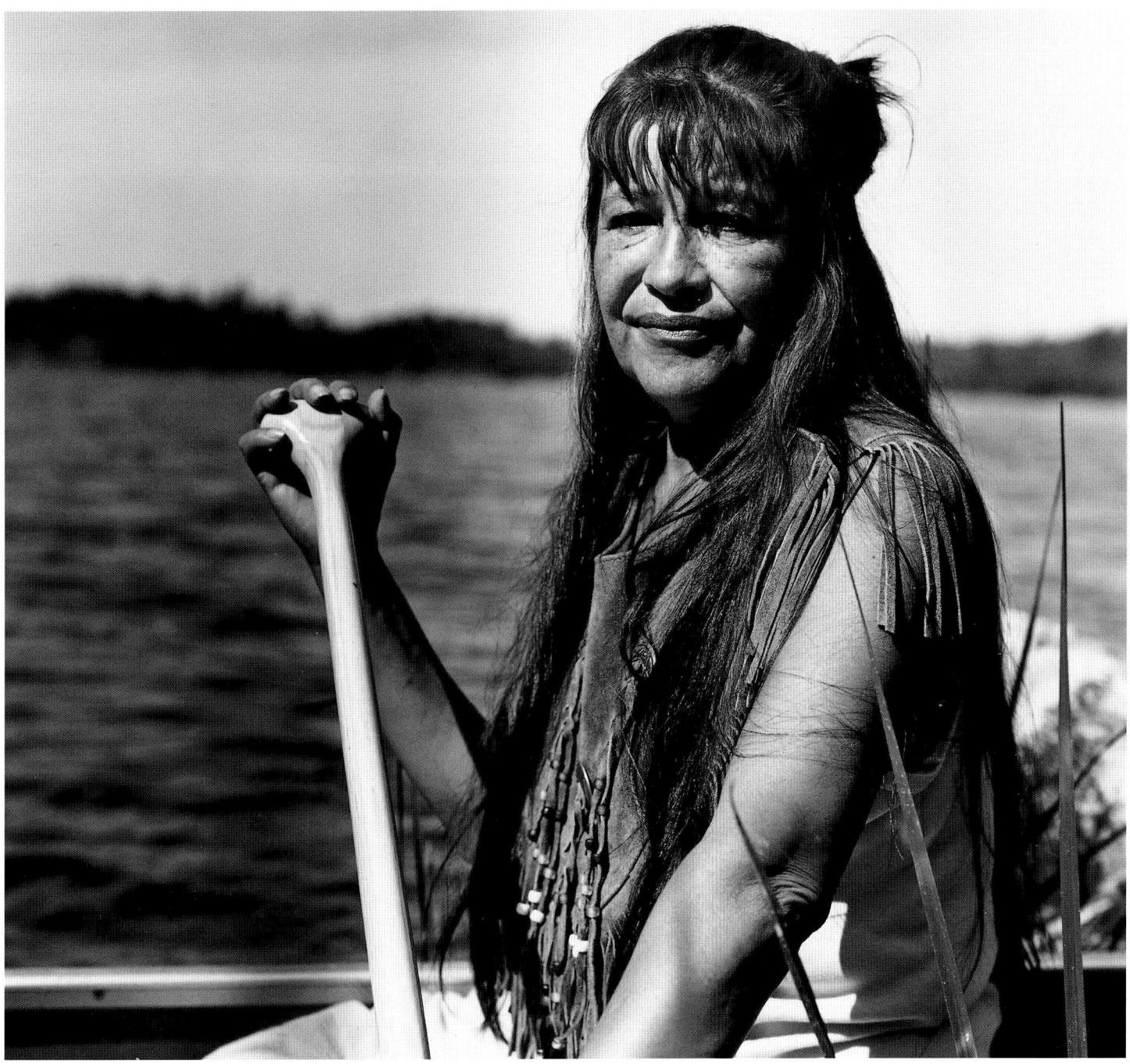

PLATE 85. Heart Warrior Chosa, artist and activist

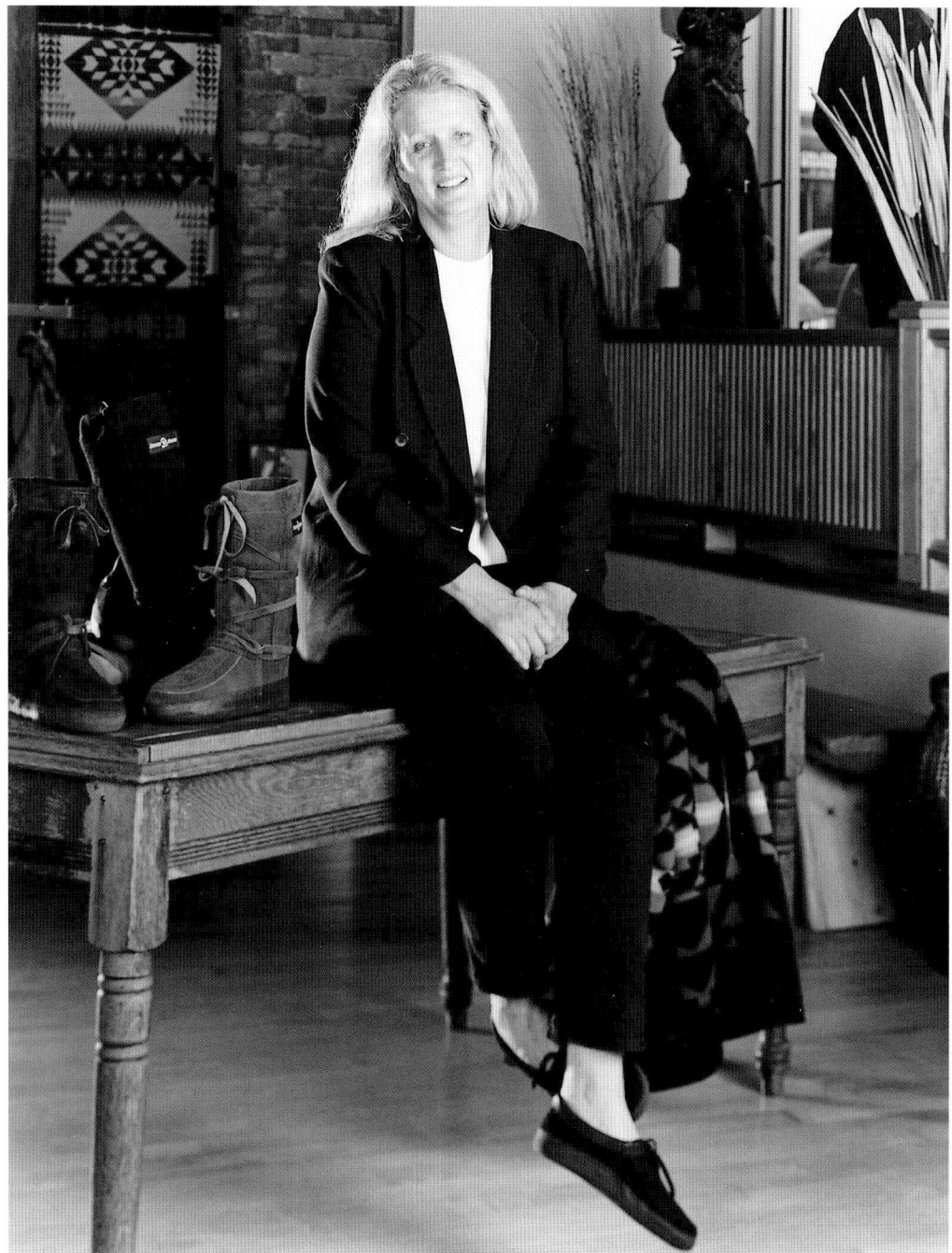

PLATE 86. Patti Steger, Steger Mukluks and Moccasins

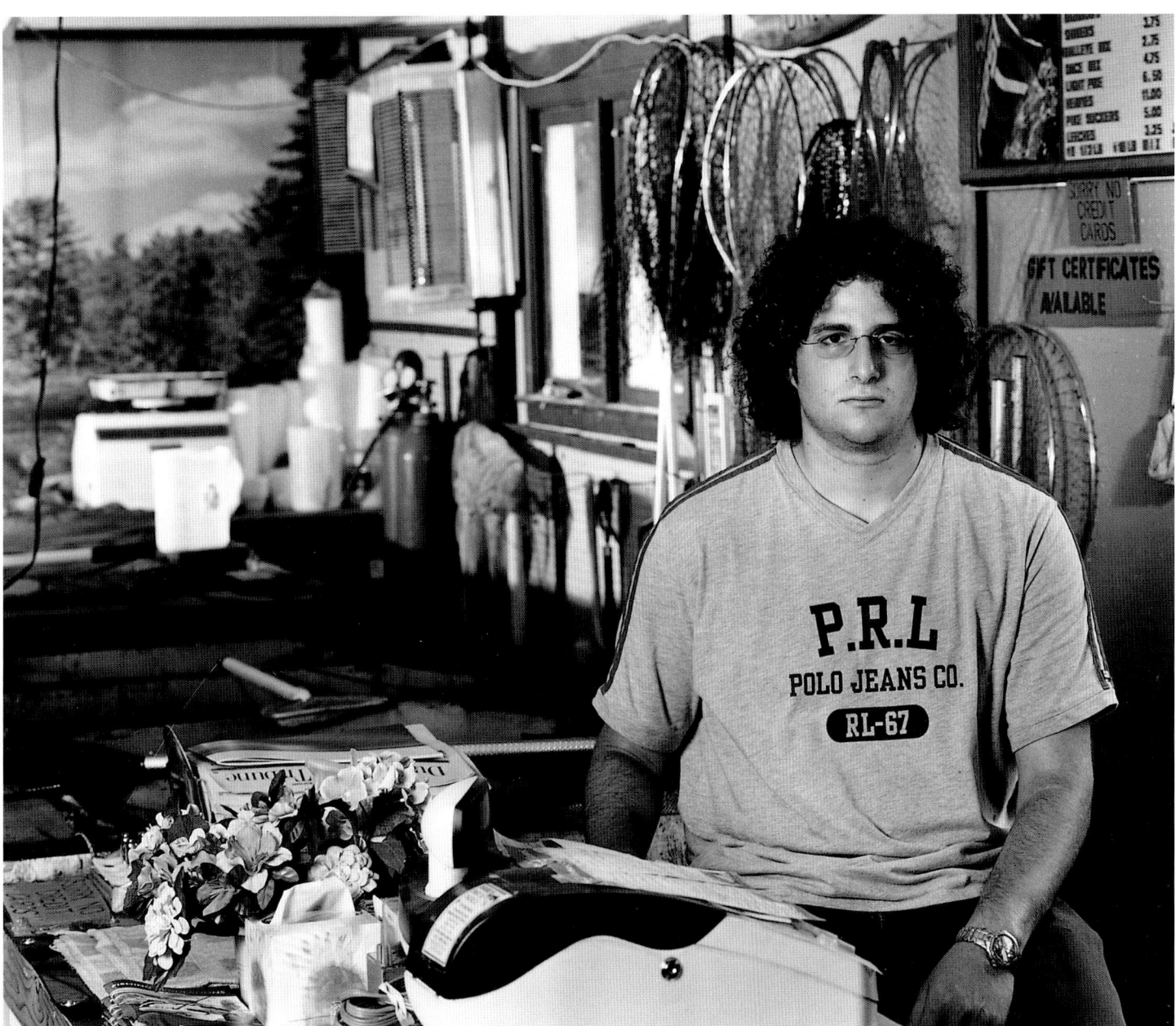

PLATE 87. Justin Pius, Babe's Bait & Tackle

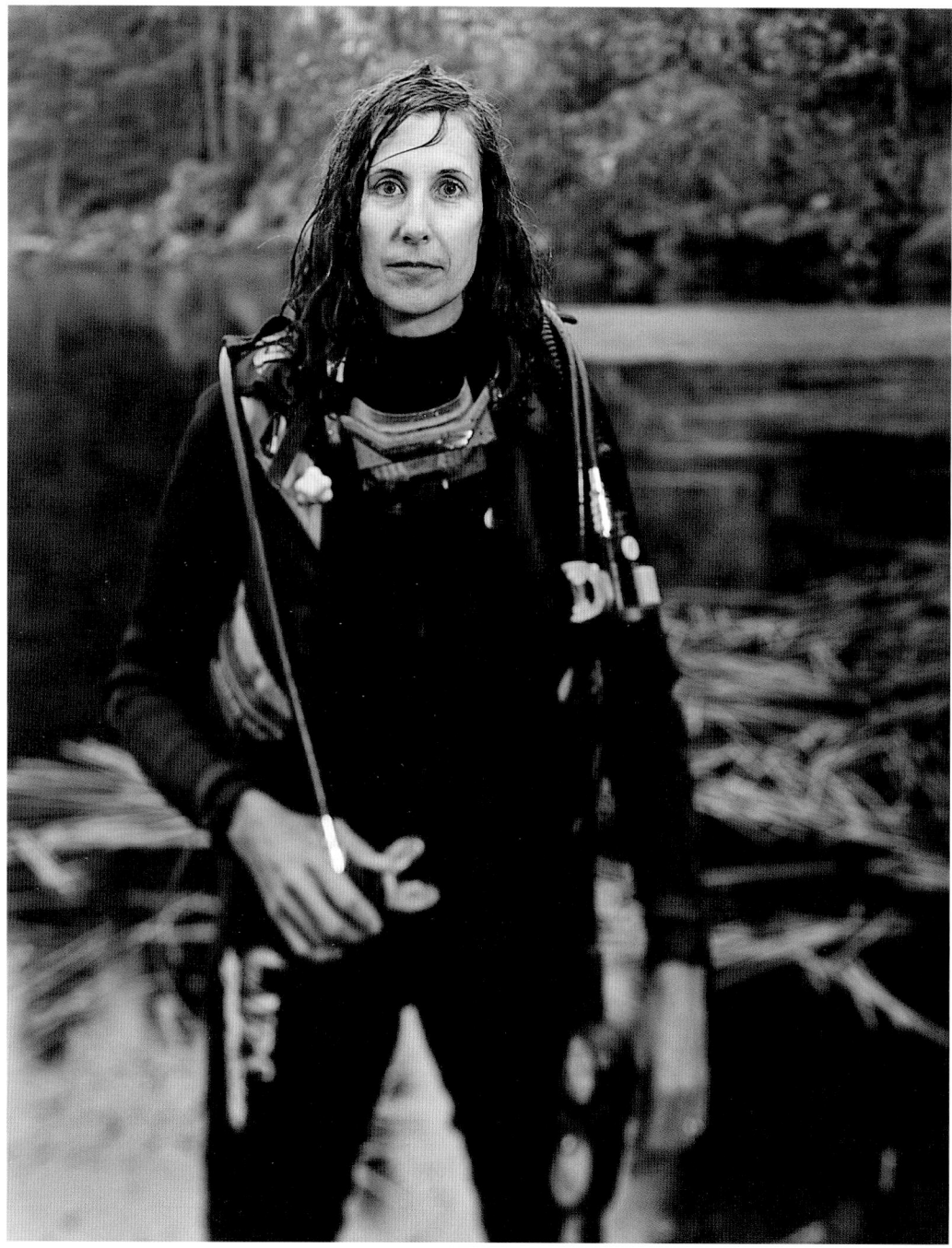

PLATE 88. Lisa Pekuri, Lisa's Upstairs Books, Piragis Northwoods Company

THE MAGIC of It All

"There's the right way, the wrong way, and the Widji way." Into the water walk three young women with a wood and canvas canoe held high above their heads. Three sets of hiking boots and socks are soaked through as the girls gently flip the canoe onto the water and step into it in well-practiced unison. This canoe will never be pulled onto rocks or dragged across sand in the manner of aluminum or Kevlar vessels—that would be counter to the Widji way. From the shore their counselor congratulates them, and the next group of three girls grabs hold of a canoe and starts to count. "One, two three, LIFT!" They are almost ready to go "on trail."

The girls are at YMCA Camp Widjiwagan just outside of Ely, and they are preparing for a twenty-one-day trip through Canada's Quetico Provincial Park.

"How far will you go each day," I ask.

"Between ten and twenty miles" is the response.

"A day? Every day?"

"We paddle from sunrise to sunset, and then pitch camp."

The term *paddle* is deceptive when it might mean cutting through whitecaps across a lake that seems more like an ocean, the rain and wind in your face and a muddy 100-rod portage waiting for you. At 16.5 feet (or roughly the length of a canoe), the rod serves as a linear measurement in the woods. Tackling a 100-rod portage, for example, means emptying your gear from your canoe and carrying it all (and your canoe, of course) through 1,650 feet of dense forest on a narrow, probably mucky path. On the other hand, "paddling" might also mean spending a sweet, sunny afternoon on a glassy lake, suspended between sky and water in a silky space of absolute perfection. Both scenarios contribute to the feeling of achievement and growth the girls gain from their trip. "I get so much stronger, so much more self-confident," one of the girls tells me. Another says, "I like disconnecting from the city and all sorts of extraneous things. You don't have a watch, you just know when the sun comes up and the sun goes down."

More than five hundred kids spend their summers on trail with Widji. It is a progressive program, with every year offering greater challenges until the most senior of the campers go on an expedition-style canoe trip in the Canadian Arctic. Joe Smith was a Widji camper before he became camp manager in 1986. He recalls his culminating forty-one-day trip far above the tree line in the Arctic Circle and the final nine-mile portage as "one of the great accomplishments of my life."

At the Voyageur Outward Bound School on Highway 1, a group of teens don their "brain buckets" and enter the high-ropes course. Like all Outward Bound challenges, this one is intended to teach these kids to solve problems and overcome doubts. They are learning that mental toughness is far more powerful than physical strength, and it definitely takes some psychological chutzpah to step onto this course. Under the reassuring guidance of Virginie Pointeau, they confront a series of daunting climbs, drops, and intersections. With shaking legs they cross the Brahma bridge and the postman's walk, traverse the monkey fists and the spaghetti lines. At last, they come down the zip line. It is over, and at least one small part of them is transformed.

At the very edge of the Boundary Waters, east of Ely on the shores of Moose Lake, a group of Boy Scouts is readying themselves for a two-week tour of duty as members of the Order of the Arrow. They are service volunteers undertaking the first major reconstruction of the Boundary Waters Canoe Area Wilderness (BWCAW) trails since they were cleared by the young men of the Civilian Conservation Corps in the 1930s. This program provides about 85 percent of the trail maintenance in the BWCAW, so there is a continuous flow of Scout teams during the summer months. Each team spends one week working—and working hard. Motors of any kind are forbidden in the 1.1 million acres of the BWCAW, so the Scouts use hand tools to repair tread, set steps to control erosion, and engineer check-dams and water bars. The work is in remote areas, but these are Honor Boy Scouts, experienced in the way of the woods. "You have to be prepared out there. No matter what happens, you're on your own for a while," says one. This is, after all, why they do it. After a week of back-breaking labor, they are free to paddle and camp as they please for another week of treasured isolation in the wilderness.

Camp Voyageur knows well how boys and the woods go together. Two generations of the Erdmann family have welcomed campers ages ten to seventeen to a cluster of small, screen-sided cabins on the shores of Farm Lake. "Camp is my passion," says Deb Erdmann, daughter of the camp's founder. "The most interesting part of this work is that every summer you have a different collection of characters. In four weeks you can see them grow right before your very eyes. They get great exercise and really good food. And their confidence within that time just soars." The boys tell me they relish the solitude of the lakes. "It's you and the canoe and that's all that matters." In an age when male teenagers are often maligned, you can feel in the air here that boyhood is celebrated for what it really is: fresh and optimistic and boundless.

I believe it is this freshness and optimism in each of us that keeps the lodges and camps around Ely in business. While hotels in other places advertise comfortable rooms and high-end services, the brochures for Ely resorts paint a picture of you at your best. Harkening back to what is often perceived as a simpler time, these are places where knotty pine paneling is not passé but offers a special sheen in the firelight by which to connect with your family and with nature. "Drop a line over the side of the houseboat while you grill a steak or sleep in the sun," tempts the Timber Bay Lodge brochure. LaTourell's Moose Lake Resort assures you that you'll "see bald eagles and osprey soaring overhead, beaver swimming near their lodges, and moose feeding in the shallow bays. You'll hear the cry of the loons and howl of the timber wolf." None of these brochures implies warm water or the absence of flies, but they do promise that you'll "sleep to the sounds of wind in the pines."

Ahto, the water god of Finnish legend, is a thief. He wants only the treasure of others, and he hoards it in his murky palace. Somewhere in these Minnesota lakes he has hidden the warmth of August afternoons and kept it forever to himself. Even on the warmest days, a dip in Ahto's dominion makes for a chilly swim. Despite the cold, scuba diver Lisa Pekuri loves the challenge of exploring the depths of Burntside Lake. "You learn to dive really well because of the amount of neoprene, the cold water, and the lack of buoyancy." The reward for Lisa? "Immense rock structures, sheer cliffs that drop as far as you can see or as cold as you want to go, the joy of three dimensions. I think that scuba diving is to be as close as I can be to God."

Up at the surface of the lake, our feet turn a ghostly whitish green as they hang off the dock at Whitshell Island and float like apparitions in the cool water. Be quiet. Shhh. Don't let the fish know we're here. But our silence is in vain as a mother merganser and her five chicks come running, yes, running, along the water, their red tufts beaming in the sunlight and their din sending every living thing scattering. Not so the great blue heron that tiptoes silently along the shoreline, eyeing us carefully with a sidelong gaze, its nervousness apparent only in the continuous shifting of its shapely neck. In the abundance of creation along this lake, he is surely my favorite, but my two sons are more enamored by the otter who stands on his hind legs staring back at them in shared fascination.

Later, after we have caught and thrown back dozens of bluegills—do we keep catching the same stupid one?—we climb the hill on the island's southern slope with empty yogurt cartons in hand. There are so many wild blueberries that we each choose a spot, sit, and stay there for half an hour, the sun shining down hard as we eat two blueberries for every one that makes it into our carton. Across a narrow inlet a beaver the size of a Labrador retriever fusses with his house, the water slipping off his back like the contrails of a jet as he moves effortlessly from the shore. I know that later the boys—both big and small—will stealthily canoe over to steal one of his carefully prepared logs. It is apparently irresistible.

With enough berries to make a pie, we wander in a sleepy daze up to the cabin to light the grill for dinner. Along the way we stop by the garden to see if we can catch the woodchuck who has built himself not just a home but a veritable condominium among the tomatoes. He has made his escape before we arrive, but I selfishly harvest every low-hanging green tomato to fry in the tradition of my West Virginia roots before he has a chance to get at them. We leave the cucumbers to him. As we climb the stairs to the deck, a red squirrel overhead chastises us at full volume. "Stay away from my pine cones!" he seems to yell as he systematically decimates a towering red pine, dropping large tufts of needles on the path as if in spite.

Reeder and Jack suddenly gasp in dismay as they discover a hummingbird lying on the porch, its heart visibly pounding through the metallic sheen of a miniature chest. It has stunned itself by flying into a window. We leave it in peace to recover, the boys keeping a distant vigil for more than an hour. At last it takes flight, buzzing like a horsefly, landing briefly in a nearby tree—so tiny! like a toy!—and then disappears.

We settle into another captive night on the island. Once dusk falls, the mainland and islands on this 7,000-acre lake become a two-dimensional palette of gray and blue. Those fortunate enough to be here through the seasons come to know the contours and notches of the tree line and can find their way on a moonlit night. But we are just visitors and will stay secure on this rock of pines until the mist clears in the morning.

The ancient Finns kept wooden carvings of *Sielulintu,* the soul-bird, next to their beds to protect their souls from being lost in the path of dreams. In their legends, the Milky Way is the path from which our souls arrive at birth, carried on the wings of the soul-bird. I remember a summer here when our boys were toddlers. As we tucked them into bed, we all heard the eerie call of the loon. The boys' eyes widened in absolute terror—there was a ghost on the lake! Perhaps they were not so wrong. The seductive tremolo and wail of the loon remind me of the soul-bird, calling us up and away, calling us back, evermore into the starlit night. It makes me tremble to think of it.

In the light of day, the northern birds seem more cheerful. We gasp in amazement at the size of the pileated woodpecker, spot the trademark "V" of the turkey vulture, feel a surge of joy in our chests at the lift of a bald eagle, sit silently to watch a kingfisher on a cattail, and startle at the sudden swoop of a downy white osprey. The loons become charming in the sunshine, some with babies tucked neatly on their backs, others disappearing under the waves and reappearing at an astonishing distance. The common loon is the state bird of Minnesota for a reason. It is truly beloved here. And it is as ancient as the landscape. Its heavy bones and set-back legs equip it for deep dives—as much as ninety feet—but render it nearly incapable of walking. It flops its way ashore to its low-lying nest and struggles for nearly a hundred feet to lift its weighty self off the water into flight.

Only the insects use their wings for spite. One day on Snowbank Lake, we inadvertently find hell on a rock, a swarm of blackflies descending in a pestilence upon our picnic. Their bites are not poisonous, but they might as well be. We jump screaming into the lake and swim quickly to our boat, yelping and complaining the whole way. The mosquitoes, of course, are vicious. I hate to mention them because it is like being a Chicagoan and hearing incessantly about Al Capone. Look at photographs in a catalog of BWCAW camping excursions, and you'll see that everyone in it is covered in huge red welts. It is not a beguiling picture, but one learns to live with the risks of DEET and go for the hard-core insect repellents.

One summer afternoon, Ann Thunhorst at Jackpine Lodge gave our sons a magical world in a large glass pickling jar—a Luna moth chrysalis, suspended tenuously from a small green stem. There were tiny bite marks from the creature's last wingless meal lined up neatly along the edge of a leaf. Here in this jar is all of nature's wonder. Oh to capture the Northwoods in a jar like that and bring it home with me. To be forever suspended between lake and sky. To resist each night the loon calling me to the path of dreams.

Instead, like so many others, we must wait eagerly for spring to pass so that we can make our way north for the summer. Embracing the coolness and settling in to the fresh, crispness of the light that seems unique to these waters. Finding the best in ourselves in the best of nature. As a young and perceptive Widji camper said to me, "This is about having your time. It's *your* time to be up here and be surrounded by the magic of it all."

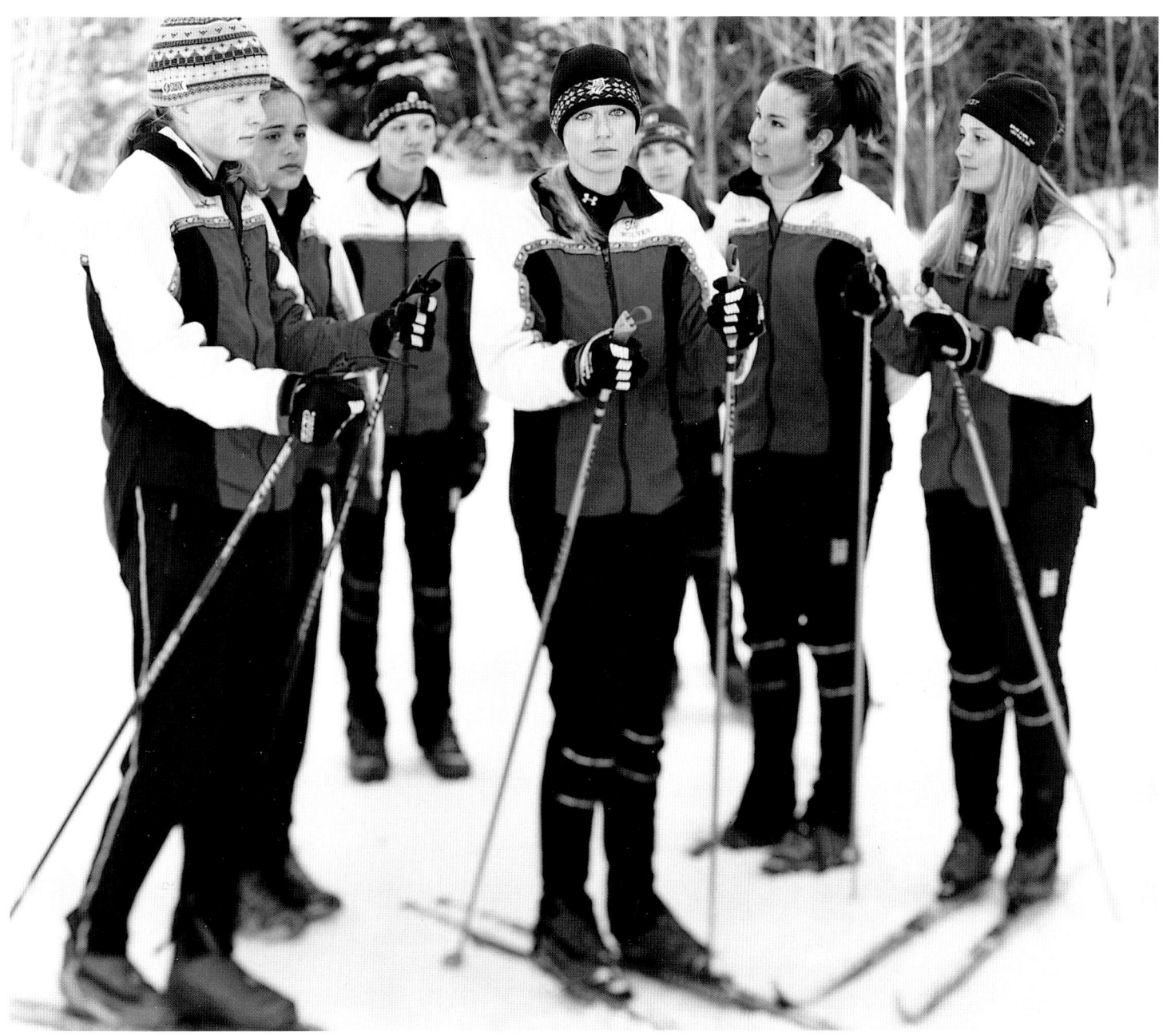

PLATE 89. The Nordic Wolves, girls' cross-country ski team, Ely Memorial High School

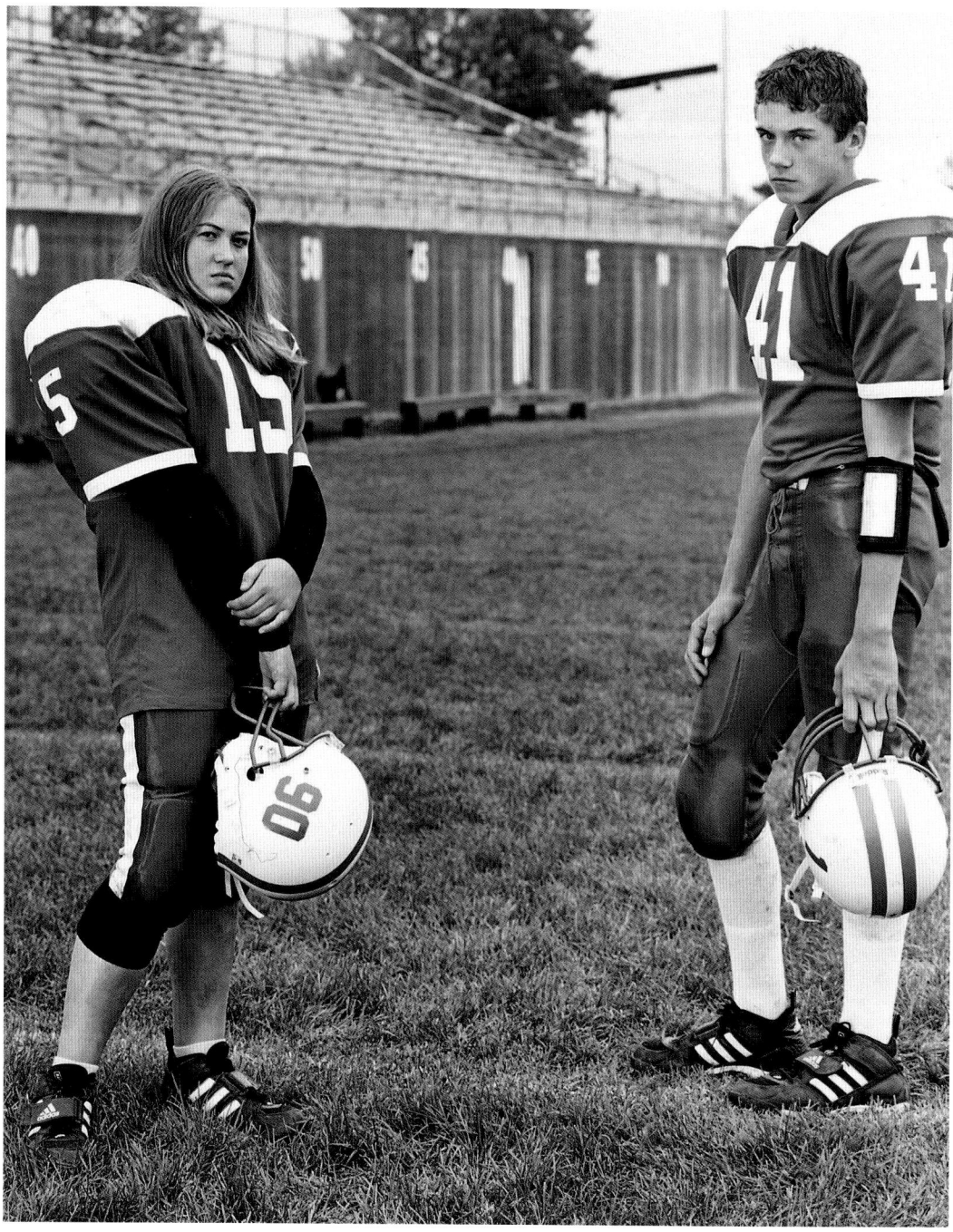

PLATE 90. Kahsha and Alex, football team, Ely Memorial High School

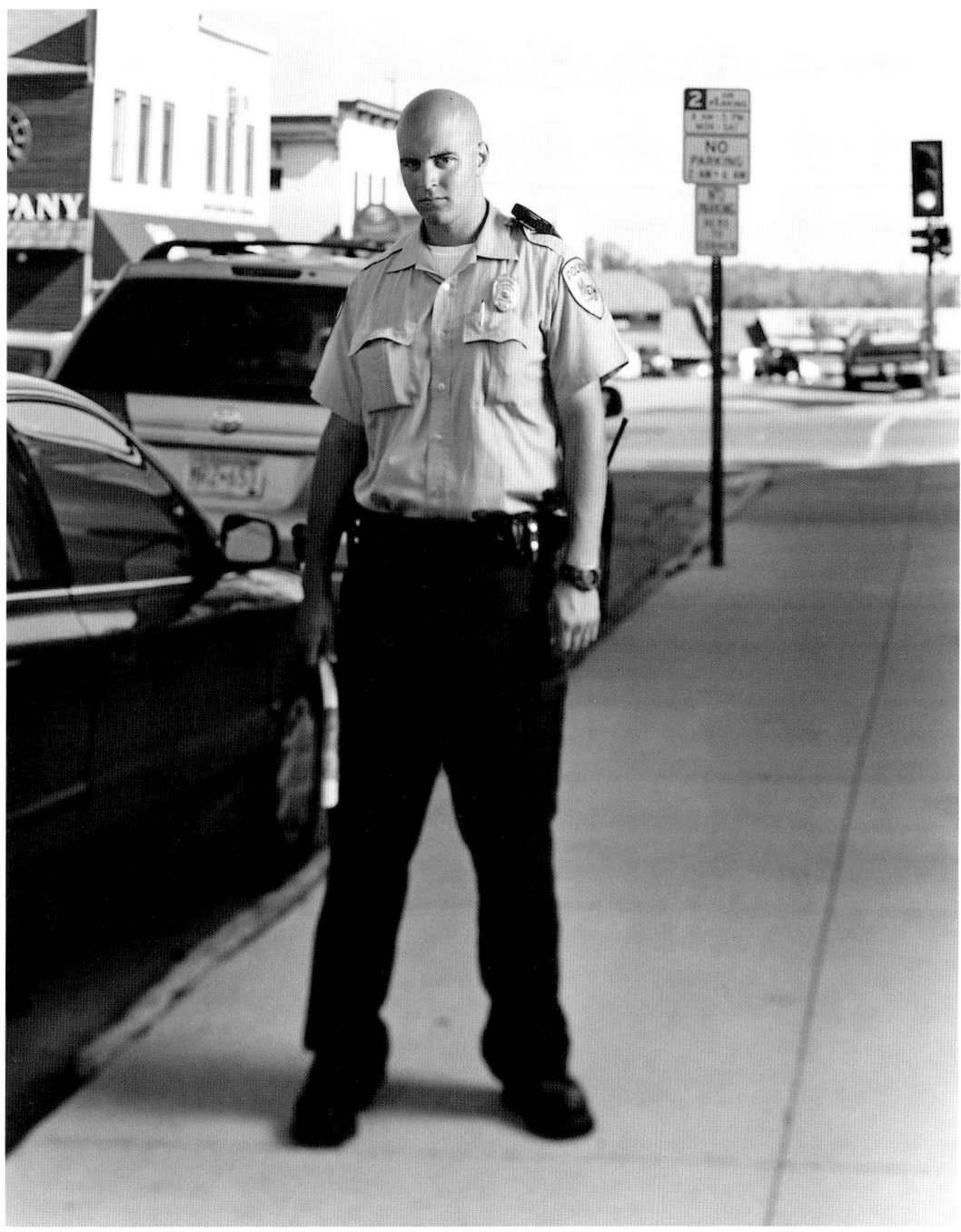

PLATE 91. George Burger, parking enforcement officer

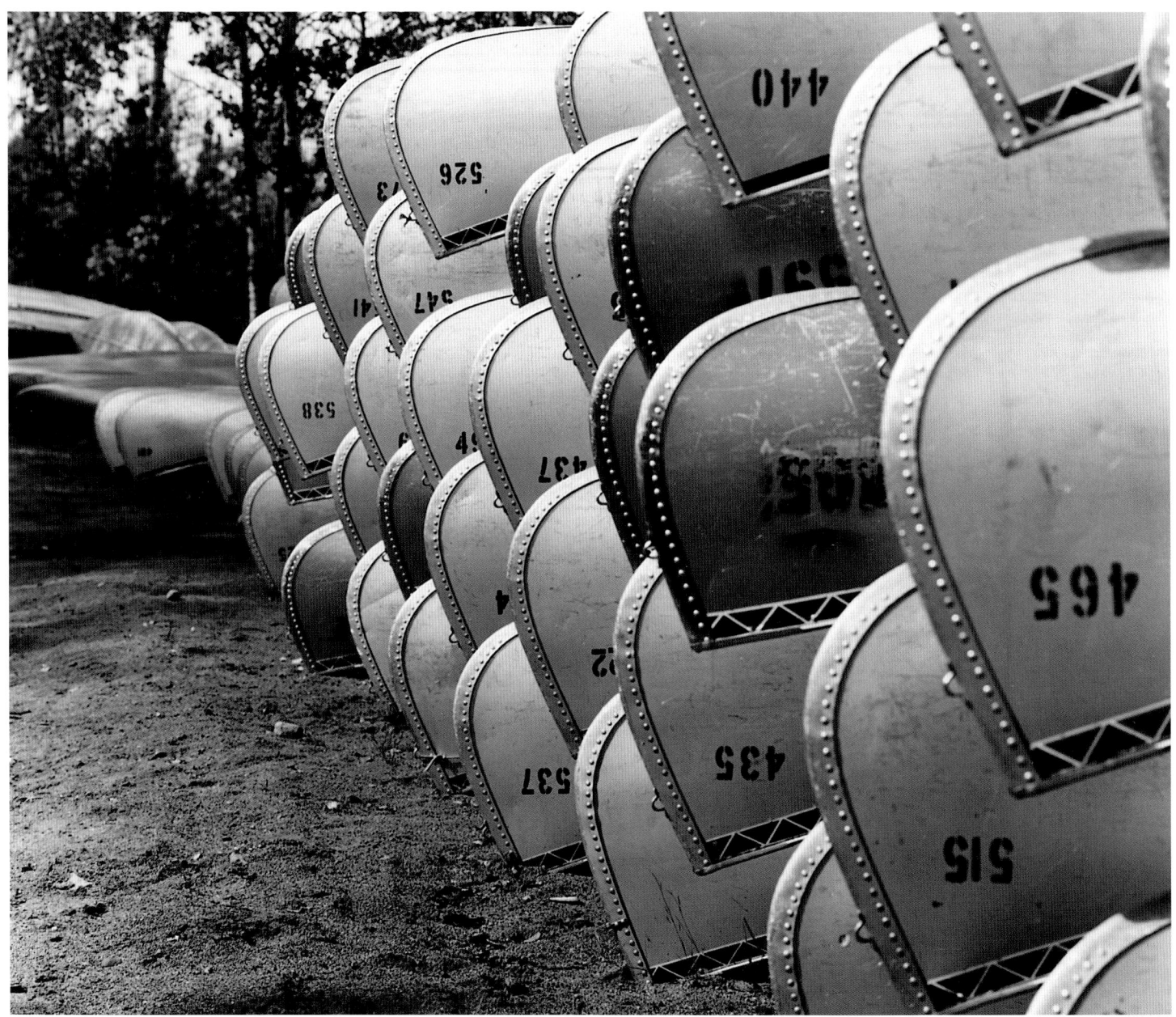

PLATE 92. Charles L. Sommers National High Adventure Base, Moose Lake

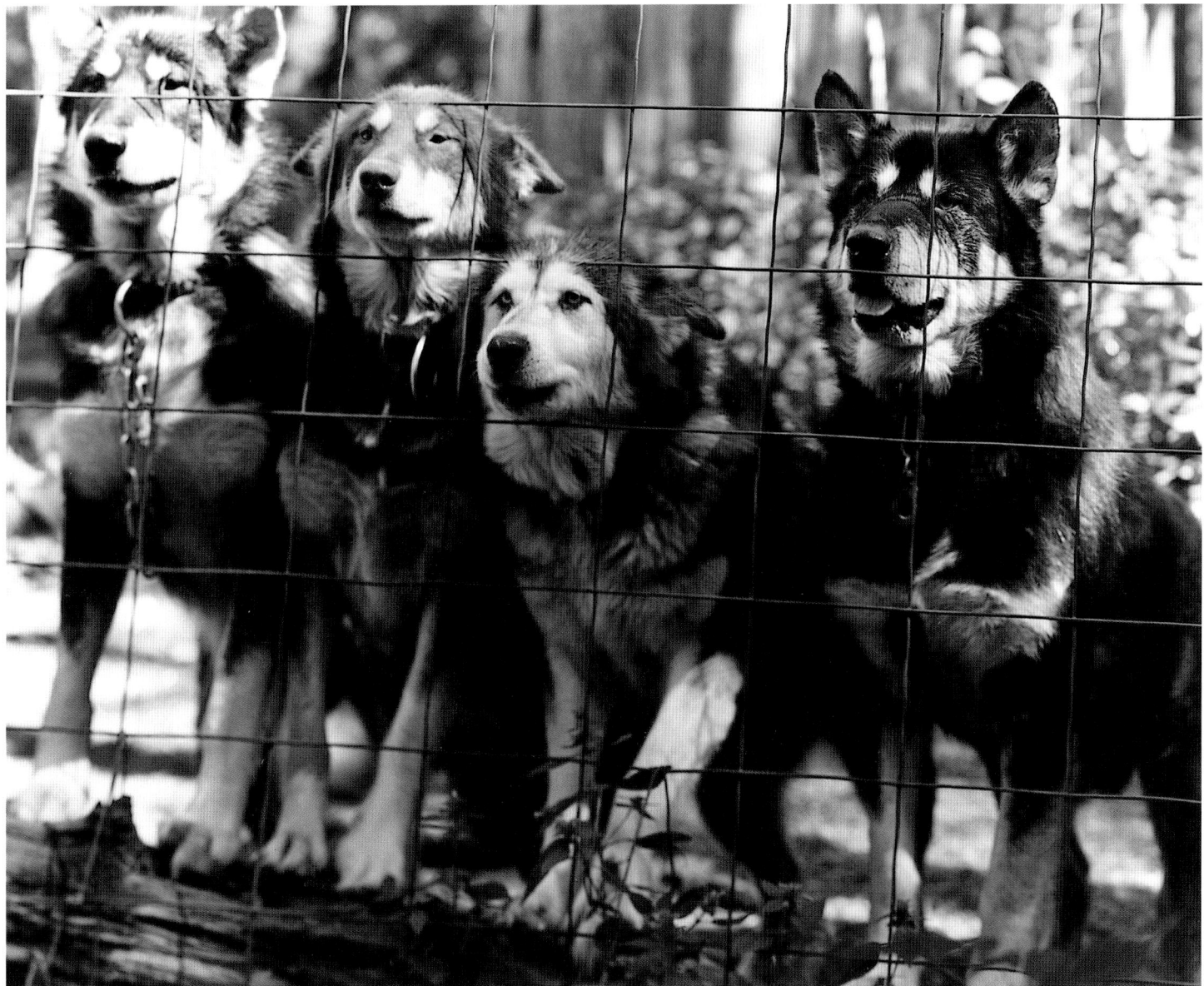

PLATE 93. Bert Hyde's sled dogs

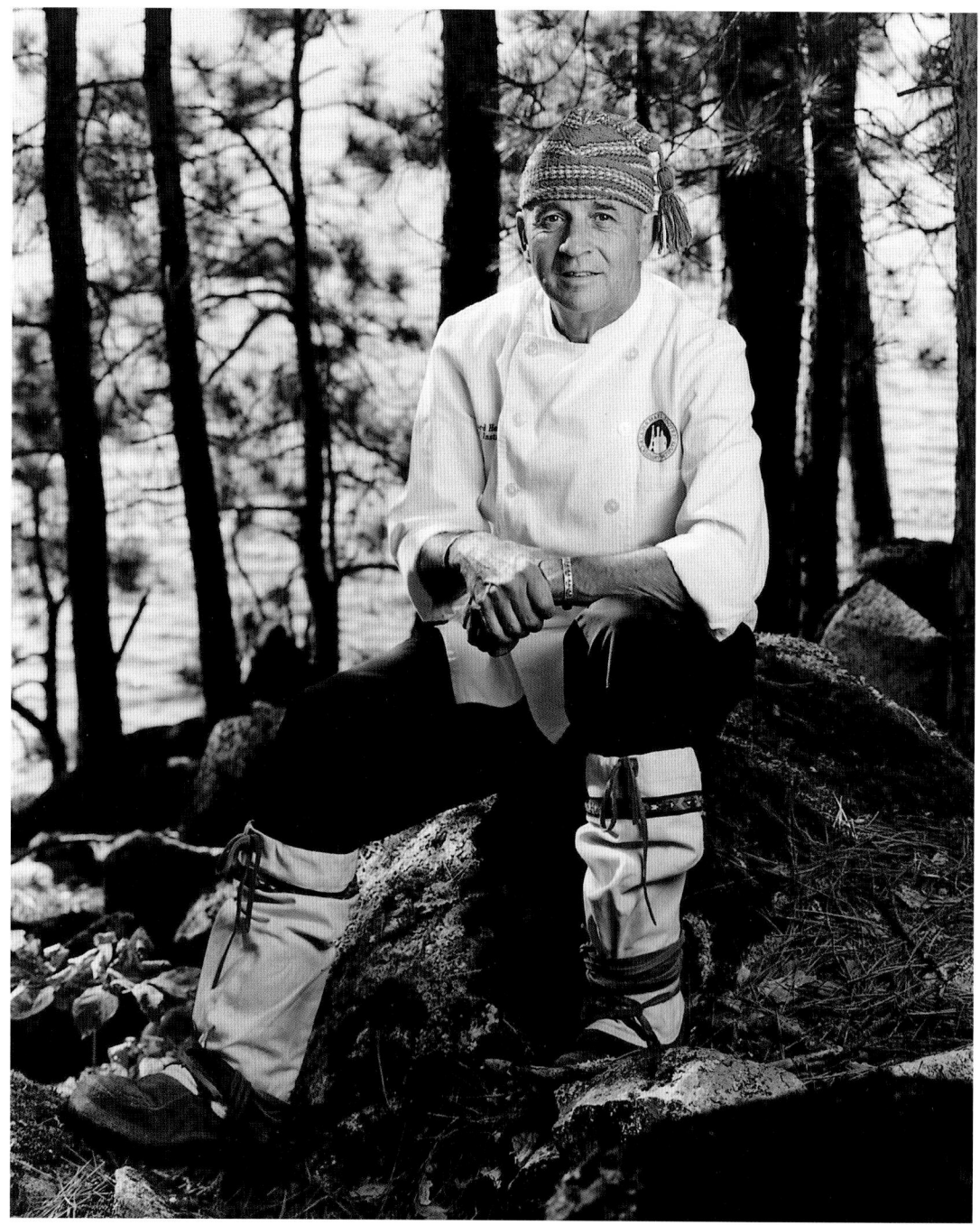

PLATE 94. Bernard Herrmann, French master chef

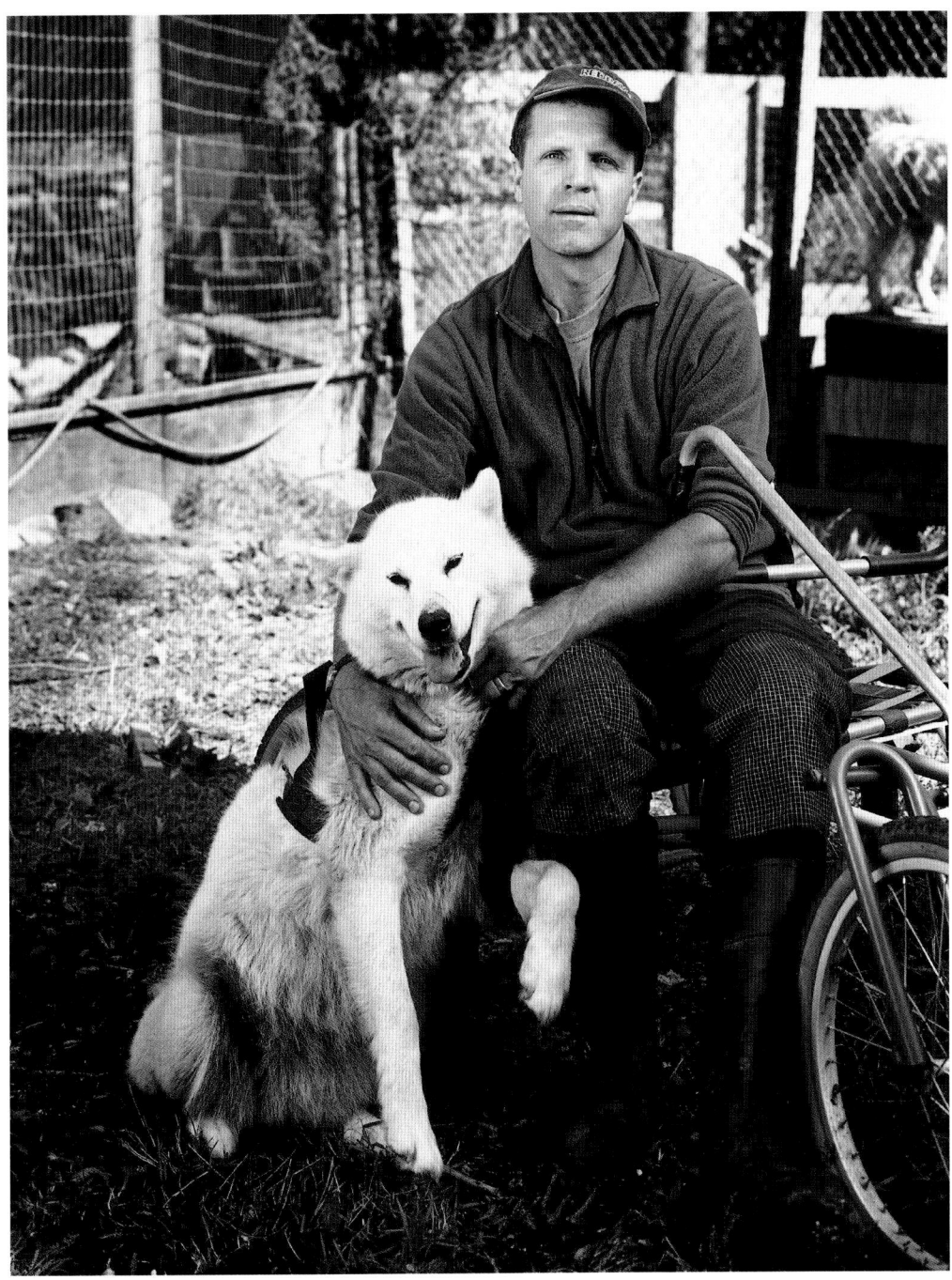

PLATE 95. Paul Schurke, arctic explorer, Wintergreen Dog Sledding Lodge

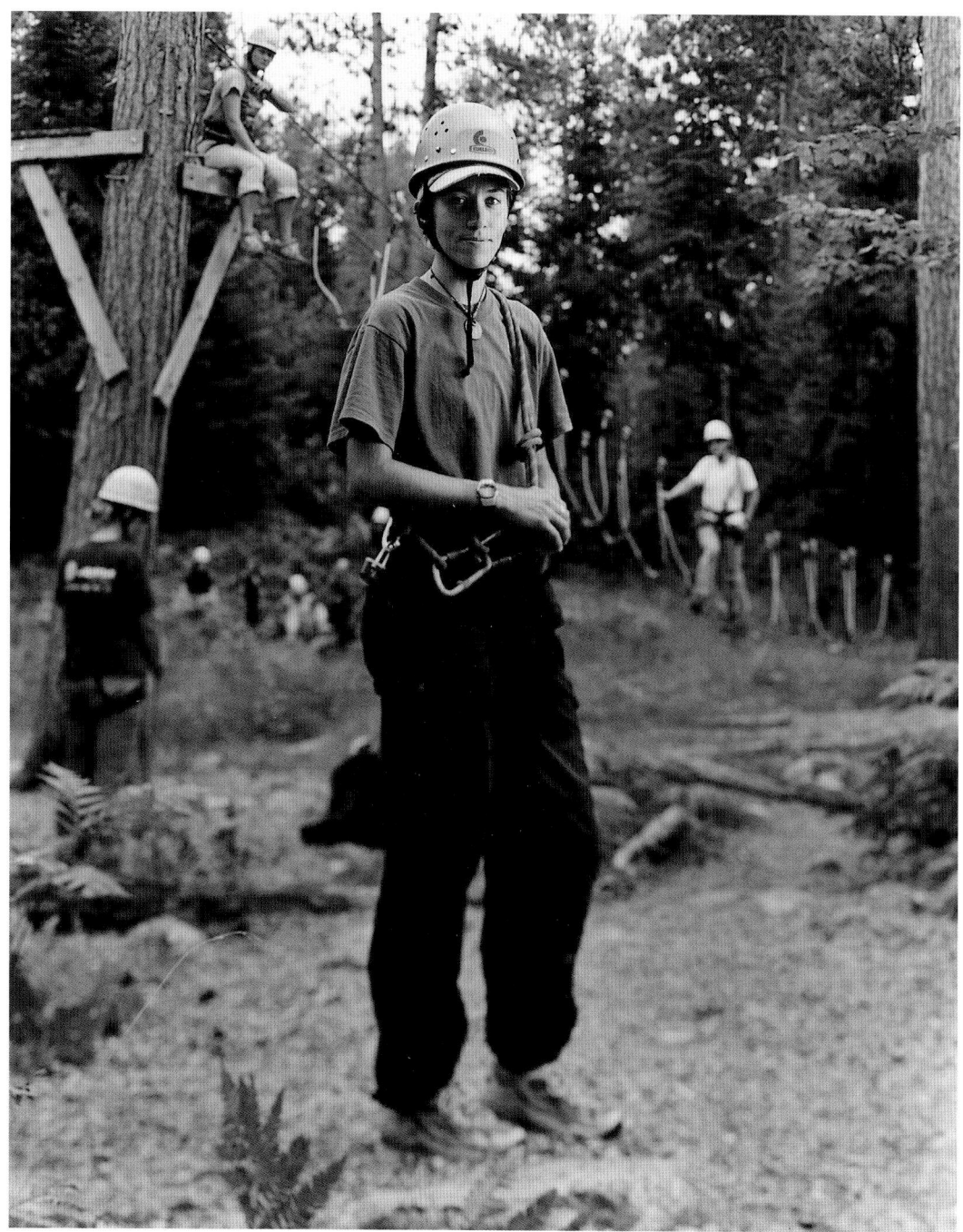

PLATE 96. Virginie Pointeau, instructor, Voyageur Outward Bound School

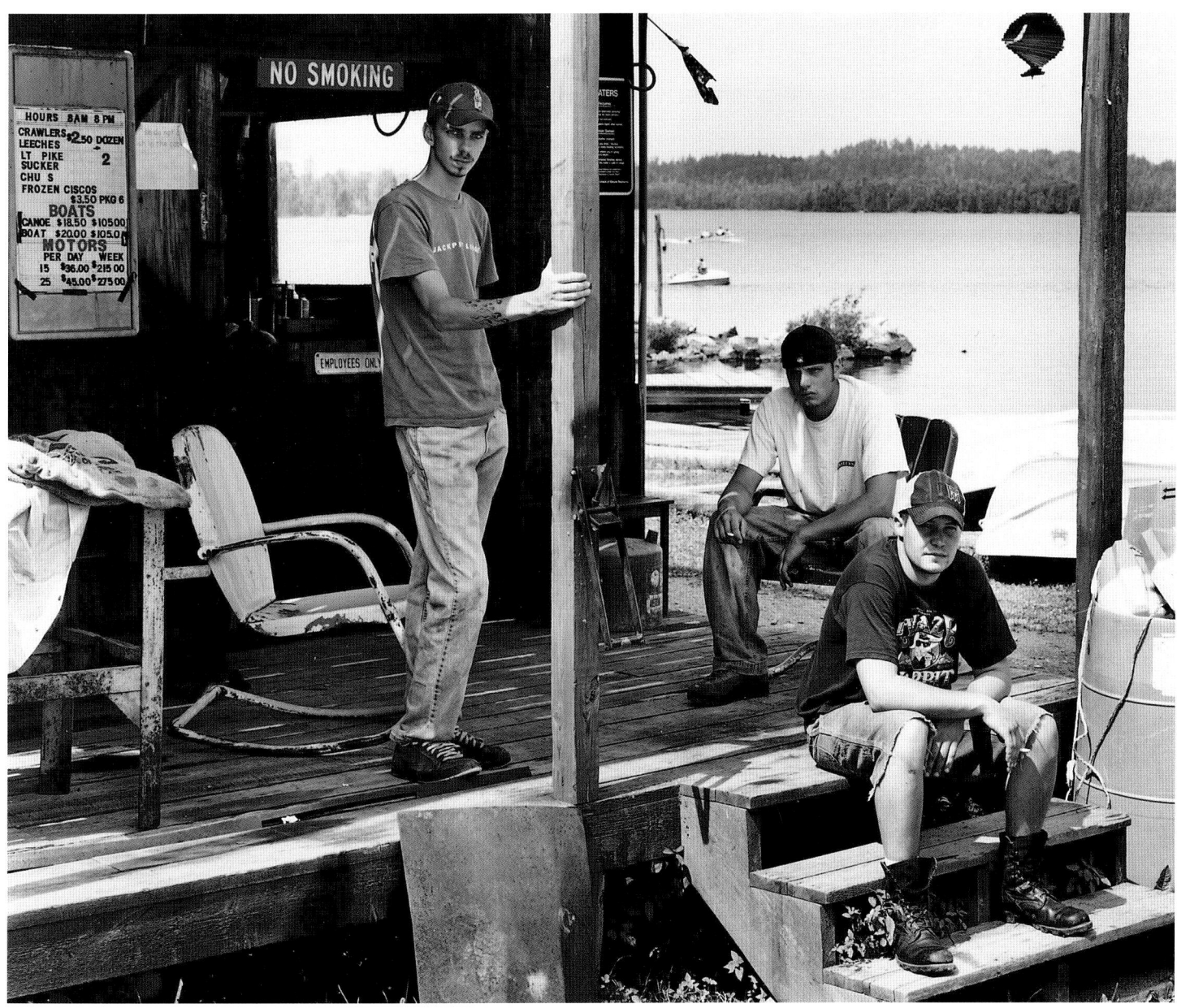

PLATE 97. Roger, Matt, and Wayne, boat hands, Jackpine Lodge

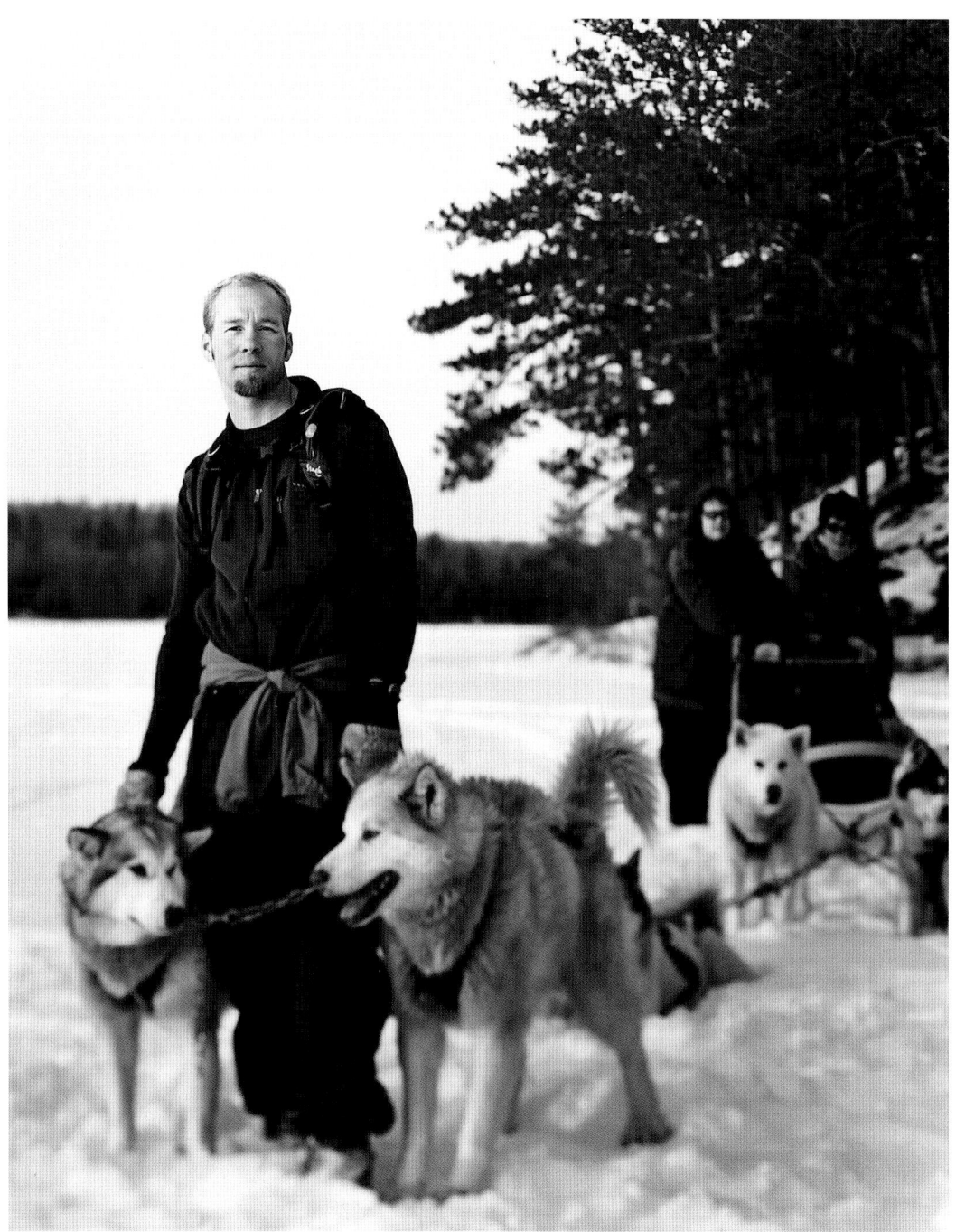

PLATE 98. Bob Nass, musher, Wintergreen Dog Sledding Lodge

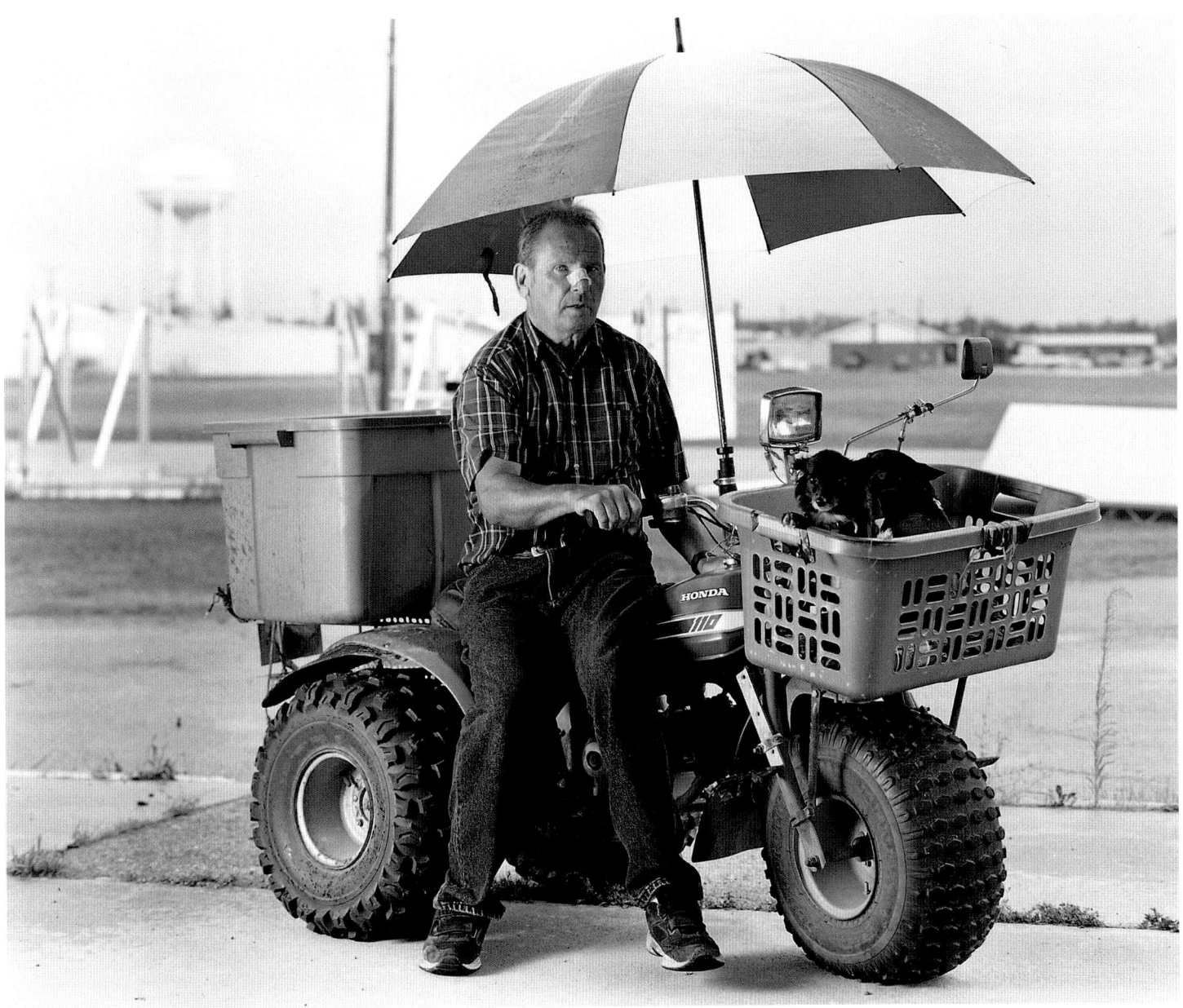

PLATE 99. Tommy Helm, retired miner and inventor, Babbitt

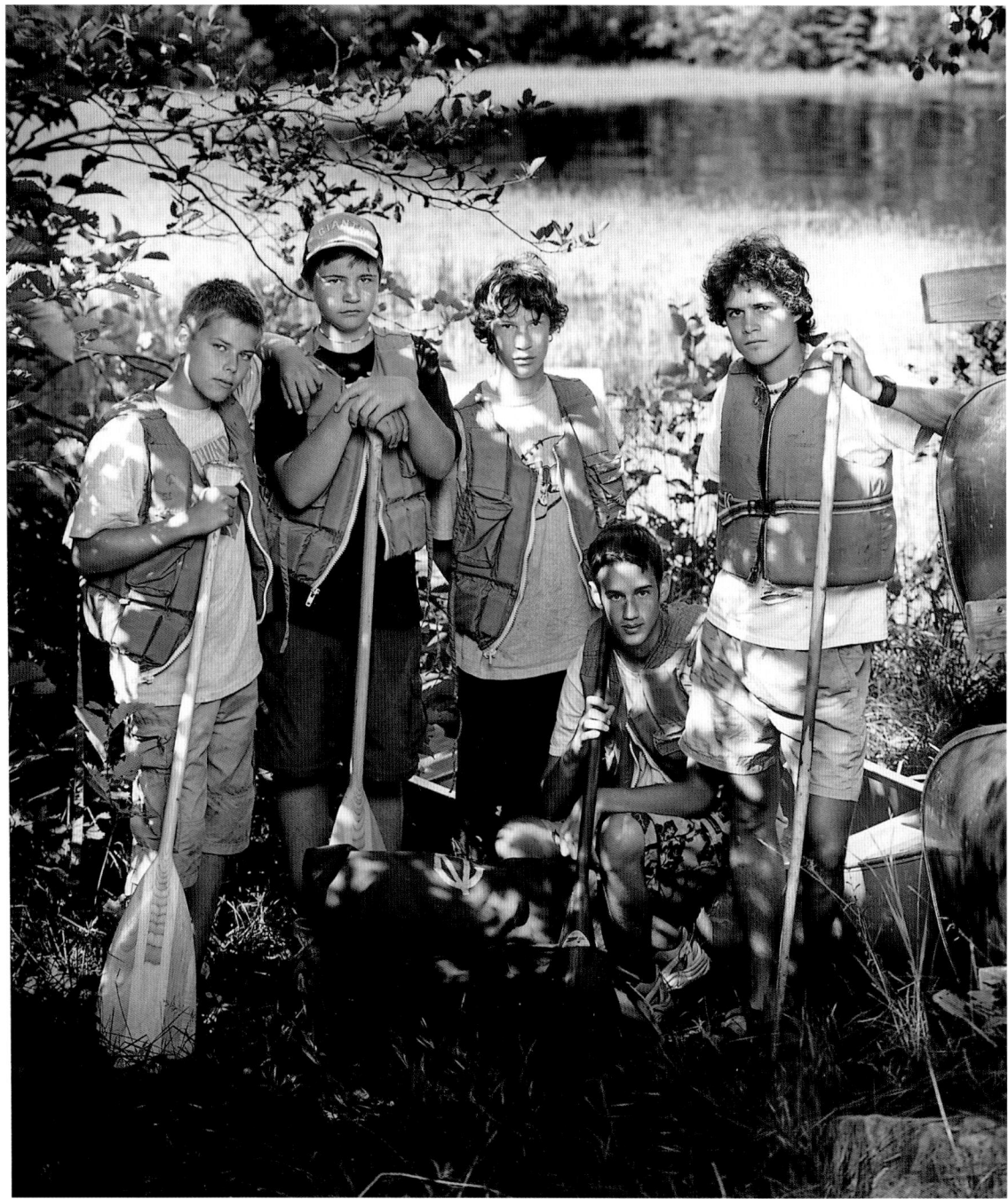

PLATE 100. Dan, Henry, Bob, Drew, Matt, Camp Voyageur

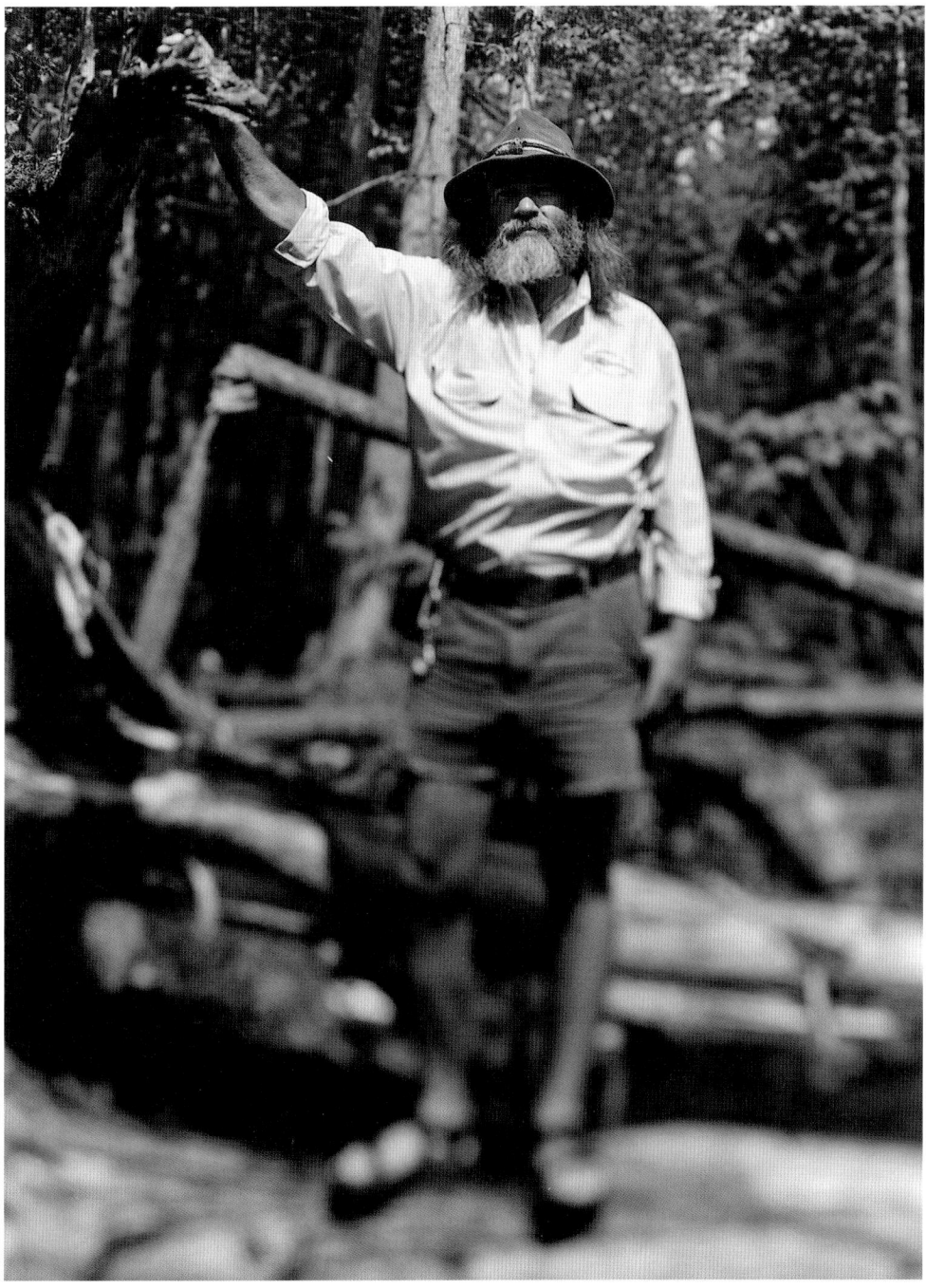

PLATE 101. Bert Hyde, wilderness ranger

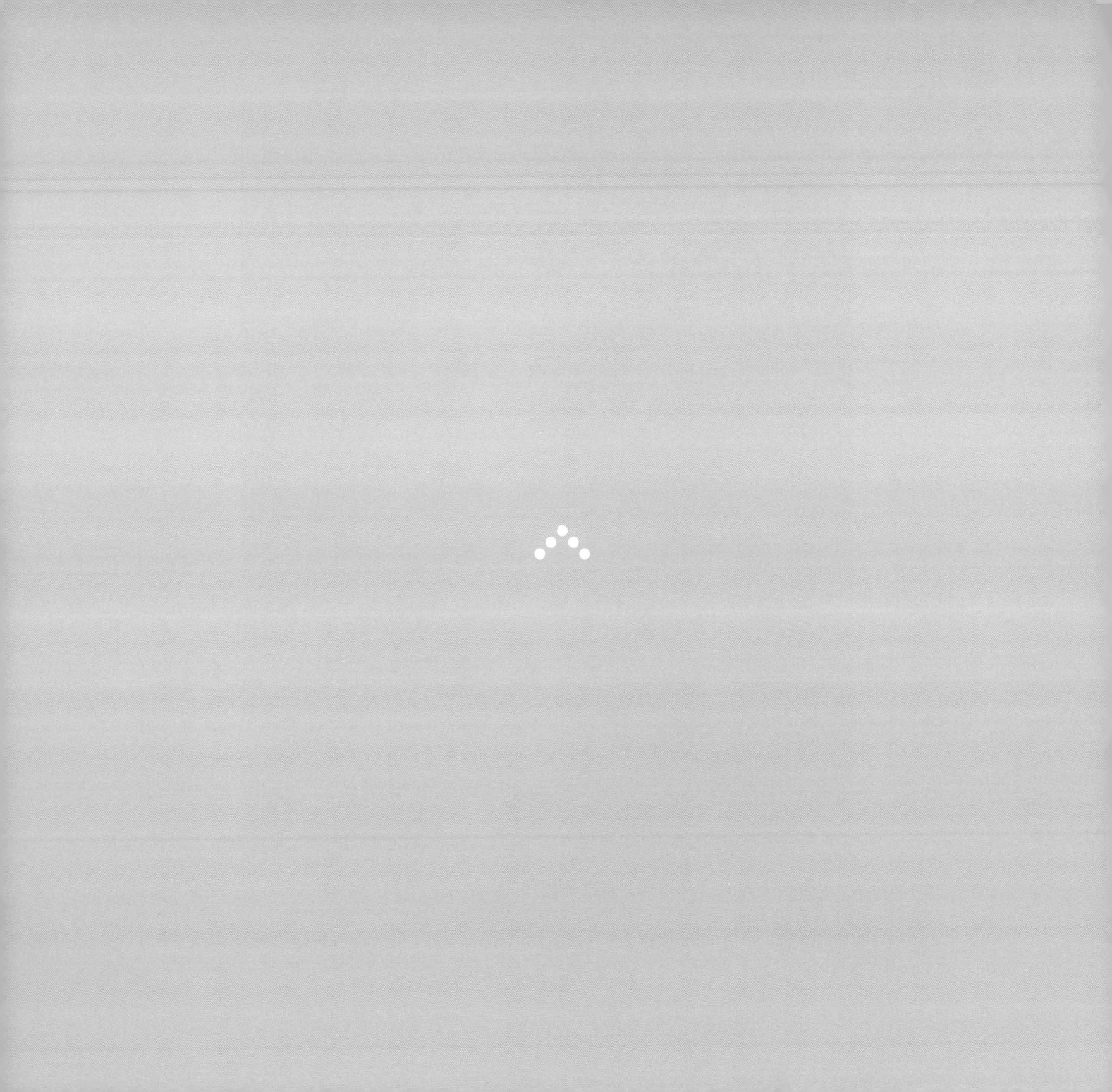

NOTES on the Portraits

PLATE 1. Steve "Rooster" Lekatz, retired miner

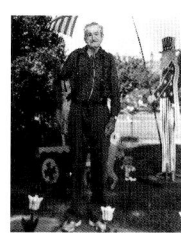

We rented a house across the street from Rooster one summer, and I could not take my eyes off his yard filled with wooden whirligigs, all of them chained together. We would see Rooster sitting in a lawn chair in his garage, visiting with friends and neighbors. I approached his daughter Gail about photographing him, and she thought it was a great idea. When we showed up to take his picture, he came outside in an old green miner's uniform—something you see a lot of around Ely—toting his oxygen tank. His emphysema makes it so that he cannot make his whirligigs anymore because of the sawdust. He was a willing and patient subject, happy to tell us about his life in Ely and to stand still as long as we needed him to.

I did not purposely include the flag in the background. When I look at all the photographs in this book, I am surprised by how many American flags appear in the images, even though we never placed one in a scene or positioned a shot specifically to incorporate it.

PLATE 2. Michele Richards and Marlene Zorman, the Chainsaw Sisters

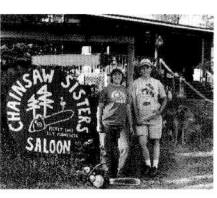

Marlene and Michele are identical twins. They studied physical education in college, at which point they decided that they did not, in fact, want to be gym teachers. Ever. So they followed a friend's lead to Ely, where they worked for the U.S. Forest Service, clearing brush with machetes and eventually working the chain saws. As Forest Service jobs diminished, they bought land from Potlatch Paper Company and set up canoe rentals and a parking lot for campers entering the Boundary Waters at Mudro Lake. The saloon came a few years later.

The twins' home-grown style of marketing has made them somewhat legendary, and rumors abound about their supposedly grouchy dispositions. So, when we drove the rough road off the Echo Trail to ask them to pose for a picture, we were a little nervous. As we walked up the wooden steps to the saloon, we agreed to just buy a beer, check it out, and leave if it didn't seem right.

It took less than sixty seconds to realize that the rumors were wrong. Michele and Marlene are a warm and welcoming pair, gently unassuming and more than a little amused by their renown. Fame is not what they intended, but as they say themselves, "at least we're not infamous."

Although the twins started the business together eighteen years ago, Michele and her husband, Mark, ran it in recent years, after Marlene got married and moved to town. Since we took this picture, the land has been purchased by the Trust for Public Land and the saloon closed so that Michele, too, can enjoy some downtime, along with a little electricity and running water.

PLATE 3. Simon and Lucy, Ely residents

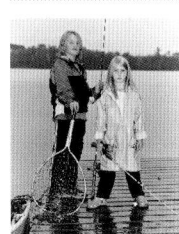

It was pouring rain when I took this shot. The kids sat in their dad's car while I set up all the equipment, covering it with plastic bags and hoping I did not get electrocuted. I got a little shelter by standing under a tree, but Simon and Lucy were drenched by the end of the session.

PLATE 4. Joe Smith and Jim Schwartz, Camp Widjiwagan

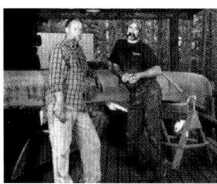

Joe Smith is the caretaker at Camp Widjiwagan and lives on-site. He and fellow worker and craftsman Jim Schwartz come across in person as the most super-content people you will ever meet. But when I took this image, it was hard to get them to reveal much of their easy-going personalities. They look as though they are holding back, which I actually kind of like. My favorite thing about this shot is all the textures—Joe's work boots and clothing, the canoe in the process of being refinished. Everything, including the guys, looks well-used and rugged, experienced and tough. A lot like Ely. Later in the project I photographed Joe again with the local men's hockey team.

PLATE 5. Joe Prijatel, retired miner and snowshoe maker

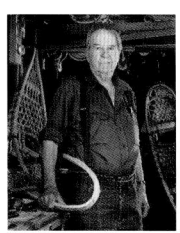

Joe's house is very typical of Ely—a four-square with siding and a tiny basement. He was so kind and patient as we took over his basement, moving snowshoes around and squeezing lighting equipment into every corner. I could not stand up straight the entire time. We had not realized that Joe was part of the Civilian Conservation Corps in his youth, before he worked as a miner. It meant a lot to talk to him about those experiences. This was early in the project, and it really helped jump-start our understanding of the history of the area while also giving us insight into the type of people who live in Ely.

PLATE 6. Peter Schmiechen, Abbie Bahnemann, and Daniel Schmiechen, Burntside Lake

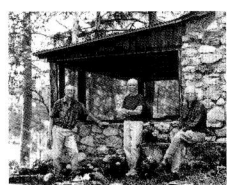

Dan is a close friend and neighbor of our cousins. Many times we have paddled to Dan's island and vice versa. He and his two siblings own a cluster of three gorgeous islands left to them by their father. All of the islands are used as idyllic vacation retreats for the extended family. It was only a few years ago that Dan and his wife, Barb, added electricity to their cabin. This picture is of the three siblings, taken in front of Peter's cabin, the original stone house built by their father with the help of the local Ojibwe Anderson family.

PLATE 7. Dennis and Bonnie Orn, Bear Island Lake

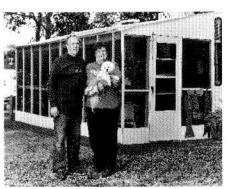

Dennis was the mayor of Babbitt for a time. He worked for the taconite plant until his retirement. He and Bonnie spend most of each summer in this mobile home on Bear Island Lake at the edge of a campsite. Every camper who pulls in will be greeted by Dennis and Bonnie, provided the two of them are not out on the lake fishing off their pontoon boat, and if the camper is lucky, he will be invited to the screen porch for homemade doughnuts on Sunday afternoon.

PLATE 8. Eric Mase, Northwoods artist, Wee Cabin Company

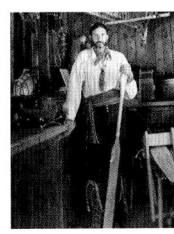

Eric grew up in Chicago but left as soon as he could. He has found an ideal life in Ely with his wife, Dayna, also an artist. Many articles and features have been written about Eric's amazing artisanship, for good reason. He uses only organic materials and ancient techniques to produce birch-bark canoes and baskets and now a collection of "wee cabins" that are the most romantic wood hideaways you can imagine. He is dressed in this photograph in the traditional costume of the French voyageurs, which he wears during his presentations about the history and craftsmanship of the people who lived in the Northwoods hundreds of years ago.

PLATE 9. Seraphine "Sludge" Rolando, retired miner, welder, and artist

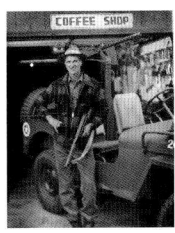

Seraphine's garage is a social gathering point, mostly for men driving pickup trucks. People come cruising down the alley, and they invariably have something to pick up or a part that needs fixing. "Sludge" is the go-to man for anything that needs welding or repair, and also for any community news. He is definitely an extrovert. Once you know Sludge a little, you know him a lot. Nothing made our kids happier on this entire project than riding down Sheridan Street in this old jeep with a replica machine gun on top.

PLATE 10. Will Steger, polar explorer, educator, and environmentalist

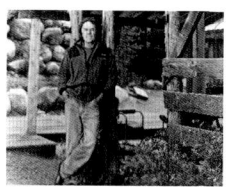

A rustic and muddy camp spreads out like a moat below world-renowned explorer Will Steger's tiny two-room cabin. This is the launching point for polar expeditions of the most dramatic kind. Waves of dogs, supplies, mechanics, carpenters, volunteers, scientists, environmentalists, and media flow in and out of this remote compound depending on Steger's current status—pre-expedition, postexpedition, or the rare times in between. Will has led such historic expeditions as the first dogsled crossing of the entire continent of Antarctica, a grueling journey of nearly four thousand miles. He has stood on both poles and faced the most unimaginable challenges. This compact and soft-spoken man has pulled dogs and team members from sheer ice crevasses, looked a dog-hungry polar bear in the eye from thirty feet, and helped pioneer Internet-based education, reaching millions with his message of environmental preservation.

PLATE 11. Jeanne Bourquin, canoe builder

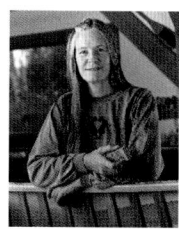

Jeanne produces up to eight of her gorgeous Otter and Lutre canoes every year. Anyone who buys a canoe from Jeanne is welcome, for the same price, to help her build it. Oftentimes, a family will join her for a few days at a critical stage in the process, thereby giving Jeanne a chance to pass along her techniques and love for canoes.

PLATE 12. Marty Stage, conservation officer, Babbitt

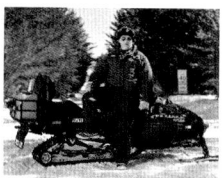

The conservation officer becomes a traffic cop in the winter, complete with radar gun and a pad of blank tickets. Snowmobiles are dangerous—more people die every year in snowmobile accidents than from firearm injuries in Minnesota. Northern Minnesota has an extensive network of designated snowmobile trails, which helps limit their environmental and aesthetic impact while still affording riders their fun. Snowmobilers, for the most part, know the drill. So, when Marty pulled over a few people while we were taking this shot, they did not put up a fight and took their warnings with good spirit.

PLATE 13. Heather and Dale "Limey" Tweit and family, Cedar Creek Mini-Golf Course

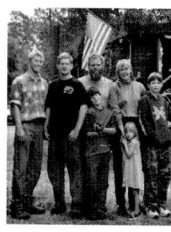

There were many photo shoots on this project that melted into long, sunny, social afternoons. This was perhaps the longest. The family photograph was taken first—an unexpected gift of a shot, as we had originally planned just to photograph Limey. The minute they were "released," the younger boys disappeared with our kids to the rear of the property to spend an afternoon shooting BBs and generally doing the things boys do in the woods. Limey fired up his forge, and while I photographed him, he rendered us an ornate backscratcher out of a piece of old refrigerator shelving. He and Heather had only been married a few years, blending their families and quickly adding their daughter, Elizabeth Grace, to the clan. A seemingly odd pairing, Limey nicknamed Heather, a computer consultant, "High Tech," and she referred to him as "Low Tech." We wandered through the mini-golf course, taking pictures of old cars and gorgeous beds of wildflowers, and tape-recording Limey's wonderful voice with its lilting British accent. By the time we left, the light had long since faded past the point of taking pictures, and we had gained yet another new set of friends.

The next winter, their car hit a patch of ice in a shaded spot along the road and ran headlong into the path of a logging truck. Heather died instantly. Almost immediately, we received phone calls from her friends in Ely asking us to please be sure to include her photo in this book as a remembrance. We are so glad to have captured a beautiful afternoon when she and Limey seemed to be at their happiest.

PLATE 14. Kurt Simer, Noah Lucarelli, Joe Smith, and Dan Olson, men's hockey league

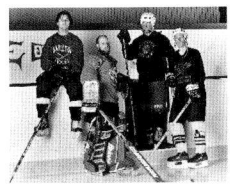

Jimi Hendrix is blaring at full volume while these guys, all of them from Minnesota or Massachusetts, glide over the ice, battling for the puck in the same way they have done since they were four or five years old. "Once it's in your blood, it's there forever," says one. These four men seem mild mannered. They tell us the goalies are the crazy ones. Joe warns parents: "Be sure you want your kid to be a goalie, because once you get the pads on, you'll never get 'em off." All these players have their teeth intact, but other scars, like a gnarly ear or two, give them away as lifelong hockey players.

PLATE 15. Kim McCluskey, owner/explorer, Worldwide Paddling Adventures

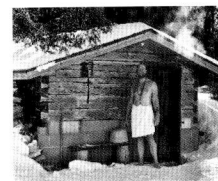

This picture is taken at the Piragis family's wood-burning sauna situated alongside a sweet meandering river west of Ely. The sauna tradition runs deep in the community and has spread far beyond those of Finnish descent, although everyone here still does pronounce it "sowna." An original wood-burning sauna requires a commitment of time to get it going, and as our Finnish friend Milli says, "saunas always burn down before they rot, the good ones do anyway."

Kim McCluskey leads adventure trips all over the globe but has a particular passion for Vietnam. He befriended three homeless girls there on an early expedition and established a nonprofit organization, Sun in My Heart Vietnamese Children's Fund, to raise money to build them a home. Once that was done, he moved on to help more Vietnamese children and led the effort to establish a school there. There have been many fundraisers in Ely to help with this work, and he has been deeply touched by the generosity of the community.

PLATE 16. "Jackpine" Bob Cary, author, artist, and one-time presidential candidate

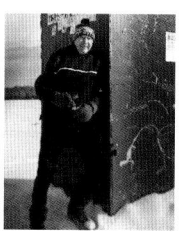

It was forty degrees below zero on the day that Bob and I met on Miners Lake. This eighty-something-year-old man arrived with his wife, Edie, and endured a bitterly cold session in which my equipment barely functioned. At the end of the shoot, I gratefully bundled myself back into the car, while Bob and Edie put on their cross-country skis and set off across the lake for some exercise.

"Jackpine" Bob Cary was a celebrity in Ely and, in fact, in the state of Minnesota. He was a longtime writer for the *Ely Echo*, the author of more than a dozen books, and an artist and illustrator. He even ran for U.S. president under the auspices of the Independent Fisherman's Party. He was a great storyteller, a drummer, and a competitive cross-country skier, and he was fluent in the Ojibwe language.

PLATE 17. Roger Nyquist, Jackpine Lodge

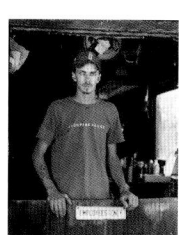

At the time this photograph was taken, Roger worked for his girlfriend's family at Jackpine Lodge, spending his entire summer at the edge of Snowbank Lake and moving into town for the winter. Jackpine was truly a classic Northwoods lodge, and most people went there for the fishing. A year or two ago, the owners sold the property, passing the title of "last resort accessible by road" along to the next resort to the west.

PLATE 18. Elli and Nancy Piragis, Ely residents

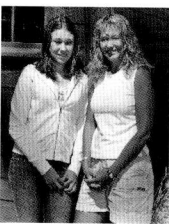

Seeing Nancy walk across one of the only tillable plots of land we have ever seen near Ely was a beautiful and unusual sight in this land of rocks and water. I knew immediately that I wanted to photograph her near her barn. She cajoled daughter Elli into joining her at the last minute. Nancy came to Ely many years ago for scientific research as a limnologist—studying bodies of freshwater. She met fellow scientist Steve Piragis; they married and determined never to leave Ely. Together they built one of the most successful outfitting companies in the area.

PLATE 19. Colton, Ely resident

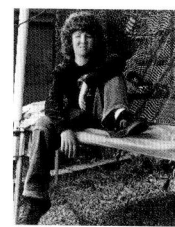

An Ely native, Colton was an extraordinarily patient subject. He was willing to work with me, staying in his pose and being super-polite for longer than most kids his age would deem reasonable.

PLATE 20. James Kurzdorfer and Ryan Jones, Mudro Lake Access Point, Boundary Waters Canoe Area Wilderness

We drove out to the Chainsaw Sisters Saloon to see if we might catch someone coming out of the Boundary

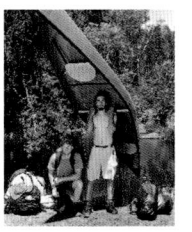Waters entry point there. We did not have a permit to get into the BWCAW ourselves, so we just sat and waited. Ryan and James were the first to appear. They had been out for twelve days and had lost their fishing pole to the murky depths on day two or three. So they "Huck-Finned" it for the rest of the trip, using sticks and string to catch their daily dinner. Ryan took his camera with him into the wilderness and was eager to get home to Colorado and develop some of the long-exposure lightning shots he had taken from the door of his tent.

PLATE 22. Robert "Jeep" LaTourell, LaTourell's Moose Lake Resort

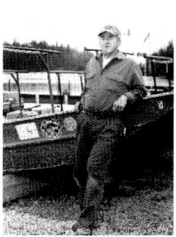Jeep's dad started this fisherman's paradise of a resort on the very borderline between the United States and Canada. Both countries' flags fly at the end of the dock. It was a close call for the family when the Boundary Waters was established and many lodges were bought out and condemned by the government. Now, they are perfectly placed right on the edge of the Boundary Waters. Jeep's twin daughters, Missy and Mindy, run one of the few motorboat portages into the protected wilderness. If you were to write a comprehensive history of this region, one of the first people to talk to would be Jeep. His knowledge of and personal connection to the wilderness and the people who have made it their livelihood are extensive.

PLATE 23. Theresa and Leonard Moreland, log peelers

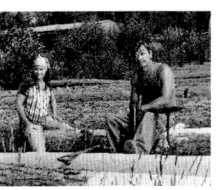Hand-peeling creates a particular sheen and texture to these fifty-foot pine logs that is highly regarded by the people who buy log homes. Theresa and Leonard use a horrifyingly sharp draw knife that they pull toward themselves with two handles. It is a great way to spend an afternoon together and make a few dollars. Like so many people in Ely, Theresa is an artist at heart. She published a book of poems and called it *Poet Unknown*. It sold twenty-five copies, which explains, says Theresa, why she called it *Poet Unknown*.

PLATE 24. Father James Scheuer, St. Anthony's Catholic Church

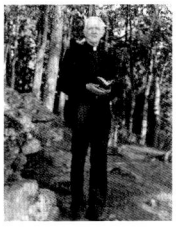Father Jim is at home in the woods. He is a passionate swimmer and loves to get his exercise in Shagawa Lake. St. Anthony's was originally a Slovenian congregation but is more mixed these days. This is the second time Father Jim has served St. Anthony's, the first time being back in the 1960s. He has served other congregations too, all of them in Minnesota.

PLATE 25. Rebecca and Carol Stouffer, Ely residents

This picture was taken in the deep woods at Carol's hand-built cabin. She and her husband seek a simple life and their children, including Rebecca, stay close to

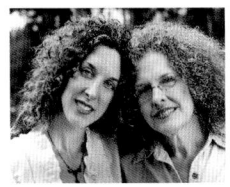 this commitment. Carol's garden is something to behold. She has a treasured collection of heirloom plants and seeds. Many people suggested that we photograph Carol and Rebecca, calling them, good-naturedly, the "ladies with the hair."

PLATE 27. Steve Johnson, wilderness guide, High Lake

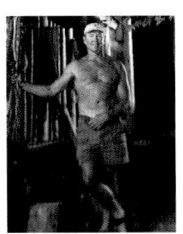 I was sitting in Chicago, watching *Extreme Homes* on television when I heard the narrator describe a cabin in Ely. It was Steve's totally-off-the-grid cabin that he had built by hand nearly thirty years ago. We found Steve's number in the phonebook and cold-called him. It was one of the project's earliest shots. We hauled our equipment a mile into the woods on Steve's ATV and found a secluded and fairly elaborate compound. In addition to his main cabin, Steve has an icehouse, a canoe-manufacturing shed, a number of tepees, and several storage buildings. Nevertheless, he spends most of his nights in a pitch tent down by the water. The name "Steve Johnson" is not entirely unusual in Minnesota, so people call him "High Lake Steve."

PLATE 28. Aaron Mellgren and Ronald Tokela, miners exploring for copper, nickel, and precious metals

Aaron and Ron are working in the woods near Babbitt on an old logging plot that has been leased for the mineral rights. The foreman drove me out there on a bumpy dirt 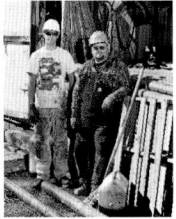 road and talked Aaron and Ron into participating in the book. It seemed like time was of the essence for these guys. They work long hours and rarely take a break. It was Aaron's first week on the job, and he was happy to be there. This is good work. No matter what the extractive industry, there are always people who are concerned about the environmental impact. It remains to be seen what Aaron and Ron's exploratory work will yield and what, if any, debates will follow.

PLATE 29. Van Conrad, at Will Steger's icehouse

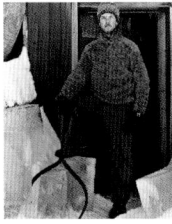 Will Steger's icehouse is a cave dug into the side of a hill and insulated with a wood and rock facade. Van is filling it up after Will's annual ice-cutting party. These icehouses really work, keeping vegetables and other perishables in a perfect, cool humidity all summer long. The ice is gorgeous, like quartz, and gets buried in sawdust, which makes it seem like hidden treasure. In early Ely days, huge blocks of ice were delivered to homes and businesses on horse-drawn sleds. Most people now use Bobcats to haul their ice up from the lake.

PLATE 31. Sylvio Boulanger, motorcycle traveler

We were packing up our photo gear in the gravel parking lot of Trader Craig's consignment store when a motorcycle rumble made us turn and catch an eyeful of Sylvio Boulanger. This leather-encased man with silver-crowned

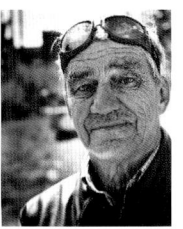
helmet and acid-yellow goggles, not to mention a most unusual face, asked us for directions, and we were so, so happy to know the way to the Echo Trail. For in return, we asked this stranger to sit for a portrait on the spot.

That he agreed would be no surprise to anyone who knows Sylvio. He is a charmer by nature, warm and exuberant, with a French Canadian accent still strong after a half century in the United States. He told us about his romance with Ruth, his wife of forty-eight years, whom he convinced to marry him after just six weeks despite their total inability to speak the same language. He talked of his three grown sons and of his life in the woods near Knife River, where he hand-builds log cabins for a living.

But mostly he talked of the open road and the satisfaction he gets from the twisted, turning highways surrounding Ely. He was sad, though, that Ruth was not with him on this trip, confined at home with a bad back. She was going to be sorry, he told us, to learn she had missed three moose grazing in the mist along the highway that very morning.

PLATE 32. Anne Swenson, owner and publisher of the *Ely Echo*

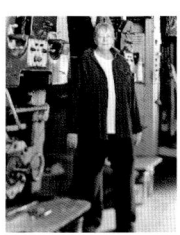
Anne moved her family here in the 1970s from Chicago. She really never intended to become a newspaper owner, publisher, columnist, and editor, but she ended up doing all of those things. And loving every minute. In the early days of the business, she personally operated these presses.

PLATE 33. Frank Salerno, mayor of Ely

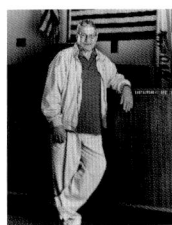
Maybe we are jaded by living in the big city, but it was truly astonishing to walk into the mayor's office, ask him to participate in a photo shoot, photograph him at city hall, and have it all work so effortlessly and smoothly. There were no permits, no approvals, no gate-keeping secretaries or schedulers. I am still amazed when I think about it. Frank is a realtor by profession, and like the long line of mayors before and after him, he served as a part-time mayor along with a small group of volunteer councilmen. When we asked Frank why he engaged in this public service, he told us how grateful he is to Ely for providing him with a wonderful home, a great place to raise his children, and a good business.

PLATE 34. Bait shop, West Sheridan Street, Ely

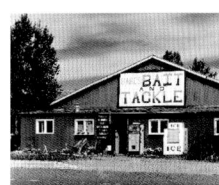
After the speed limit on Highway 169 changes to thirty miles per hour and you pull into Ely, the first thing you see is this bait shop. It is so familiar, and we all say, "yes, we're here at last."

PLATE 35. "Trader Craig" Loughery, radio host and auctioneer

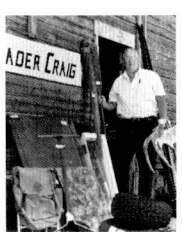

It's doubtful that Trader Craig ever kissed the Blarney Stone, but he most certainly has the gift of the gab. He can sell just about anything to anybody. We almost bought a sitar while photographing him but somehow managed to resist. In addition to running his consignment store, he hosts a daily morning radio show called the *End of the Road Trading Post.* Craig's grandparents left Europe early in the twentieth century with their sights set on Minnesota. They indentured their services on the East Coast for passage and found themselves with a growing family before they had a chance to settle their debt and head west. Craig feels that by putting down roots in Ely he finished the journey for them.

PLATE 36. Pat Loe, seaplane pilot, U.S. Forest Service

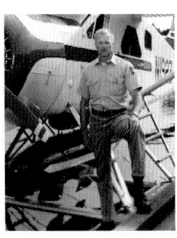

Ely native Pat Loe honed his piloting skills in the Alaskan bush before assuming a highly coveted post at the U.S. Forest Service's only seaplane base. There are just four lucky pilots who call Ely's Shagawa Lake home, and they have the skies to themselves thanks to the Boundary Waters' air ban signed into effect by President Truman in 1951. An enormously controversial piece of legislation, the effects of the air ban still reverberate among the families whose resorts and commercial flying enterprises were rendered obsolete when private planes were prohibited in the designated roadless areas.

Pat and his colleagues fly a fleet of beautiful 1959 DeHavilland Beavers, shiny silver and red prop planes that are incredibly versatile. They are equipped with floats in the summer and skis in the winter. They rescue campers, put out fires, stock lakes with fish, and often carry scientists and photographers to track wolves, lynx, and other animals. It is a rite of passage for Ely children to make it across a path of scattered and slippery rocks to a small island in Shagawa Lake where the seaplane base's windsock flutters atop its pole. If they are lucky, they get there just as the sparkling floats of one of the Beavers lift into the air amid a tremendous sputtering and whirring, and they hold their breaths as the plane barely skims the tops of the trees.

PLATE 37. Joe Seliga, canoe builder

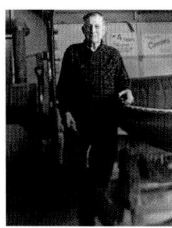

This was one of the first photographs I took for this project, and it remains one of my favorites. It was important to me to photograph Joe. He is a genuine celebrity in Ely, and having met him a few times, I knew he would make a great picture. He was in his early nineties at the time and was enjoying his sixty-fourth year of canoe building. The Seliga wood and canvas canoe is known far and wide among paddlers for its quality and craftsmanship. Each one of the more than 650 canoes that he built during his career was hand-crafted in this garage behind his house in Ely. For many years, his wife, Nora, worked alongside him. Around the time I took this picture, local photographer Deborah Sussex had just completed a full-color hardback book about Joe and his work. Joe was really proud of that book and enjoyed the sense of celebrity it gave him.

This was one of the more difficult images in the book for me to print because I had thrown the bottom of the picture so out of focus. This, combined with the darkness of the tone, tends to really exaggerate imperfections. The low camera angle is deceptive, giving diminutive Joe a larger-than-life presence in keeping with his reputation and character.

PLATE 38. Henry Held, Henry's Shoe Repair

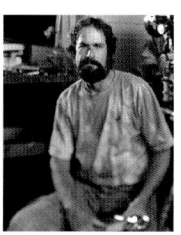

Henry chides me that I made him look so mean in this photograph. He really isn't mean, but he didn't enjoy having his picture taken, and it shows. Henry has been a purveyor of moosehide products and, according to his Web site, "battling entropy" since 1973. His shop is a fixture on Sheridan Street.

PLATE 39. Lori Schmidt, wolf curator, International Wolf Center

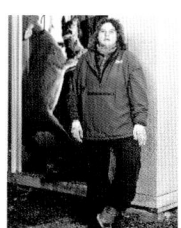

The International Wolf Center is a major tourist attraction in Ely and enjoys a worldwide membership base. There are several resident wolves, some on exhibit and some "retired." Lori is in charge of the care and well-being of the wolves and is photographed here with some of their food. Apparently, captive wolves are loathe to eat processed food, so Lori and the folks in Ely routinely scrape up roadkill and store it in this freezer for the wolves.

PLATE 41. Seliga Canoe, canoe restoration class, Camp Widjiwagan

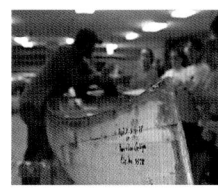

I was watching Jim Schwartz teach a canoe repair class at Camp Widjiwagan when I noticed this hand-written marking on one of the more than forty Joe Seliga canoes in service at the camp. I had already photographed Joe Seliga but had not realized that he marked each and every canoe in felt-tipped pen under the canvas. This one reads: Built 5-14-88 by Nora & Joe Seliga, Ely, MN 55731. After Nora passed away, he included her name and the dates of her birth and death on every canoe. You can see in the lower right corner that this particular canoe is marked W132, which identifies it as a Widji canoe. This was the first, and one of the few, digital pictures I took for the project.

PLATE 42. Three generations of the Anderson family, Anderson's Resort, Burntside Lake

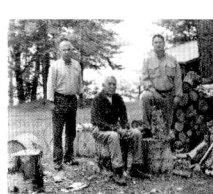

The Andersons are an extensive and long-standing Ojibwe family in this part of Minnesota. This particular branch of the family runs a seven-cabin resort on the east arm of Burntside Lake. John Senior told us the story of how his mother, Mary Anderson, was born along the shores of this lake. The older men are members of the Bois Forte Band of Ojibwe, which has had a reservation at Nett Lake and Lake Vermilion since the mid-1800s.

PLATE 43. Chuck Dayton, environmental attorney

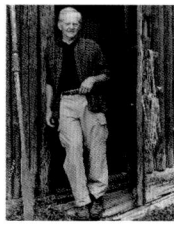

A Chicago colleague opened the door to meeting Chuck, a pivotal player in the early days of establishing the BWCAW. The Dayton family, which includes four sons in Chuck's generation, has long-standing ties to Ely. They still own and enjoy the property from which the family once ran an outfitting and lodge operation. An award-winning attorney, Chuck has turned much of his attention from environmental issues specific to Minnesota to the larger challenges of sustainable energy and global warming.

PLATE 44. Ann Chapek, forestry student, Vermilion Community College

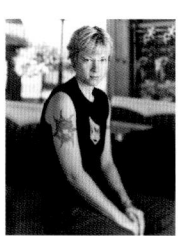

We met and photographed Ann when she was working at the Ely Surf Shop, an establishment that is now closed but used to attract our kids like a magnet because it sold skateboards. The first place in town to offer Wi-Fi, it was our office away from home. Ann was consistently sweet to our boys, and I wanted to capture the complexity of her appearance.

PLATE 45. Susan Schurke, owner, Wintergreen Designs

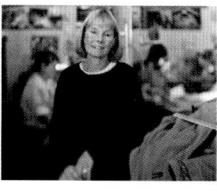

Sue's apparel designs were tested and perfected in the field by her husband, polar explorer Paul Schurke. The company started twenty-one years ago after Sue found that their expedition clothes had a commercial market. For many years now, Wintergreen has been a major presence on Sheridan Street, occupying the better part of a block and keeping more than forty locals employed. Sue, Paul, and their three children also run Wintergreen Dog Sledding Lodge on White Iron Lake.

PLATE 46. Jim Brandenburg, photographer and filmmaker

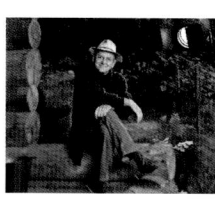

Jim Brandenburg's curiosity and energy have afforded him several careers—filmmaker, musician, photographer, editor, writer—but he is most known for the stunning nature photographs he publishes in books and *National Geographic* as a means to engender reverence for the wilderness. A lifelong obsession with animals brought him to Ely nearly three decades ago, seeking the raw and wild places that attract wolves, the most elusive of his photographic subjects and the ones that ultimately brought him fame. Millions have seen his images, now taken with the most high-tech digital equipment, but he sees them as fundamentally primitive. Cave paintings that tell an ageless story.

This picture is taken in the deep woodland setting of Jim's sauna, a rustic and natural landscape. In the background is a 2,000-watt movie light that I had hauled up to Ely just for this shoot. I wanted to expose the process of the lighting to play up the contrast between Jim's use of ambient light in his nature photography and the highly manipulated process that I use to create artificial light in my work. There can be a certain amount of tension when one photographer photographs another, but Jim set me at ease, and it was a pleasure to work with him.

PLATE 47. Pat Zupancich, Zup's Market

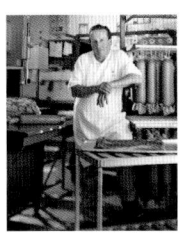

Zup's Market first opened in Ely in 1915, serving sausages and brats to miners and loggers. Today they offer the same specialties to tourists and locals in six stores around the area, including in Babbitt and Tower. Apparently Zup's family recipes, such as Thursday's hot bologna, have a universal and timeless appeal. Pat started working in the store in 1957 alongside his cousins, where they all learned butchery from their fathers and uncles. Nowadays the Zupancich boys go to school to learn the trade. A few have left Ely, but most stay. Pat says it never occurred to him to do anything other than stay in Ely and enter the business. The summers are especially busy because of the influx of tourists, but Pat makes sure to get out of the office early once the Vikings' season starts.

PLATE 48. Pam Freeman and Bernard Herrmann, Mantel House kitchen

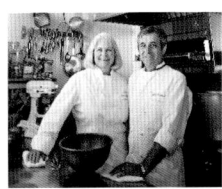

Bernard is a celebrated third-generation French master chef who has managed the kitchens of some of the most prestigious restaurants in the world. Pam, also a certified chef, was a student of his when they both lived in Dallas. She and her husband introduced him to the treasures of Ely, and Bernard was hooked. He left the big city for a life of fishing and low-key cooking. For a while, they ran the Mantel House Restaurant together, but at the time of this picture they were embarking on other enterprises.

When I showed up to take this picture, I was reminded of all those commercial shoots where I had been instructed to take a photograph in an almost impossible setting, except this time it was my own doing. The kitchen had very little room to move, and everywhere I would try to place a light, it would be in view of the camera. Pam and Bernard were very patient as I moved and moved and then moved again every piece of equipment I had brought with me.

PLATE 49. Pat Surface, Eli Bissonett, Robin Anders, and Rob Mattson, musicians

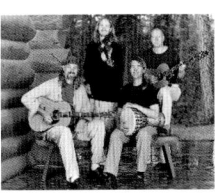

This photograph could read like the beginning of a fairy story—it was a dark, rainy day in the deep, deep forest. That is great for a story, but it makes for a really difficult photograph. The light levels were so low that I couldn't pick up any ambient light at all. Combined with the rain and the cold, it might as well have been the middle of the night. I do have a great Polaroid outtake of Ann and the boys sitting on the bench, looking pretty wet and miserable. Thankfully, Eli's mother, Milli, was there and kept us all warm and happy with tea and the best Scandinavian cookies we have ever eaten.

The music scene in Ely is really rich. These four musicians sometimes play together, sometimes with other musicians, and sometimes solo. During the summer Blueberry Festival, you will hear them in every configuration and see them selling their CDs to huge crowds.

PLATE 50. Kahsha, Ely resident

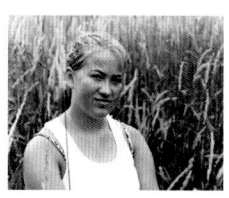

It was only fitting to photograph Kahsha in the outdoors seeing as she was raised in the woods, miles from the nearest road. For a long time, she kept her own sled dogs, but was in the process of selling them off when this picture was taken. She had decided to move into town to attend the Ely public schools after being homeschooled for many years. Her wilderness upbringing has contributed to her ability to make up her own mind and take on responsibilities far beyond her years. You will see her later in this book in her high-school football uniform.

PLATE 51. Cortney and Bailey, Timber Bay Lodge, Babbitt

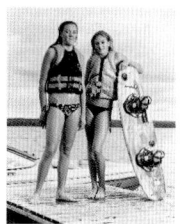

It was a cloudy, cold morning when we took this shot at Birch Lake. I asked the girls, "Do you mind getting wet to make the picture more realistic?" "No problem," they said and jumped right into the lake. I am sure the water was painfully cold, but these sisters didn't whine at all. I have never worked with a professional model who would do something like that without complaint.

PLATE 52. Dr. Frank Udovich, dentist

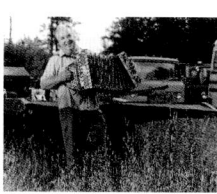

I heard about Doc Udovich as the accordion-playing dentist with a huge collection of really big stuff, and I just had to get his picture. He grew up "on the range" in Chisholm, Minnesota, where his dad had settled as a child in 1913. His grandfather and father both worked the mines, and they told him in no uncertain terms, "You're going to college." Frank came to Ely in 1965 to set up practice but was surprised and worried when the Pioneer Mine closed two years later. It turns out that his business was not affected, and he still finds it hard to limit his patient load. He works strange hours to accommodate the needs of his working neighbors and often barters his dental services for things he needs or wants. Sometimes he will receive an addition to his collection of large machinery like school buses, tractors, and fire trucks; other times he will get something welded or repaired. Frank's instrument is a Mervar accordion manufactured by immigrant Slovenians in the Cleveland area.

PLATE 53. **Wendy and Amber Schlueter, Babbitt**

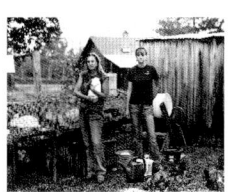

This is one of my favorite images in the project. It demonstrates to me so perfectly the contrasts in people's lives and the misperceptions that some of us have of small-town residents. Wendy has an absolute passion for animals and is shown here taking care of her rabbits. She might just as easily have been photographed with her horses, ducks, chickens, dogs, kittens, or perhaps even an orphaned fawn or two. While this country, casual life is her passion, she is also a professional for the City of Babbitt and transforms into a businesswoman in the blink of an eye. Amber, too, loves animals and the country setting but has spent several years as a professional fashion model in Manhattan.

PLATES 54 AND 55. **Camp Widjiwagan, Burntside Lake**

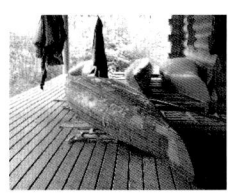

It was really great to load up our equipment on a pontoon boat and putter from our cousins' island on Burntside Lake over to Camp Widjiwagan for this shoot. What a commute. When we got to Widji, the girls showed us the storeroom in which they were preparing for a twenty-one-day trip in Canada's Quetico Provincial Park. We

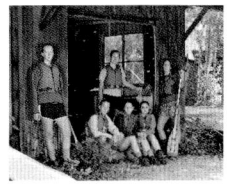

were amazed that these young people had to be so organized. If they failed to pack anything at all, they would just have to do without it. For three straight weeks, they would be about as remote as a person can get in today's world.

PLATE 56. **East Sheridan Street, Ely**

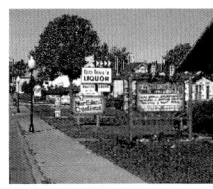

This scene reminds me of my summer vacations as a kid. It is so typical of the Northwoods and could be any town in northern Minnesota, Wisconsin, or the Upper Peninsula of Michigan.

PLATE 57. **Babbitt Conservation Club**

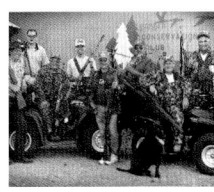

The forty acres that the Babbitt Conservation Club calls home is leased from the City of Babbitt for a dollar a year. The primary purpose of the club is shooting—skeet and trap—but the property is also used for bird watching and other community activities.

PLATE 58. **Bruce Kainz, logger**

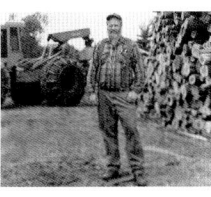

Third-generation logger Bruce Kainz is a lumberjack in every sense of the word, although his trade has abandoned the axe and now employs an amazing machine that grasps a tree, clips it easily at its base, lifts and strips it of bark in one motion, and loads it directly onto a truck—all in a matter of minutes. Unlike his predecessors in Minnesota's legendary logging camps, Bruce works almost entirely alone. When asked what he likes to do in his spare time, Bruce, a grandfather of nine, says he likes to fish or take a walk in the woods and look at trees.

PLATE 59. Robyn Bertelsen, lunch lady, Ely Public Schools

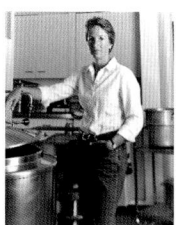

When our friend Deb Pettit suggested we photograph Robyn, her use of the term *lunch lady* conjured images from my childhood of large, cranky women who seemed to have a loathing for food. Therefore, I was pleasantly surprised when I met Robyn. "Food," she says, "is my bliss." She has worked as a short-order cook and a sous chef. Like many in Ely, she has also done sewing for Wintergreen Designs and Steger Mukluks. She started at the school in 1997 and feeds literally every kid in the Ely school system between the hours of 10:48 a.m. and 12:30 p.m. She and her team make their own gravy and mashed potatoes to go with the pork steak. "The best part of my job is that I know every kid in town," says Robyn. "I see them every day."

PLATE 60. Dave Serena, Ken Schlueter, Tony Serena, fish house, Snowbank Lake

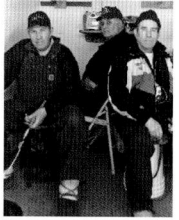

This photograph was taken in Ken Schlueter's icehouse on Snowbank Lake in early March. The icehouse is basically a trailer with tread metal on the corners and aluminum siding. It has a heater, a kitchen counter and cabinet, a TV, and two rows of openings in the floor through which Ken and his friends use a power auger to drill holes through three feet of ice. The lake trout they fish for are reputed to taste better in the winter, when the water is colder.

PLATE 61. TB & the Blasters, rock band

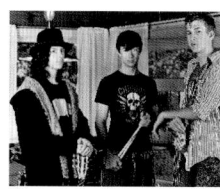

Our friend Dayna Mase arranged this photograph with one of the band members who works with her at Piragis Northwoods Company. All are high-school students, and they are fortunate that one of their parents lets them practice in their little fishing cabin next to a lake.

PLATE 62. Steve Piragis, owner, Piragis Northwoods Company

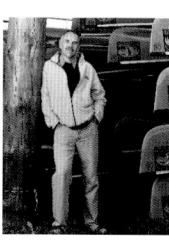

Steve was first a scientist but entered the business world by selling woodstoves out of his garage. Before he knew it, he and his wife were running a major outfitting company. Piragis

Northwoods Company is a dominant presence on the west side of town. Over the years they have added travel services, a bookstore, and a gift shop to their offerings. They are adjacent to the Chocolate Moose restaurant, and their shared "front yard" is a common gathering place for tourists. Our favorite event is the annual loon calling contest at Piragis, which our young cousins Lydia and Reed have won several times.

PLATE 63. Frana Cherico, owner, Miners' Inn

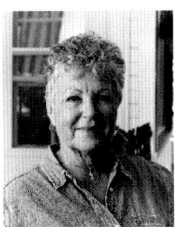

Frana's father came to join his older sister in Ely when he was just fourteen years old, leaving his parents behind in Yugoslavia. He never saw them again. He served as the deputy sheriff of St. Louis County from 1923 to 1965, and he lived to be ninety-four. Frana owns the Miners' Inn, a homey bed and breakfast with an impressive collection of mining artifacts. She loved growing up in Ely and loves living here now. She is an artist and a painter. On the day we photographed her, Frana gave us the first ripe tomato from her gorgeous garden, an extraordinary gift in a climate with a growing season as brief as Ely's.

PLATE 64. Headframe of Pioneer Mine, Ely

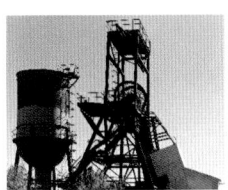

The Trezona Trail, named for an early mine supervisor, winds for five miles around Miners Lake on the north end of Ely. The lake was formed by the flooding of the original open pit of the Pioneer Mine and the collapse of its underground sections, as well as several other underground mines. As you walk the Trezona Trail, you will come across the headframe and water tower of the mine's "B" shaft, built in 1909. This shaft was once used for hoisting Ely's incredibly rich iron ore out from the depths directly onto rail cars that would carry it to Lake Superior and on to the steel mills across the Great Lakes. The Pioneer Mine closed in 1967 after producing more than forty-one million tons of ore. New methods of steel production had rendered the high quality of Ely's ore unnecessary and the cost of underground mining prohibitive.

PLATE 65. Pete Pastika, mine engineer, Babbitt

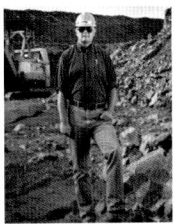

The sheer size of this mining operation and the associated equipment is impossible to capture in a photograph. Standing at the edge of Babbitt's taconite mine is like looking at a bunch of Tonka trucks in a sandbox. Taconite is a low-grade iron ore extracted from rock. Pete drove us down into the mine, and we struggled for a time to find a spot in which we could fit an entire piece of equipment into the frame. The loader behind him is so huge that a full-size truck would not even come close to skimming the bottom of the main cab area. We are actually really, really far away from it.

PLATE 66. Dan Olson, Ely Ice Center

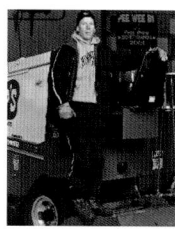

The Ely Ice Center is almost constantly abuzz with activity during the winter months. Situated behind the high school, classes of children come over for phys. ed.—some of them obviously experienced and others still hesitant despite the fact that they live half their lives surrounded by ice. The locker room is dark and a little scary, masses of children digging around trying on mismatched skates to find the right pair. In the afternoons and evenings, various hockey leagues come and go. We managed to find a brief hour in which the place was quiet to take this shot. Finding the rink freshly groomed and totally empty, our kids took a running leap in their boots and slid across the ice in their snow pants. While we unrolled extension cords, they kept Dan's dog Ruger happy by throwing hockey pucks across the rink.

Dan went to Vermilion Community College and chose to stay in Ely. He spends the winter managing the Ice Center and the summers doing masonry work. Like so many people here, he seems content with a slow pace of life, enjoying the outdoors and the people who surround him. As we pulled away from the rink after the shot, a group of pink-faced elementary students chanted happily to him, "Dan, Dan the Zamboni Man."

PLATE 67. Dr. Lynn Rogers, North American Bear Center

The North American Bear Center recently opened on the west end of Ely on Highway 169, a mirror to the 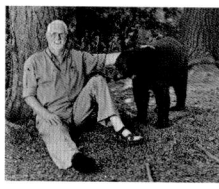 International Wolf Center on the other side of town. This is the fulfillment of a longtime dream for Lynn, an internationally recognized bear researcher, and many members of this community. Both organizations play an essential educational role, helping campers and tourists understand the healthy realities of living with wolves and bears, and dispelling the myth of man-eating carnivores lurking in the woods. Chances are good you will see a black bear at some point during a wilderness experience. Lynn's ambition is that you will respond appropriately, not endangering yourself or the animal. We took this picture of him and a juvenile bear at his own research center farther west of Ely. He has collared several wild bears in the area and can summon them fairly easily with some cooing and a handful of dates.

PLATE 68. Bonnie Anderson with Kj and Derek, owner, Britton's Café

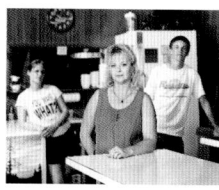

Bonnie tells the story of how when she walked through her dark restaurant at 4 a.m., headed for the kitchen to make fresh doughnuts, she stopped short behind the row of bar stools along the counter. She couldn't believe it, but one of the stools was missing. Unscrewed from its base, the red vinyl and chrome seat was gone. Who would take a bar stool? The mystery was solved a few hours later when a regular customer returned with the repaired stool in hand—unbeknownst to Bonnie, it had been squeaking for days.

That is how it is at Britton's. Bonnie has owned the place for ten years, but the Britton family ran it for twenty-six years before that. Many folks regard the place as their own, establishing squatters' rights at specific bar stools and stopping in up to four times a day. The menu varies daily, but the home-cooked feel remains the same. The customers treat Bonnie well because she treats them well. When fishing season starts, she will even open the place early to make sure her regulars beat everyone else out to the lake.

PLATE 69. **Ryan, Jeff, and Philip, Charles L. Sommers National High Adventure Base, Boy Scouts of America, Moose Lake**

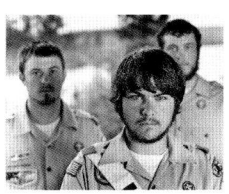

These guys were getting ready to head into the Boundary Waters for a week of trail maintenance as members of the Boy Scouts' Order of the Arrow. After that, they would get a week to themselves to explore and camp as they pleased. The Order of the Arrow is open only to kids who have participated in a rigorous qualification process. They definitely know what they are doing in the woods.

They were not nearly as comfortable in front of a camera. It was a rainy day, so we set up in a picnic shelter overlooking Moose Lake. It took a while to run electrical cords from the main building, so the boys had a long time to think about the shot and get more and more uncomfortable about it. Sometimes this kind of tension can really make a picture, so I decided to play on that and bring them in closer to the camera. In the end, it is the intensity of their faces that makes me like this image so much. I also like the aesthetic that results from not worrying about everyone being completely in the shot or whether people are in focus. Letting go of these restrictions gives me more room to create an interesting structure in the photograph.

PLATE 70. **Ken Schlueter, retired conservation officer, Babbitt**

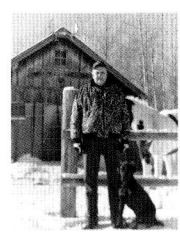

Years ago we spent a couple of summers in cabin 9 at Timber Bay Lodge. I asked owner Ron Rykken if he might recommend a fishing guide, and he gave Ken Schlueter a call. We set up a time for him to meet me and my son Reeder, who was maybe four years old at the time. We set out early in the morning, and it was close to midnight when we returned. Although Ann had been worried, Ron had reassured her that "if they're with Kenny, they're just fine." And we were. After a long day of successful fishing, Ken took Reeder and me to his country home in Babbitt, where he cleaned all the fish. His wife, Wendy, earned a lifelong friend by showing Reeder her menagerie of baby bunnies, kittens, chickens, horses, ducks, and more. I was sold when Ken took me into his basement rec room, and there was a refrigerator with a beer tap in it.

That was the start of a lasting friendship between our families and, in fact, the true beginning of this book. It was Ken who inspired to me to capture the faces and stories in this community. And it was Ken who opened the door to many of the people who chose to participate.

Wendy was just as supportive, feeding us, entertaining our kids, and always offering a cheerful welcome when we returned to Babbitt. Their daughter Crystal, who is now in the Navy's Honor Guard in Washington, DC, also cared for our kids many times and their elder daughter, Amber, participated in the project as a subject.

Ken was a conservation officer for many years in Babbitt and knows pretty much everyone and everything in the area. He got a degree in biology, but he says it was his large stature that probably landed him a spot in the highly competitive C.O. program. Now retired, he serves as one of the best fishing and hunting guides around.

PLATE 71. Brian Kainz, log home builder, Winton

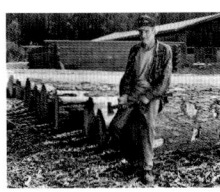

I really wanted to represent the log-building industry in this project. Log homes are so traditional here, a classic structure in the area, and there are a lot of great craftsmen. Brian Kainz descends from the Kainz brothers, who had a successful sawmill in Winton. This shot was also a good opportunity to represent Winton, which was, after all, a bigger town than Ely a hundred years ago. Brian's brother Bruce, a logger, also appears in this book. It is a little ironic that Brian looks so forbidding here. He is a really gentle, kind guy.

PLATE 72. Chris Maher and Aaron Chick, trappers

I called Aaron to arrange this picture, and he said he would take me out to a beaver house. I naively thought a beaver house was some kind of small hunting lodge

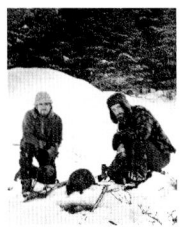

or shack where we might see Aaron's traps and a collection of pelts. We met Chris and Aaron on a very snowy day in a parking lot. They helped me haul a generator about two hundred yards through the snow, and we emerged onto a lake next to a white mound. By beaver house, Aaron had meant beaver lodge. We were so totally clueless, such city slickers!

We watched as the two men tended their traps and pulled a dead beaver from one of them. It was amazing to be so connected to a tradition that has been in these parts for hundreds and hundreds of years. At the beginning of that day we didn't know what we were doing, but I will tell you that we were really, really glad we were doing it. It was these kinds of enlightening surprises that made the project so meaningful and so fun for us.

PLATE 73. Jonathan, Damien, and Ashlee, students, Vermilion Community College

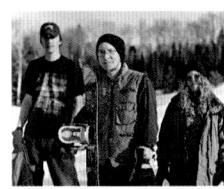

Hidden Valley, just east of Ely, is an old ski-jumping training center. The jump is defunct now, but the framework still rises high above the landscape. There are extensive Nordic trails through the woods, but only a couple of hills for snowboarding. There are no lifts or fees or anything because the place is officially closed down, but we saw Jonathan, Damien, and Ashlee trekking up the slopes on foot, boarding down, and then trekking up again. We asked them if they would pose for a shot, and they agreed.

PLATE 75. Chip Hanson, veterinarian

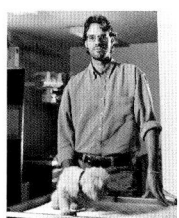

The little dog that Chip is caring for in this photo is just one of twelve thousand dogs in his practice. A few thousand of those are sled dogs. After all, a single owner can have up to a hundred in his or her kennel. Some are Alaskan huskies, Paul Schurke has Canadian Inuit dogs, and some mushers might use a mix of other breeds. Chip says they are among the healthiest dogs he sees, in large part because mushers are renowned for developing highly specialized diets for their dogs, and also because they are bred entirely for health and performance. When he is called out to a dog yard, it is usually for vaccinations or sports-related injuries. A really sick dog will be brought to Chip's office. He sees a lot of dogs who have eaten rocks because they can get so bored in the summer–the antithesis of their active and joyful winter life. And the dog yard can be a rough place. When two sled dogs get in a fight, it can be pretty vicious. "Thankfully," says Chip, "dogs are incredible healers; much better healers than us."

Although dogs are definitely the mainstay of Chip's practice, he gets plenty of variety to make life interesting. He has treated loons, foxes, eagles, and more. Whenever you see a strange wildlife story in the local paper, Chip's name seems to be involved. A bear gets hit by a car, a cougar attacks a horse, Chip gets a call. After that cougar incident, he said he felt more than a tingle or two on the back of his neck during his evening ski sessions on the Hidden Valley Nordic trails, directly behind the property where the cougar attack occurred.

PLATE 77. Milli Salmela Bissonett, Finnish radio host and designer

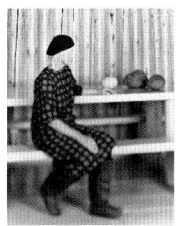

All four of Milli's grandparents were born in Finland. They settled in Embarrass and on the Pipe River near Tower. "They were always a people of the earth," she says. "They were farmers, musicians, artisans. They did everything. To label them as doing only one thing doesn't capture it." The same could be said of Milli, who is a musician, chef, mother, radio host, promoter of the arts, and so much more. She is a talented designer and worked for many years in Finland for the creator of Marimekko fabrics. For this shoot, she chose to wear a dress made from the "Northern Witch" design, manufactured with an expensive silk-screening process that pushes the ink through the material so that the pattern appears on both sides. She is also wearing a pair of authentic Finnish boots, the toe tips curved up to accommodate ski straps. Milli collected the rocks and placed them on the table and chose to sit in front of the vertical log wall.

PLATE 78. Bill and Barb Godlin, artisans

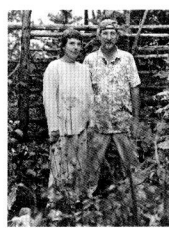

Bill and Barb are woodworkers and gardeners. In yards, at lodges, and on private properties all around Ely you will find their handiwork in the form of elaborate landscapes, sweet little gardens, gorgeous boathouses, and even small sleeping cabins. Their home is set high on a ridge over a small lake, and you feel like a prince or princess in an enchanted castle when you look out the window of one of the turrets in their house. They work together to create a magical environment for themselves and for those who are smart enough to retain their services.

PLATE 79. Marvin Lamppa, Iron Range historian, Babbitt

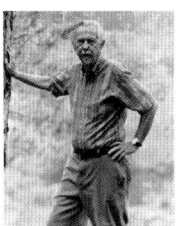

Marv Lamppa is a renowned mine historian—a recognized expert on the fascinating story of the Iron Range. His passion is finding ghost towns left behind long ago, after the ore resource had been extracted and the miners moved on. Marv has counted at least 130 such ghost towns and has given voice to shadows—the people who lived here, worked here, and left here—through his books, teaching, television documentaries, and the establishment of the archives at the Iron Range Research Center. This particular photograph was taken of Marv standing at the very edge of Section Thirty, an iron-ore mine that operated east of Ely for fourteen years but now sits as a precarious cavity in the middle of the woods.

PLATE 81. Ely Steam Sauna

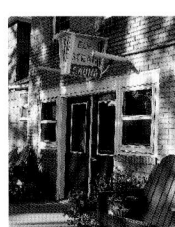

Dennis Orn poked his head into the cabin we were renting at Timber Wolf Lodge one summer and asked Ann, "Do you think Andrew would like to join me and the guys at the sauna tonight?" She unhesitatingly replied, "Well, of course he would, Dennis. What time should he be there?" So, thanks to my wife's sense of humor and, I must say, commitment to research, I was obliged to enter a hot, steamy room with a bunch of men I hardly knew, naked.

Let me say that you have to go to the Ely Steam Sauna sometime, just to see it. Its heating system is an amazing network of old radiators, and there are rows of benches lined up against the walls. I asked Dennis where I should sit, and he said, "down low." I was the youngest guy there by a long shot, but the top bench was filled with eighty-year-olds. Two of them got into an argument over some detail of local history, and one of them stormed out in a temper.

The owner of the establishment is a guy named Rick, whom I photographed—*twice*. The first time I photographed him there was a light leak in the camera. So I arranged to photograph him again. His back was out, but he did the shot anyway, in a lot of pain. I had reloaded film in the car on a bumpy road, and it made the dust and static awful. The negative was totally ruined. So, this is an official apology to Rick that he is not in the book. I just could not call him a third time, so I took this picture instead. I have never messed up two shots on the same person in my life.

PLATE 82. Ann Thunhorst, Jackpine Lodge

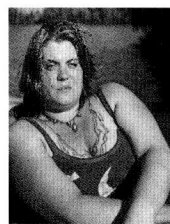

When our youngest son fell and split his lip in the pool room at Jackpine Lodge, a flurry of women swept him into the kitchen and healed him with love and popsicles. He was thereafter an official adoptee of the Jackpine Lodge family and their longtime employee Ann Thunhorst. An Ely local, Ann worked at the lodge for nearly ten years of summers, starting at the age of fifteen and ending only when the property was sold a few years ago. This was not Ann's favorite picture that we took of her. I had taken others of her, featuring the fabulous tattoos on her back, but they just failed to capture the strength of character and directness that we so like about her.

PLATE 83. Oscar Kenig, Ely resident

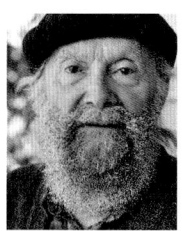

Oscar is well into his nineties but lives alone and spends much of his time out and about in Ely. He eats lunch regularly at the Northern Grounds and chats for hours with his friends and neighbors. According to some people, he is "the most learned man in Ely." Obviously, Oscar has a wonderful face, so I wanted to capture it up close. The more time I spent with him, the more entranced I became with the character of his eyes and the translucency of his skin.

PLATE 84. Sigurd Olson's cabin, Listening Point, Burntside Lake

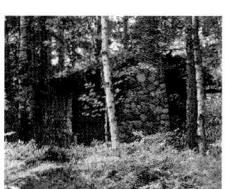

Sigurd Olson's memory is nigh on sacred to many people. He was an outdoorsman, a guide, a teacher, a prolific writer, and a committed advocate for the wilderness. He served as president of the Wilderness Society and the National Parks Association, and he played a key role in the 1964 Wilderness Act, establishing the national wilderness preservation system. For all those who adored him, there were as many in Ely who despised him for his work to ban air traffic over the Superior National Forest and for his role in the final passage of the Boundary Waters Canoe Area Wilderness Act. Whatever one thinks of him and his work, he was undeniably a key character in the history of Ely. His beautiful private retreat on Burntside Lake is now managed and protected by the Listening Point Foundation in order to further Olson's message of wilderness preservation.

PLATE 85. Heart Warrior Chosa, artist and activist

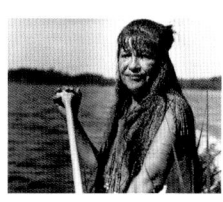

In 1990, Heart Warrior ran for the office of governor of Minnesota under the auspices of the Earth-RIGHT party. She didn't win, but it gave her a chance to advocate for the environment, women's issues, and the rights of Native Americans. Much of her world view is described in her book *Seven Chalk Hills*, in which she writes about her experience in a Catholic boarding school as a child. She is a writer, painter, weaver, interpreter, and so many other things, so we let Heart Warrior decide how she wanted to be represented in this photograph. She was really clear that she preferred the idea of being pictured in a canoe in traditional dress.

PLATE 86. Patti Steger, Steger Mukluks and Moccasins

The traditional Native American "mukluk" is perfect for the dry snow of the north. The supple, only partially

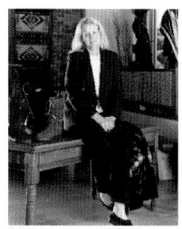waterproof moosehide is durable, and the wool liners are completely and utterly toasty. You will see Patti's mukluks on people in Aspen and Telluride, and on the locals of Babbitt and Ely. Patti was once married to polar explorer Will Steger and still actively supports his expedition work through fund-raisers and publicity. Her store is a high-end boutique on Sheridan Street, but people of all kinds flock here for the warmest and most comfortable winter foot wear you can find.

PLATE 87. Justin Pius, Babe's Bait & Tackle

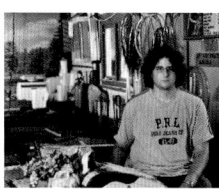As we worked on and off to photograph Justin at the bait shop, we learned quickly what it takes to do his job—patience and an encyclopedic knowledge of fishing in the area. A continuous stream of people, most of them tourists, came in for their fishing licenses with a list of detailed questions about lures, bait, depth, timing, and more. It took forever to finally get the picture between the customers, some of whom occupied up to fifteen minutes of his time. That's what he is there for, so we waited patiently, and our admiration for the local bait shop workers all across town grew by the minute.

PLATE 88. Lisa Pekuri, Lisa's Upstairs Books, Piragis Northwoods Company

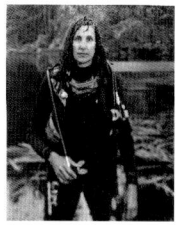Lisa is the manager, more of a curator really, of Lisa's Upstairs Books, an offshoot of the successful Piragis Northwoods Company. It is a careful collection of works including how-to's on dogsledding and bass fishing, historic compilations about the Ely area, charming children's books by local authors, and more nature and adventure books than you can imagine. The entire effect is so thoroughly appropriate to place that you feel you have arrived in the Northwoods just as truly as if you were standing on a glacier-carved rock overlooking Burntside Lake.

And if you were at Burntside, or any other lake, you might come across Lisa in her diving gear, looking deeper than most for the true meaning of these woods. What does she see there? Bass, trout, old cabins, beer cans, and, she says, on the good days she gets a glimpse of God.

PLATE 89. The Nordic Wolves, girls' cross-country ski team, Ely Memorial High School

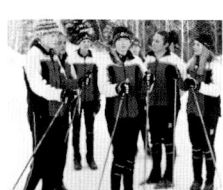These girls are among the best skiers in Minnesota and even in the country. After this picture was taken, three of them headed to compete in the Junior Olympics. Ely sends a few kids there almost every season. Even though it doesn't look like it, this picture is lit artificially

with two strobe heads. I covered them with soft boxes, which reduces the harshness of the lights. As usual, this required that we drag a generator across the snow and into the woods.

PLATE 90. Kahsha and Alex, football team, Ely Memorial High School

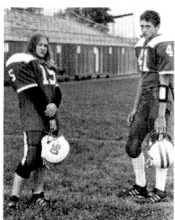

Kahsha is not, as you might assume, a kicker. She is a linebacker and participates to her fullest in the high-school football games, making tackles and yelling instructions to her teammates. Alex is the quarterback. Together, they made a good effort on this rainy, crummy day but didn't capture the win.

PLATE 91. George Burger, parking enforcement officer

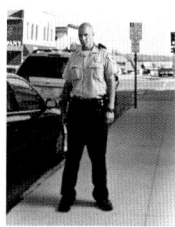

George is referred to as the "chalk cop." He walks up and down Sheridan Street, marking tires and issuing tickets to cars that have exceeded the two-hour limit. Most of the store owners hate this policy, wanting tourists to park freely for as long as they want to shop. And, of course, the people getting tickets don't like it either. George, however, maintains an extraordinarily calm demeanor, even in the face of the occasional irate shopper.

I photographed him in open shade using a fast shutter speed and a strobe. This took most of the natural daylight out of the shot and let me create dark shadows on George's face. The intimidating nature of the shot really has more to do with how his position is regarded in town. On a personal level, he is a quiet, nice guy who races snowmobiles and deejays at parties when he is not working the parking patrol shift.

PLATE 93. Bert Hyde's sled dogs

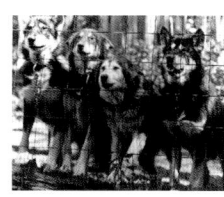

If you have never seen a pack of sled dogs eat, I would not recommend it unless you have a strong stomach. Bert took us into the dog yard, our youngest son riding in safety atop his shoulders, and we stood back as Bert poured chow into two large metal bins. The dogs have established a clear hierarchy of who eats first, but to us humans, it seems like a free-for-all with more than a dozen furry sides heaving as they lunge into the bins as if they have never eaten before. We have seen Wintergreen Dog Sledding Lodge owner Paul Schurke dip a shovel into a box of lard and feed his dogs huge chunks of it. It is a noisy, smelly, wild affair.

PLATE 94. Bernard Herrmann, French master chef

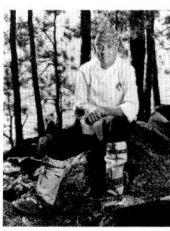

Bernard followed in the footsteps of his father and grandfather and became a French master chef in 1978. It is testament to his love for the outdoors that he gave up a high-powered career and settled here in Ely, where he can fish as often as he likes. It is great for the tourists and campers who come here because they can eat like kings thanks to Bernard. He cooks for Wintergreen Dog

Sledding Lodge and for Camp Voyageur. At the latter, he says the boys are reluctant at first to try some of his dishes, but by the end of camp they will be asking him, "What's that herb in the salad, Bernard?"

PLATE 95. Paul Schurke, arctic explorer, Wintergreen Dog Sledding Lodge

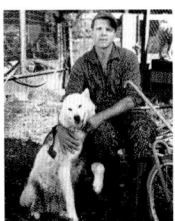

"Getting people together and breaking barriers." This is how Paul describes his personal mission. A few summers ago, we talked with Paul and his eldest daughter as they were packing up to lead a Wilderness Inquiry canoe expedition into the Canadian forest. They were going to take a group of physically disabled people on a train journey and simply ask the conductor to drop them off at a remote point along the track. After a multiday journey, in which the participants would develop a completely new sense of self-reliance, they would make their way back to the tracks and wait for a train to come by. Paul founded Wilderness Inquiry years ago but gave up administrative responsibilities so he could move to Ely and establish his dogsledding business. Creating access to the wilderness experience is a commitment he will never relinquish, so he guides these trips whenever he can.

Similarly, he has opened doors for the Inuit families he has befriended in the Arctic Circle. In the 1980s, he led a 1,200-mile, two-month cultural journey between Siberia and Alaska at the time when the Bering Strait was still firmly closed to travel, a diplomatic effort that led to the opening of the strait to native travel. He continues to make journeys north to take people on what he calls "cultural adventures," building connections and breaking barriers the whole way.

Paul is perhaps most famous for his fifty-five-day, record-setting journey to the North Pole with Will Steger in which they accomplished the first confirmed unsupported journey there by dogsled. It was a life-changing experience from which he has drawn the personal strength and fortitude to achieve so much, not least of which is the success of Wintergreen Dog Sledding Lodge here in Ely.

PLATE 96. Virginie Pointeau, instructor, Voyageur Outward Bound School

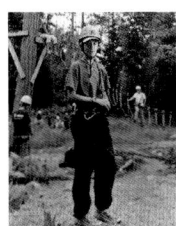

This Outward Bound School is set on a gorgeous plot of land southeast of Ely and offers dogsledding, canoeing, camping, hiking and myriad other outdoor activities. All are intended to build resilience and enhance problem-solving skills, often among groups of teens. Virginie was spending the summer instructing here and is pictured preparing to lead a group on the ropes course.

PLATE 97. Roger, Matt, and Wayne, boat hands, Jackpine Lodge

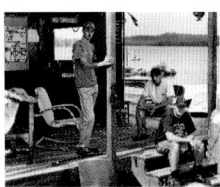

This picture was taken during one of the last summers that Jackpine Lodge operated at the edge of Snowbank Lake. The staff, like these three guys, worked hard but seemed to always have a few minutes to enjoy the pristine environment. It is exclusively summer work—the season starts in May and ends in September—so these guys all returned to town jobs or went back to school for the winter months.

The best few dollars I ever spent paid Roger to clean our fish after a successful day on Snowbank Lake. Every bone was gone, and he had left a perfect little square of scales on each fish so you could see what kind of fish they were. But the best part was when he chased our sons with the eyeballs.

PLATE 98. Bob Nass, musher, Wintergreen Dog Sledding Lodge

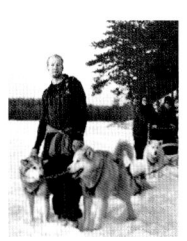

Bob and his wife travel from their West Coast home to spend a few months in the winter working at Wintergreen. Bob works the dogs, and his wife helps in the lodge. The Schurkes' operation is incredibly well orchestrated. We showed up to photograph Bob and the team and were kept informed minute by minute of Bob's whereabouts by walkie-talkie. However, the light was fading fast at the end of the day, and by the time Bob arrived in front of my camera, I only had time to expose a few shots and it was over. The curve of the sled, Bob's positioning, the relationship to the point of land, all happened naturally in the rush of the setting sun.

PLATE 99. Tommy Helm, retired miner and inventor, Babbitt

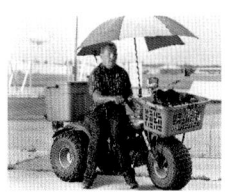

Tommy was an exploration miner in Babbitt for more than thirty years. He is now retired and spends his days inventing stuff. His latest craze is kites, and you will see him out flying them in all kinds of weather. He is photographed here with his loyal dogs Fluffy and Minnie. They were born on a fifty-degrees-below-zero day and are now nine years old. Tommy says, "They've rode with me since they were 3 months old. They're like backseat drivers."

PLATE 100. Dan, Henry, Bob, Drew, Matt, Camp Voyageur

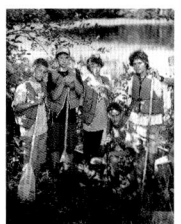

This was the last day of a month-long camp session, and these campers had done some serious canoeing and wilderness camping during that time. Matt, the guy on the right, is the counselor.

I wanted the dappled light through the trees, but it was a real challenge to keep up with the position of the sun. Ann and Reeder were holding branches back and then pushing them forward to manage the brightness on the boys' faces. We would have everything set, then everything would change. This is typical of shooting outside. You are always trying to slow down the light. The ratio between shadow and highlight can only go so far. There is a fine line between dappled and disaster.

PLATE 101. Bert Hyde, wilderness ranger

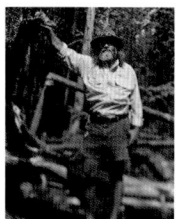

Bert Hyde is the kind of man who races through the summer forest as though on cloud slippers, so silent that the woods seem raucous around him. For months each year he serves as a wilderness ranger, carving trails, grooming campsites, and checking up on campers in the BWCAW. The rest of his days are spent "off the grid" in his deep-woods homestead with wife, Johnnie, and daughter Kahsha. Bert says he is self-sufficient because he is cheap, but it is hard to imagine that economic considerations alone would lead a man to raise a family in the deepest wilderness with no electricity or running water, many miles from the nearest paved road.

Life in this family settlement is governed by the seasons. Winters are occupied preparing for summer, hand-cutting four tons of ice from the lake and storing it under layers of sawdust in an insulated icehouse. Summers are spent preparing fuel for winter, cord upon cord of wood curing in the shed, wild rice harvested into a canoe. Bert's sled dogs are ever present, their ears bloody in summer from the relentless deerflies, everything within them awaiting winter, when once again Bert will move like a spirit through the woods with only the soft scrape of sled runners and the panting of dogs to give him away.

Andrew Goldman is a freelance commercial photographer. His clients include ESPN and Playboy Enterprises, and his photographs have appeared on more than forty magazine covers. **Ann Goldman** is a freelance writer and presenter whose professional background is in museum and nonprofit management. They live in Boulder, Colorado, with their two sons.

The work of award-winning nature photographer **Jim Brandenburg** has been featured in *National Geographic* magazine since 1978. His many books include *Chased by the Light* and *Looking for the Summer*. He lives near Ely, Minnesota, where his work can be seen at Brandenburg Gallery.